Conviction

Editor: NORMAN MACKENZIE

PETER SHORE

BRIAN ABEL-SMITH

RAYMOND WILLIAMS

PETER TOWNSEND

RICHARD HOGGART

CONVICTION

NIGEL CALDER

HUGH THOMAS

PETER MARRIS

MERVYN JONES

PAUL JOHNSON

IRIS MURDOCH

1959 : MacGibbon & Kee : LONDON

© MACGIBBON & KEE 1958

First published 1958

Second Impression 1959

Set in 10 point Pilgrim
Printed and made in Great Britain at
the Saint Ann's Press, Altrincham

Contents

NORMAN MACKENZIE

After the stalemate state

THIS IS THE MIDDLE of my journey: on
that the actuary's table and the biblical span agree. Half-way. As I
look back over the journey I see that it falls into definite stages. The
first begins with the clearest of my childhood memories—a file of
troops trying to force a bus through a picket-line. That was 1926.
Along the years after that I remember other landmarks, all personal
but all increasingly political : the dole queue—a conventional symbol, but one you never forget—that I passed on the way to school;
the Friday evenings that I spent with two school friends, going
down the ill-lit streets cramped between the railway arches and the
docks collecting money for Spanish medical aid from families that
had barely enough to pay the rent-collector next morning; the first
practice with the balloons; and then the superb September afternoon when all that ended, and the Thames was a golden fire-break
between two walls of flame. For me, that was the real beginning of
the war, the next stage. Of that I say only that it was more a time
of hope, of fellow-feeling, than of destruction—an optimism that
reached its climax on a July morning when I boarded a bus near
Blackfriars Bridge and the conductor asked me if I knew the election results. I told him; he stopped the bus, called down the driver,
and the two of them literally danced in the road. Somewhere in the
years after that the optimism withered; this period was the fourth,
in which we created the stalemate state, that curious interval in our
social history, in which there was no way back to the world which
had guttered out into war yet no clear way forward to a really new
society.

As I recall these stages I realize that I am old enough to remember
and young enough to hope. That, perhaps, is one reason why I am
a Socialist, for memory and hope are the two qualities which blend
into a Socialist conviction. That, too, may be why Socialism has
been unfashionable among those who have grown up during and

since the war : they have no memory, and no one has given them much reason to hope.

Need it be so? Can we break out of the stalemate state and make a new beginning? I believe we can—and so do my friends who have contributed to this book. But first we must understand what has happened to us, marry memory to hope again.

I have not written a formal introduction to the pages which follow. There is no need for it. All of us have stated simply, from our own experience, what we dislike about our present condition, and what we believe can be done to alter and improve it. What we have in common can be expressed in these words : conviction, and a sense of direction. It is worth while to think clearly, believe honestly, act decisively. It is worth while, because only so can we give meaning to our lives and purpose to our society.

Franklin Roosevelt used to divide his supporters into two groups—those who backed him before the Chicago convention which gave him the presidential nomination in 1932, and those who came to him 'after Chicago'. There is a similar division in British policies between those who worked for 1945 and those who inherited it. It is an important gap, in memory, experience and feeling. Jimmy Porter put his finger on it when he said : 'I suppose people of our generation aren't able to die for good causes any longer. We had all that done for us, in the thirties and forties when we were still kids.' It is a gap I suddenly appreciated when I was talking to a university Labour Club, and someone asked me if I could say something about the Popular Front. I slipped into the answer, but as I spoke I sensed that to these undergraduates such names as Jarrow, Guernica and Munich were no more than yellowing newspaper clips, a Picasso picture, a scrap of newsreel film. Spain was as distant from them as the Russian revolution had seemed to me at their age; their memories of the 1945 general election were as fragmentary as were mine, in 1938, of the 1926 general strike. Someone said caustically in the discussion : 'We aren't interested in the thirties. The only people who talk about them are those who lived in them.' And yet, round those events, round our reaction to them, there is now the glow of legend.

No wonder that those who grew up in the war and its aftermath resent our complex and dangerous world, and look back not in anger but in nostalgia to an heroic age when things seemed simpler, the causes good and clean. Some of them, no doubt, would have liked to be there in Hyde Park when repeated baton charges broke up a demonstration of 100,000 unemployed, at Cable Street when Mosley's march was stopped; they would have enjoyed, perhaps, the canvass on wet nights to collect signatures for the Peace Ballot. I cannot now guess where on the Left they would have found a spiritual home: heaven knows, the choice then was wide enough. But they would have had a sense of belonging, that there was something to be done and that they could have some part in doing it. There is a world of difference between a Porter addressing a dole queue and Porter nagging his wife, between a young man who believes he has an answer and a young man who throws away the posh papers in disgust because no one has an answer, between the dissenter who flatly declares that he is a Socialist and the rebel for whom politics has almost become a dirty word.

Time is a lens which exaggerates the light and the dark. But, though much of the thirties was really a grey world, there were great causes—and they engulfed people with a passion that could sustain them through one defeat after another. Even if there was anger at the defeats, there was also hope—hope that war could be averted, or that if it could not be averted it would at least end in the destruction of Fascism, hope that one day the reckoning would come with the hard-faced men who ground down the unemployed, starved Jarrow and dined Ribbentrop, hope that it would all end with a new social order to replace the capitalist system that led to poverty at home and war abroad. That was the larger, the long-term hope. Meanwhile the pieces of politics seemed to fit into an intelligible pattern.

Is is easy, of course, to forget how few were engaged, how little was in fact achieved. The Labour Party in Parliament was a struggling minority; public opinion was lethargic; too many people were panicked by 1931, corrupted by the Silver Jubilee, lulled by appeasement. But those who were on the Left felt that they possessed the key which would in time unlock all doors for them. It was not that they were all Marxists, though dogmatic Marxism was just as important as the apparent success of the Soviet Union in giving the

9

Communists an intellectual appeal out of all proportion to their numbers. It was that the broad propositions of Marxism seemed true enough. Capitalism, in Europe and the United States, was in a state of chronic crisis; the ruling class was reactionary and inept; imperialism, and the rivalry between great capitalist powers, seemed a valid explanation of the drift to war. So, as you read in one Left Book Club volume after another, each of us had to take our stand in the coming struggle for power. It did not greatly matter on which barricade you chose to fight. Was it against unemployment, the malnutrition that cursed half our population, the educational system that turned out weedy boys and girls half-literate at fourteen to ferret for dead-end jobs? Was it to give some decency to the people who squandered their lives in the slums of London, Liverpool, Leeds and Glasgow? The enemy was clear, and full in view. Was it for sanctions against Mussolini's Italy, for arms for Spain? Once again, you had the same answer: Chamberlain Must Go! Was Litvinov's offer of collective security spurned, were Britain and France bribing Hitler to turn to the East? It seemed so. Very well: Join the Popular Front! All out on May Day! Underlying all this, the assumption behind the slogans, was the belief that it mattered what British governments said or did, that a victory for any one of these causes could have a decisive impact, not only upon our own future, but on the fate of Europe. It did matter.

Is this only my own form of nostalgia? I can forgive anyone who has come to politics since the war for saying, with hindsight, that this was a naïve belief. Hindsight, indeed, has made many of those who once spent themselves in these campaigns wonder if they were right, or as right as they then felt. But I cannot share this scepticism. Despite the modern fashion for rewriting history, no one has yet managed to whitewash the Tory thirties. Their essential tragedy lay in the fact that Britain was still a power of the first rank, with great material resources, and yet its government was as unwilling or unable to save democracy abroad as it was to provide a good life for our people at home. Those who ruled Britain in the thirties were Top People. The United States wallowed in depression: its economic collapse had fatally upset the precarious balance of the world, but it had not yet come to redress that balance. Russia was in the grip of the kulak famine, the rigours of the first two Five Year

Plans, and the terror of the great purges. China was no more than a notion of geography, a prey equally to the Japanese and internal civil war. India apart, colonial nationalism could be ignored—the Middle East, Africa and large parts of Asia were still held quite comfortably by the imperial powers. Europe was the centre of the world stage, and Britain was cast in the leading role. And the Top People muffed it. That was self-evident at the time; and that is why the causes of the thirties were relatively simply and consequently so attractive. If you were asked what was wrong, you knew. If you were asked what should be done about it, you produced a petition, a membership card, or a leaflet advertising the mass meeting next Sunday afternoon.

Things are not so simple now. For years we have lacked causes— or should I say that for years we have been unable to recognize them? It does not matter which way you put it. Something happened to paralyse both passion and action. True, there were causes. To me, the peril of nuclear war seems just as great a threat as Hitler's form of genocide. I feel that some kind of agreement between East and West is just as urgent as collective security seemed in the thirties. I detest concepts of racial superiority. Much of Britain is still slum, still squalid, and even those parts of it that remain unspoiled are falling into the hands of the subtopians. I am appalled by the poverty that remains among the aged and the chronic sick, by the gross overcrowding of our State schools, by our overloaded and inadequate hospitals, our archaic prisons, blue-laws and sexual attitudes that are a relic of pre-Freudian prejudice, by the triviality of our newspapers. I do not like a society in which the Establishment is riddled by snobbery and false values. And in all this I know that I am not alone, nor am I alone in saying this. But many who have complained most, like Sir Orlando Drought in Trollope's novel *The Prime Minister*, that 'everything is dead' in politics, have somehow lacked the effort of will to liven everything up. They felt restless, perhaps, cynical more often; but too often they talked themselves into a mood of resignation and retreated into private worlds.

What explains this change? One reason, I believe, is that so much of what was happening seemed irrelevant to these private worlds—

and we have had to wait until we again heard the shouting under the window to realize that, out there, it was still real and unpleasant and dreadfully our concern. I think this mood, in part, reflects the long retreat of Britain from the first rank of world powers. Almost all our politicians, and most of the voting public, had their ideas and attitudes fashioned in a different age, and it has not been easy for them to adjust, to learn a new part for which there is no script and for which the words and actions must be improvised. It is easier to fall back upon the old clichés. It is this that has given such an air of irrelevance to so much of British politics since 1945, that has made people less sure what ought to be done, and what can be done, than they were when Westminster was one of the hinges upon which fate turned and when a shift in British policy—or a change in the balance of our political parties—might have had decisive results. It is a painful process of adjustment, and it is often humiliating, as so many discovered for the first time in that final futile fling of imperialism at Suez. Yet there is no help for it. Two world wars, punctuated by a great depression, have made it impossible for the British to compete on equal terms with America or Russia, or even to hold what they have. And there is nothing ahead but disaster if our leaders go on striking postures the country lacks the muscle to sustain.

Of course, Britain still has influence, still resources. But this country has become much more dependent on the whims and interests of others over whom we have little or no control. And you cannot arouse much enthusiasm, or move people to action, for causes that seem either irrelevant or unreal. One may deplore some aspects of American diplomacy—the flinty recalcitrance of Mr Dulles, for instance, or the non-recognition of Peking—or condemn the Soviet intervention in Hungary. But demonstrations in Trafalgar Square are not likely to have more than the most marginal effect on opinion in Congress or on the decisions made in the Kremlin. 'Force America and Russia to give up the bomb' was a slogan used in mid-1958: it shows that this misunderstanding persists. It is only when there is some plain relation between cause and result that the crust of apathy is broken. The Anglo-French war against Egypt was a case in point. It was *our* Government that was responsible, *our* troops that were committing aggression. So the wave of protest was both morally justified and politically relevant, and there was again a straightforward cause: Eden Must Go! Or consider the origins of the campaign against the H-bomb that suddenly took fire at the end of 1957. For some years it has been clear that a nuclear war would mean the extinction of civilized life in this country, even that the continuation of nuclear tests was a grave if undefined hazard. But despite the anxiety that any thinking person must have felt the public was lethargic. The problem was beyond us—or so it seemed. Would agitation in Britain stop the manufacture of nuclear weapons in New Mexico or Siberia, or the tests of Eniwetok or in Kamschatka? Then came the flash of protest. What caused it? The discovery that American bombers armed with nuclear weapons were flying on operational patrols from bases in this country: the cold statement that it was impossible to protect the civilian population of Britain against nuclear attack; and the decision that made such attack more likely—a chain of offensive missile bases along our eastern coast. Each of these issues raised complicated questions about the purpose of the Western alliance, and our part in it; about the value of the deterrent; and about Anglo-American relations. But they seemed to be within the jurisdiction of the British Government, and so protest could thus be relevant and perhaps effective.

Still, that is not the whole story, at least so far as the Left is concerned. Something else happened after 1945. Before, and during the war, the Left could comfortably marry two convictions: the threat to peace came from the Fascist aggressors, and the cause of peace and progress was championed by the Soviet Union. For all the known peculiarities of Stalin's Russia and the contortions of the Comintern, the Left commonly assumed that the Communists were on the right side. True, there was a sticky patch between 1939 and 1941, but there was then a second honeymoon until the Cold War began. But once there was a Cold War—how it started and why is another confusing question—the easy propositions of the thirties no longer seemed to make sense, and the Left was without a simple integrated answer to world problems. The world was divided into two systems of power, and that division cut right across the old lines of belief. Those who could not wholeheartedly back either system became the odd men out. It was impossible, for both political and emotional reasons, for anyone on the Left to feel happy about the course of anti-Communism in the West, to accept Chiang Kai-shek, or Syngman Rhee, or Bao Dai, as allies, to endorse the over-simple slogan that the 'free world' was in mortal danger of Soviet aggression, or to become an enthusiast for the rearmament of Germany only six years after the survivors were rescued from Belsen and Buchenwald. But it was equally impossible, in the face of the evidence, to insist any longer that 'there are no enemies to the Left' : in Russia, Stalinism was reaching its climax; in eastern Europe, the revolution from above was being ruthlessly imposed at immense cost and with staggering mistakes; and, all over the world, Communists were promoting 'peace' movements which did nothing but echo the current line of Soviet diplomacy. Understandably, the Left became fragmented and confused.

This was true in an even wider context than foreign policy. For to the degree that the apparent success of the Soviet Union in the thirties—and its military power in the forties—had provided a psychological crutch for the Left, so the reaction to Stalinism created disillusion and dismay. More than it had realized the Left had drawn strength from its belief that Russia 'had gone over into the future'. If, for those who have the benefit of hindsight, this merely suggests that the Left was simple-minded, I beg them to go back and read the newspapers and books of the thirties to understand why this should have been so. There was more to this belief than the compensation that impotence finds vicariously in potency : it was based upon the conviction that, whatever its faults, the Soviet Union had proved conclusively that 'Socialism' could work. Thus, Socialism was equated with Soviet Communism—and the power of the equation was not really diminished by qualifications about the peculiar historical conditions of Russia. The Left profited from that equation in the thirties. In the post-war years the equation was read the other way : no one can yet assess how much damage was done to the notion of Socialism because it became identified with the distortions and, in many respects, profoundly anti-Socialist perversions of Stalin's Russia. I do not suggest that it was merely the Left that became demoralized : the public as a whole became distrustful of any course, however innocuous and well-intentioned, that might seem in the end to lead to a totalitarian tyranny, to create the equality of the slave-camp in the name of human brotherhood, and to establish a society that was devoid of moral judgment because it had become the instrument of historical necessity.

All these are external reasons for apathy. But what happened here at home to change us? How did things go wrong? Anyway, what is wrong?

There is one answer to these questions that is facile and insidious. It is the theory of the English Disease. We are, so the argument runs, suffering from a national malaise, a form of political sclerosis brought on by the exertions of the war and the compulsive search for comfort and security that followed it. The trouble, we are told, is that we are taxed to death and molly-coddled into the grave; that we are dominated by the Americans, outwitted by the Russians, defied by Egyptians and Cypriots, outsold by Germans; that our workers have become clock-watchers, that the greed of the trade unions is the cause of inflation, and that our Civil Servants are bureaucratic slaves to Parkinson's Law. So, say the cynics, we have lost our pride and our ambition, and even the pleasures of life have become tatty and unsatisfying. John Bull died at Dunkirk, and his place has has been taken by Archie Rice, well-intentioned, incompetent and desperately bored. Where, in this England, is there a place for the ambitious man with fresh ideas? Nowhere: there is no incentive for him to get on, or to seek opportunity for his children, and it is better to get out to Canada or Australia while there is still a chance, leaving the decaying family home to the deadbeats who have taken it over. Let them sit around, while the rain comes through the roof, reading the headlines that chronicle our descent from greatness and turning from them with a yawn to check the pool coupons or to blur their eyes and minds on the seventeen-inch telly.

You've heard all this, haven't you? You've even said some of it, haven't you? For it has enough substance in it to make it glitter attractively, as the clever counterfeit mixes silver with the dross. But it is a forgery, minted by the middle class and circulated assiduously by those who have managed to climb, since the war, into the middle class. Of all those I dislike, it is the phoney disillusioned patriot I dislike the most, the man who moans of the grandeur that was Rickmansworth and the glory that was Cheam, morally insensi-

tive and intellectually lazy, who believes that the world in general
and the British working class in particular owe him a living. What
he really means, when he talks of the English Disease, is the failure
of post-war Britain to give him the rewards he was brought up to
consider his due.

If this were all, I would not mind. But such a sense of frustration
is not confined to the middle class—that is why some of its resent-
ments can gain general currency. Too many who should have
known better have been complacent, unwilling to ask what are
the real choices that face us or the true cost of pursuing them. The
world has been going to hell around them, and they have done too
little about it, because it has been more comfortable to drift. This,
I believe, is the peculiar quality of this generation's crime against
itself and its children. It has been indifferent, caught up in the
problems and the satisfactions of a private world. I think it was
a Soviet novelist who wrote a book called *The Revolt of the
Indifferent*; anyway, its maxim sticks in my mind. 'Do not fear
your friends,' he said. 'They can only betray you. Do not fear your
enemies. They can only defeat you. But fear the indifferent, for it
is their indifference that makes it possible for your friends to betray
you and your enemies to defeat you.' A Communist society—
indeed, any authoritarian régime—forces indifference upon the
mass of the population as an act of policy. Indifference is almost a
social virtue. If you are indifferent, and work hard, you get a medal,
or a holiday at a rest home, or a larger apartment. The only condition is that you do not ask awkward questions or otherwise make
life difficult for the party bosses who remain bosses because you
are indifferent. But we have not had indifference thrust upon us:
we have acquired it, and we have accepted it because it makes less
trouble, not for our bosses, but for ourselves. Its classic symptom
is the question: Why bother?

Why, indeed, when there is a failure of morals? Am I my
brother's timekeeper, his teacher, his healer, his town-planner? Not
if I can help it, Jack. Nothing is for nothing, nothing is for free.
I'll look after you, Jack, when you look after me. Do you give up
because you are betrayed, or defeated? No. It is because nobody
cares. But it is not because nobody dreams any more. Oh, no. We
are full of dreams, but they are dreams of a vanished past, because

nostalgia is the opium of the people. The Germans do not look back
—behind them are only cruelty, ruins, collapse. The Russians do
not look back—the future cannot be worse than the past. The
Americans do not look back—the future has always seemed better
than the present. But our ruling class turns away to that old faith
in God, Crown and Empire, the Victorian Trinity, at once secure
and omnipotent; our middle class turns away to the creature com-
forts that went with world power, cheap labour at home and even
cheaper labour abroad; and even the working class, which knew
that it was ill-used, exploited and denied its rights, had at least the
New Jerusalem to set against its poverty and its impotence.

For the Britain in which we have been living has lacked hope as
it lacked anger. Our society has become a caucus race without great
rewards or punishments but with small prizes for everyone. The
businessman has his expense account, his car on the firm; there are
prestige jobs for members of the old ruling class who find themselves at a loose end; the middle class have the Health Service and
washing-machines; the worker's family has its television set; all of
us have that warming, cosy, huggable symbol of our nostalgia—
the Happy Family, the ultimate in advertising. The monarchy today
is unimportant, benign, and utterly irrelevant to anything that
matters; but it has become the central pillar of the new Establishment. Round it cluster the modern Barnacles of all the Circumlocu-
tion Offices—The Tame Men, the masters of the soft phrase and
the indecisive policy, holding the good jobs in government departments, running our radio and television programmes and our newspapers, making speeches, fixing things up, doing a good job of
public relations to persuade us that we have all arrived, or that
enough of us have arrived to make Gilbert's point: 'When everyone is somebody, then no one's anybody.' Their watchword is
Humbug, and their aim is Compromise. They would have us
qualify, rub off the sharp edges of life, forget what it is like to love
or hate passionately, to praise honestly or condemn with conviction. They make hypocrisy the condition of success, plain speech
a gross indiscretion, and mediocrity the most useful of all the
talents. They would have us be genteel, bowing and scraping in
meaningless rituals that bear no relation to the real problems that
face us—the H-bomb, the sputnik, Arab nationalism, and all the

other jokers that history has added to the pack. What good is it for them to keep on assuring us that we are on the threshold of a New Elizabethan Age in which we shall again reap rich harvests, while they make us indifferent to the future by feeding us the seed corn? But do not blame them only, for we all are guilty. We let them get away with it, because we know that much of the past was intolerable and because we have been willing to settle for a present that may be unexciting but is tolerable and bearable.

I put this question to those who must answer it. Why do we let them get away with it? Why does the new Establishment ride upon our backs? It is not enough to say that we were betrayed or defeated, and that the Tories came back. We allowed them to come back because we misread the banner under which we marched on that sunny July morning in 1945. We thought it bore the device: 'Let Us Face The Future'. In fact it read: 'Let Us Solve The Problems Of The Past'. It was not an unworthy mistake, or one that could easily have been avoided. Nor do I minimize what was achieved. But it is now quite clear that the programme on which the Attlee Government worked so hard was designed in its essentials to liquidate arrears, to create the social and economic pattern which was the alternative to Baldwin's England. In this, despite the difficulties caused by the war, but also helped by the post-war mood, it largely succeeded. More, even this limited and overdue reform made such a difference to our economy that we have ever since been living off the proceeds. But it did not create what Mr Anthony Crosland calls a 'post-capitalist' society, still less a half-way house to Socialism. What it did was to marry social reform to a capitalist boom, and thus create a society far better than anything we had known before: the old causes withered, and the fire died in bellies that had at last been filled. Those who have grown up since the war, within the cocoon of full employment, may feel frustrated. But what is their frustration compared to the satisfaction that the post-war years brought to those who spent a lifetime of struggle for the objectives that were achieved after 1945? They gave Jarrow work, and India freedom. They narrowed the spectrum of poverty and wealth. They provided new homes, new factories, new social services. What more, they ask, could be needed than an improved version of contemporary Britain?

No more, if you are content with this society of paradoxes, this stalemate state. For it is a remarkable achievement. It incorporates much of the social machinery from the Socialist catalogue, but its motive power remains private gain; it has made the distribution of income less unequal, but it has not really changed the distribution of wealth; it employs the rhetoric of democracy, but it has placed power increasingly in the hands of non-responsible oligarchs and their bureaucratic subordinates; it talks of equality, but observes the rituals of class; it offers somewhat greater educational opportunity to the children of the working class, but the price of admission is surrender to the values and objectives derived from the needs of Victorian capitalism; it has improved the status of women, but it has found no way of tapping the reservoir of energy and trained ability thus created; and though, at last, we have one vote for every man and woman, it has made the ordinary voter more sceptical about the value of that vote and increasingly cynical about party politics. It has made Tories the reluctant servants of the Welfare Society, and Socialists into pillars of the Establishment. It is in many ways more moral, more humane, than any society we have known, and yet it has made too many of us morally indifferent. It was created as the climax to a century of Socialist effort, but among its successes must be counted a paralysis of Socialist thinking.

As I look at this society—if you want a clumsy sociological name for it you might try 'social-bureaucratic State capitalism'—I cannot help recalling the vision of William Morris. I do not mean the golden fancy of *News From Nowhere*: this flash of insight comes from an essay he wrote towards the end of his life in which he asked whether the Fabian-style reforms then coming in vogue might not 'dull the efforts of the whole class of workers towards the winning of a real society of equals'. As he suggested, 'the Society of Inequality might . . . accept the quasi-Socialist machinery and work it for the upholding of that society, in a somewhat shorn condition, maybe, but a safe one. . . . The workers themselves better treated, better organized, helping to govern themselves, but with no more pretence of real equality with the rich, nor any more hope for it, than they have now'. In such a society, said Morris, we should be satisfied with some outward show of Socialism, joined to 'an increase in prosperity to satisfy the cravings of men who do not know what the pleasures of life might be if they treated their own capacities and the resources of nature reasonably, with the intention and expectation of being happy'.

This seems to me a fair description of the stalemate state, and it has come about for precisely the reasons that Morris foresaw. When we have a Conservative Party and a party of reform that accept the balance of great interests we are bound to be committed to negations and indecision. Each side can march us to the polls to keep the other side out; each side can mobilize grievances rather than aspirations; each side will fear decision, because decision may lose votes. For the aim is stability, a system in which the Establishment is tolerated because it no longer behaves like a ruling class at bay, and in which some of the claims of the working class are met because it does not seek to dispossess the Establishment altogether. But such stability is by its nature more favourable to the Conservative interest: one may lop off branches from the tree of the Establishment, but while its roots remain undisturbed it will send out new limbs. As Morris pointed out, 'the tremendous organization of civilized commercial society'—his phrase for what we call the Establishment—can play a game of cat-and-mouse with reformers as long as they accept its rules for the game of politics. It does not require a policy: its purpose is to avoid change or to limit the extent of change when it is unavoidable. It has great reserves of power, and a remarkable ability to absorb the shock of reform. Above all, except in times of crisis, it enjoys the benefit of the doubt. In office, or in opposition, it can depend upon social inertia, upon all the instincts and agencies which two hundred years of the acquisitive society have developed as the defences of property, privilege and inequality.

The Labour movement has no such natural reserves. What it has achieved, either by industrial or political action, is the result of struggle, of the use of what Professor Galbraith has called 'the countervailing power'. By employing the processes of democracy it has modified our society and improved its own position until it is now too powerful to be destroyed without tearing society apart.

But though it may escape destruction, it can become the prisoner of the Establishment.

This, indeed, is why the Labour Party has found it so difficult to break out of the bridgehead that it wedged into the acquisitive society in 1945. For to the extent that it made Britain a more tolerable place in which to live, it made the electorate more tolerant: by its own success it seemed to diminish both the case for further change and the public desire for it. There are policy-makers in the Labour Party who fear that a more radical pro-gramme, however satisfying to the sentiments of the rank-and-file, might simply cost the party the next election because it would appear captious, dogmatic and irrelevant to marginal voters. That is one part of the dilemma that has plagued the party since 1950. But the other part is equally important. Without a Socialist pur-pose that is renewed in each generation, a radical party is bound to appear colourless, timid, sclerotic, a collection of professional politicians waiting to inherit office because of the blunders of the Government. Until the Labour Party solves that dilemma—and I believe that the disintegration of the stalemate state as a result of internal stresses and external pressure has already begun—it is bound to mark time and to lose time that we cannot afford to lose.

So much for the past. Will the future be different, or can we make it different? Can we avoid the Age of the Oligarchs, and defeat the faceless men of power? I believe we can. But we must know why we want to do this before we can say how we propose to do it. That means, first, we must regain confidence in man's ability to control the social and technical machinery he has himself created. This I put as the central Socialist objective. And the second is closely related to it. It is the belief that it is co-operation rather than conflict that gives dignity and purpose to our lives. The acquisitive society is based upon an ethic which runs directly counter to these two principles, and it is its denial of them that, fundamentally, makes me a Socialist, that makes me ask what life could be like if we treated our own capacities and the resources of nature reasonably, with the intention and the expectation of being happy.

These are general terms, and something more than this is required from those who call themselves Socialists in this generation. As I look back on the thirties, I realize how much was put in sweeping statements and how little was spelt out in detail. It was enough, perhaps, to say that planning would eliminate unemployment, without describing what plans would do it, how they would be drawn up, who would enforce them; to say that public ownership would transform our industries, without showing how, precisely, it would transform them, and to what effect; to say that social legislation would abolish inequality, without carefully considering how the roots of inequality might remain alive. I take only three examples to make the point. Consider, next, the vastly different problems that we face, now that we know more about the complex nature of modern industrial society—the contrast between our daily life and the possibilities that headlong scientific advance has created, the relationship between planning and human behaviour, the sociology of giant enterprises, the attitude of managerial *élites*, the conflict between the desire to consume and the need to invest, the complex relation between social welfare and our concepts of morality and liberty. Consider, too, the difficulty of enlisting the willing co-operation and intelligent effort of the technicians and specialists upon whom success in tackling these problems depends. And, finally, consider how hard it will be to change the values—and here I think of human relationships as well as of the vast 'cultural' machine which shapes them—ingrained by our experience of living in the acquisitive society. No wonder that is seems easier to stumble along the path of pragmatic reform, hoping that the next Labour Government, or the one after that, will somehow legislate us into a hygienic paradise.

Yet the difficult alternative is the right one, and in choosing it we recognize that to this generation belongs the responsibility of the transition. More than ever before we have the material resources, and the means of expanding and applying them, which can remake our life in this country and the life of the millions who exist at the margin all over the world. We can choose to do that, or we can choose indifference. The contributors to this book have made their choice.

In the room at the top

I N NOVEMBER 1956 I was chosen by the Halifax Labour Party as their prospective candidate. Thereafter, until I moved to London a few months ago, every third weekend I travelled from my home in Harlow to my new constituency.

It was a strange journey. I was travelling, not just from Essex to the West Riding but between two industrial revolutions, between two centuries. I left behind me a New Town, one of a dozen or so that have been built in post-war Britain; a town of steel and glass, concrete and plastic, shining with light and colour. Seven hours later I arrived in a town of sombre stone and brick, blackened by time and smoke; a town of tall factory chimneys and church spires. It was a journey from the new world of planning and welfare to the old world that capitalism had built.

It was a journey, too, between two sorts of politics. In Halifax, the greater part of Socialism is the physical re-equipment of society; new houses and schools, slum clearance, modern factories, even bathrooms and kitchens—the needs that made the Labour Party a mass movement. In Harlow there were practical problems too: house building was outpacing the schools, rents were much too high, bus services inadequate. But one felt that these were growing pains, problems that would in the reasonably near future find their solutions. At root, politics were already, or would soon be, about something different: about human relationships more than social amenities, about power rather than poverty.

Harlow and Halifax are extreme contrasts. But all over Britain a new mid-twentieth-century society is coming vigorously to life. It is not just bricks and mortar that mark the change. Our way of life is being profoundly transformed. Full employment and the post-war break-through in science and technology have been the outstanding events. But there have been others, too, scarcely less important. Living standards have risen. More people have modern houses, motor cars, washing machines, vacuum cleaners, and this will continue as long as—but how long?—full employment lasts. Clever but poor children have now a better chance of getting a decent education. The State is more involved in the welfare of its citizens and more active in the regulation of the economy. Tax rates are high and are said to redistribute income.

Industry too is changing. New industries such as atomic energy, oil refining and air transport have grown up, while old industries such as coal mining and textiles are clearly in decline. With the new industries come new products, new methods, a change even in the nature of work. In organization and structure there have been major developments too. The family business has been replaced by the giant corporation as the dominant institution in the economy. Moreover, the tempo of change appears to be increasing. Scarcely a week passes without one of our leading corporations proclaiming some fresh advance in industrial technology and science.

The emergence from all these changes of a new mid-twentieth-century society poses questions, creates problems. Of one at least my journeys from Harlow to Halifax made me acutely conscious. The unevenness of contemporary development has greatly increased the complexity of British politics. Policies that seem right in one set of circumstances may be wrong or irrelevant in another. To assert that 'things have changed' may be taken in Harlow as a simple statement of fact, in Halifax as a sign of complacency. Always now, if one is not to be misunderstood, it is necessary to explain which society, the old or the new, one is talking about.

But while the past and its problems will be with us for many decades, it is the new, emergent society that commands attention. Clearly we are moving into unfamiliar territory and many of the old landmarks that have guided us in the past are, one by one, dipping down behind the horizon. To map the new political landscape has become, therefore, a most urgent task. For unless we know where we are, unless we know the direction in which new forces are taking us, we can be no more than the creatures of events.

What kind of society then are we creating? Is it, as different writers have suggested, a Welfare State or an Opportunity State, a Mixed Economy or a Post-Capitalist Society? Should we call the 'system' Statism, or Last Stage Capitalism, or what?

Of two things at least we can be certain: that the emerging post-war society is significantly different from pre-war and that whatever else it may be it is not and is not tending towards a Socialist society.

In 1939 James Burnham wrote the *Managerial Revolution*. Initially well received—in Britain it earned a large Pelican edition —it is now probably one of the least read and certainly one of the least fashionable works of political analysis in the English language. There are several reasons for this. The later works and conduct of the author did not add to his reputation for sagacity. But more important, the theory itself has always been anathema to those to whom it was principally addressed—to Socialists because the arrival of a 'managerial class' on the stage of history is a denial of a century's hopes and promise; to property owners because the management class is felt to be a potential threat, a 'Trojan Horse', smuggled into the citadel of private property.

Whatever the reason, its eclipse is a pity: for the *Managerial Revolution* is, in spite of weaknesses, an important and suggestive book which throws out certain essential clues to the understanding of our new society.

Burnham began by restating the familiar Socialist analysis of capitalist society: that its decisive division lies between those who own and control the means of production and those who do not; between the employers who buy other people's labour and the employees who must sell their own.

From this division springs the typical class and power structure of a capitalist society. To the men of property accrue the rewards of ownership, the status and power of decision makers; to the propertyless, the insecurity, low rewards and inferior status of those who depend on others for their means of life.

Burnham, moreover, shared the Socialist faith in the coming collapse of capitalism. Its fundamental instability, its endemic unemployment, as well as its injustices, would eventually prove intolerable to the rest of society and the whole system would ultimately be swept away.

But by whom? It is at this point that Burnham and orthodox Marxists sharply diverge. To the latter, it is the exploited class, the working class, which is both the agent of change and its chief beneficiary. Its historic task is to break down the economic and political power of the property-owning class, to replace private ownership of the means of production with public or State ownership and to reorganize society in the interests of the masses.

Burnham's heresy—and contribution to political thought—was not to deny the breakdown of capitalism nor even the replacement of private by public ownership, but to assert that a new class, the managers—and not the proletariat—would be both the agents of change and its chief beneficiaries.

On what was this prediction based? Mainly, as Burnham argued it, on the evidence of two major developments in the contemporary world: first, the conspicuous failure of the working class and its political and industrial organizations to make an effective challenge to organized power; and secondly, the vigorous growth, within the institution of private ownership itself, of a non-owning managerial class in direct physical control of the means of production.

Burnham saw the growth of the managerial class as a worldwide development—in Germany and Russia, the United States and elsewhere. Communism, Fascism and Nazism were, in his view, simply the new ideologies which the managerial classes used to legitimize or rationalize their own rule.

Two of Burnham's caveats need to be recalled. He was careful to explain that his use of the phrase 'managerial revolution' did not imply a sudden seizure of power but rather—as we speak of an 'industrial revolution'—an historical trend which, when full grown, would radically transform the economic and power structure of industrial society. And he was careful, too, to make the point that in the capitalist democracies the managers were not yet in control; they were simply on their way.

Burnham's analysis has been strongly criticized and there is much of it that I do not myself accept. In particular, the managers are, in the British context, not so much a new ruling class as—if social background and outlook are the tests—the old ruling class in a new occupational role. Moreover, although the interests of the managerial and the property-owning groups often diverge, there is no fundamental antagonism which would lead the former to actively seek the abolition of private property rights.

Yet, allowing for these and other objections, the central thesis of the *Managerial Revolution* has survived the years remarkably well. For it is surely incontrovertible that a transfer of power is taking place in modern industry : that the new controllers rather than the old owners of property are its chief beneficiaries and that society, in its goals and organization, increasingly reflects the needs of managerial man.

In industry itself the corroborative evidence is inescapable. No facet of our changing society is so arresting as the rapid and continuing concentration of economic power under the aegis of the great corporations. In the advanced industrial countries it is a general phenomenon. Professor Galbraith's saying that the controllers of American industry 'could be seated comfortably in almost any neighbourhood motion picture theatre' is equally true of Germany, France, Canada, South Africa and Britain. Indeed the statistical pictures are nearly identical. In the U.K. as in the U.S. a few hundred of the largest corporations now control the bulk of industry and finance.

This is a remarkable development. Only thirty years ago such firms as Unilever and I.C.I. were considered as atypical giants, mountain peaks, towering above the foothills of the capitalist economy. Today in practically every trade, service and industry, giant firms are firmly established. Thus, in this short span of years, the giant firms have become the dominant and typical institutions in the economy.

Since the main sources of scientific research, of capital and of managerial skill, out of which the future must be built, are now firmly controlled by the great corporations, no reversal of the trend can reasonably be expected. Indeed we seem already to be moving on to a new stage in which the giant firm is itself superseded by the still larger consortium or group.

It is, of course, the emergence of the large corporation that has first created and then enlarged the numbers and power of the managerial class. Their basic functions are to administer, organize and co-ordinate the corporation's affairs. As these increase in number and range, as modern technology becomes more complex and as the great corporations simply continue their growth, so the managers thrive and their numbers multiply. A single firm, Unilever, can now boast of 27,000 management men.

The managers are often described as an officer class and this is in many ways an apt analogy. There is between the works manager and the managing director the same vast stretch of authority and function that separates the subaltern from the general. In the corporate no less than the service world, privilege and power are organized on strictly hierarchical lines. The type of car, the size of the office, the pile of the carpet, all denote the exact status of the managerial man. It has been said of one great firm that you can even measure a man's position by the manner in which he receives his afternoon tea : he gets it from the trolley; he is given a cup and a saucer; he has it on a tray. On it goes, with meticulous discrimination, to the pinnacle where a secretary pours from silver jugs. But while the managers themselves are so nicely distinguished, one from another, by rank and power, they are as a group still more clearly differentiated in status and rewards from the men they command.

Inevitably, the managers develop an *esprit de corps*, a common outlook. The community of work interest spills over into social life. The corporation which gives so much becomes the main focus of interest and loyalty.

Inevitably, too, their power over corporate enterprise has greatly increased. At the highest levels, the skills, contacts and expert knowledge of the top managers are now essential. In the Board Room itself—especially after the Founder's death—the corporate managers take hold of the reins of power. More and more those who run the affairs of our great corporations are drawn from the cadres of professional managers. Like the high commands of the Civil and Armed Services the Board Rooms are increasingly manned by wholetime experts with long years of service behind them.

I do not wish to exaggerate the speed with which this process is being accomplished. There remain, of course, many large firms under total or partial family control and there are, too, in the Board Room—and these will stay—the representatives of the financial institutions: the pension funds, the investment trusts, the men from the Pru and the Pearl. But the trend is strongly in favour of the management men, whether they be corporate or institutional managers—and it is strongly against continued family or individual control.

These then are the men who control the giant firms, who make the big decisions in industry, who decide the shape of the economy and its pace of advance. In so far, therefore, as industry remains the place of power in our society, these men are the power holders.

While the top managers are tightening their control over the great corporations, the power of their nominal masters, the general body of shareholders, is clearly weakening. In one sense this is part of the general trend within all large organizations—the big union, the big co-operative society, the major political party, as well as the large corporation—in which power, along with expertise, concentrates in the hands of permanent officials. As the number of shareholders multiplies—and the giant corporation numbers its owners in tens of thousands—their ability to exercise individual influence or even collective control steadily weakens. This is exemplified in the typical company A.G.M. Perhaps twenty or thirty shareholders will turn up, perhaps a question or two will be asked. Then the report is adopted, the dividend approved, the directors reappointed—and that, unless a Sir Bernard Docker is in the chair, is all.

But the great corporations have not only escaped the control of their own shareholders, they are becoming increasingly independent of the whole property-owning class. For much the larger part of the new capital they need for replacement and expansion is not now borrowed from the private investor, it is self-generated. Through their monopolistic or semi-monopolistic control of prices, the great corporations are able to accumulate most of the capital they need. To an increasing extent, too, the State is prepared to assist in capital formation—through depreciation allowances, through investment allowances, through special finance corporations. And, if outside capital is needed, the Board can turn not only to the private shareholder but to the institutions and other corporations.

In the large corporations, therefore, the shareholder is not only losing control, he is ceasing to be necessary. In the earlier stages of capitalism he performed two great roles: he provided the money and he shouldered the risk. Today both functions can be, and increasingly are, performed without him.

Loss of function and loss of control point inescapably to the long-term decline of the shareholding class. Just over five years ago, reflecting the change in the power relationships of owners and controllers in modern industry, Mr Harold Wincott addressed the Institute of Directors in these touching words: 'I feel most strongly that anything—and I mean anything—that can be done to improve the status of the shareholder, anything that makes him feel important and wanted and a desirable and respected member of the community should be a worthy objective of company directors.'

But, of course, the acid test is reward. Are shareholders getting more or less than they did? The answer, in spite of a substantial recovery during the past seven years of Conservative rule, is unmistakably less. That is to say, their share of the national income is considerably smaller than it was in 1938; dividends, in real terms, have actually fallen and share values, in spite of capital gains, are in real terms far lower than they were before the war. Yet this decline in shareholders' rewards has taken place during a period in which the real value of industrial property has increased by at least fifty per cent.

We are of course dealing in long-term movements. Pocket handkerchiefs can be put away, for the shareholding class, though no longer increasing its wealth, has the vast accumulation of one hundred and fifty years of industrial growth on which to draw. Furthermore, within the body of shareholders, astute individuals still have ample opportunities to amass great personal wealth.

To what conclusions does this analysis lead? I would argue first that a transfer of power is taking place within the large corporations from the body of individual shareholders to the corporate and institutional managers. I would argue, too, that the top managers have interests which are separate from those of the titular owners. The managers are in the first place interested in the aggrandizement of the corporation, for their own ambitions can only be gratified through corporate growth. In the second place the rewards of top managers increasingly depend on the salaries, fees, emoluments and perks to which they are entitled by virtue of their employment. Unless they are also men of great wealth, the size of the dividend is ceasing to be a matter of major personal concern. To the share-holder, on the other hand, dividends and capital gains are of over-riding importance. From these differences there can spring and does spring a conflict of interest between the controllers and owners of the modern corporation.

But it does *not* follow that, under managerial control, the motiva-tions of economic activity have significantly altered. The corporate manager no less than the individual shareholder or the old captain of industry is out to maximize profits. Such differences as there are arise only as to how the profits should be allocated.

Nor does it follow that their use of economic power will be in any sense more responsible. All it means is that the corporate as distinct from the individual interest will normally be paramount.

Finally, as we shall now see, this shift of power does not lead, nor can it be expected to lead, to greater equality, to a more rational economic system, to the decline of class institutions or the demo-cratization of power.

Ruling groups do not long deny themselves the rewards of power. If, therefore, a kind of palace revolution is in fact taking place in modern industry, the supremacy of the new managerial *élite* will sooner or later reveal itself in the enjoyment and organization of privilege. Indeed the magnitude of its privileges can be taken as a rough index of its power.

There are in fact numerous signs in contemporary Britain that privilege is attaching itself to the managerial class. To describe it is one thing, but to quantify it is another, for our statistical apparatus records far more accurately old forms of property income than the new forms of managerial reward.

Consequently, our statistics give an entirely misleading impres-sion of the state of privilege generally. For example, national in-come, Inland Revenue and estate duty figures purport to show, res-pectively, the shares of broad classes in the total national income, the difference between incomes before and after tax and the size of personal fortunes at the time of death. Using these sources only it would be easy to demonstrate that, over the past two decades, a great movement towards equality has taken place : that the share of wage earners has greatly increased; that large incomes, after income and surtax, have been drastically reduced; that the age of great personal fortunes is passing away.

Translated into ways of living, the figures suggest a society in which conspicuous consumption can no longer be the day-to-day expectations of a privileged class but only the occasional indulgence of those who, like honeymoon couples, must live for much the greater part of their lives at far more modest levels. But patently this is not so. The Savoy Grill has its regular clientele; the first-class airlines are full; the waiting lists at the expensive public schools grow longer; the Silver Wraiths, the Pullmans and the Sapphires with their uniformed chauffeurs purr in ever increasing numbers along the London approach roads. Country houses may change hands but very few fall into disuse.

Much of the apparent contradiction between statistical and visual evidence can be resolved in the single phrase : 'tax avoidance'. The privilege is real enough. What has changed is mainly the *methods* by which it is financed and, to a lesser extent, the class of persons who enjoy it. In the past, the finance of privilege was undertaken by individuals from the dividends, interest and other income which as property owners they received. Since companies paid out in dividends the greater part of their profits and since income tax was low, the flow of wealth from the point where it was created—the workshop or the farm—to the property owner was virtually unchecked. Once received, it flowed out again, according to individual preference, to purchase privilege in its different forms.

Today, the flow of wealth is interrupted at two points. First, there now stand between the profits of production and the owners of property the managerial men. Their interests, although not dramatically opposed to those of the property owners, are, as we have seen, sufficiently distinct to push a substantial part of corporate funds into new channels which benefit themselves. Second, taxation now erects a high dam between corporate wealth and its enjoyment by property owners. The effects of these developments on the shareholders' rewards is to turn what was once a torrent of wealth into a much more modest stream. Yet productive wealth, dammed up in company reserves, grows larger. It is this that now falls under the exclusive control of the corporate managers.

Thus we have in fact a new facet of income redistribution—not the movement of resources from the well-to-do to the less well off, or from the citizen to the State, of which we have heard so much—but from the private individual to the private corporation. It is a change of immense importance. In less than two decades there has been a fivefold increase in retained profits, an enormous enrichment of corporate funds. From this there springs one of the distinguishing features of a managerial society—the corporate finance of privilege.

So far two stages in its development can be discerned. First, there is the use of corporate funds to supplement management incomes, to compensate the chosen for the tax encroachments of the State. There are many forms such aid can take : the provision of pensions, cars, expense allowances, interest-free loans, etc.—the shape being determined by the provisions of the tax code. All this is a familiar and widespread feature of our new society. A recent estimate of corporate expenditure on consumer goods reaches a total of not less than £500,000,000 a year. A third of all new cars, a quarter of travel expenditure and five per cent of drinks are now bought on business accounts.

But the second stage goes much further. Here the lives of the individual and of the corporation are in certain crucial respects integrated. The country house and the flat in town are owned by the corporation but used by the individual; the chauffeur, the butler and the gardener serve the individual but are now maintained on the company pay roll. The corporation owns its own cars, its yacht, its country club, even its aeroplane; but all are used by its senior employees. The place of work itself becomes increasingly luxurious. As the *Financial Times* reviewer of one recently constructed office block puts it :

Much attention has been devoted to interior decoration. . . .
In the conference room the rear wall is ancona walnut panelling and the flank walls are treated with white emulsion paint. The fitted carpet is of charcoal grey colour. The artificial lighting is by means of a luminated ceiling. . . .
In the ante-room the rear wall is in burr eucalyptus panelling, while the flank walls are, again, white emulsion paint. The fitted carpet is mist blue, while the wall lights and pendant fittings are in peony red.
In the luncheon room purpose-made furniture includes again a

bench seat in French walnut, a dining-table in makore to seat twenty-five, a side table also in makore and a sideboard ten feet long in mahogany and French walnut.

All these rooms have venetian blinds and dressed curtains, which impart an additional note of richness and decorative quality to the interiors of this building.

As for the directors' offices—'agreeable places in which to conduct important business'—the illustration shows—'. . . besides the chandeliers already mentioned, wall brackets, also carved gilt, the handsome desk, side table and bookcase, with single chairs in Chippendale and late eighteenth-century period'.

In short, the standard and way of life of the manager have become part of the standard and way of life of the corporation. All these expenditures, it will be noted, are not for the enjoyment of the shareholders but for the management men.

What we are witnessing surely is the rise of a new order which in certain respects is far closer to medieval society than to the capitalism of the past two hundred years. Indeed the closest analogy to the modern corporation is a survival from pre-capitalist days— the Church. In its heyday the Church was the great owner of wealth, of land, schools, hospitals and palaces. Its high functionaries wielded great power not only in their own domains but in the wider society of which they formed so large a part. They also enjoyed the wealth and privilege which their property conferred. But, and this is the key resemblance, the Princes of the Church did not own the property they enjoyed : they simply controlled it. This in turn often enabled them to amass considerable personal wealth. But even the most extensive private fortunes were negligible compared with the vast corporate wealth of the Church.

It is the same with the top managers today. They own only a small fraction of corporate wealth but they have access to it all. They may be rich in their own right but their power and influence rests on their ability to use corporate wealth for purposes of their choice.

If this is correct then it will be clear why present techniques for redistributing wealth are bound to fail. For modern taxation is based upon the fundamental assumption that wealth is individually owned. The harder, therefore, the State presses upon individual wealth and individual privilege, the more rapidly will corporate wealth and corporate privilege grow.

Philosophers have long envisaged an 'open society' in which by severe and impartial tests of native ability, the ruling group would in each generation be freshly recruited. Our own society makes earnest, but mainly abortive, attempts to achieve this goal. While the rules of democratic selection are applied, the results continue to disappoint. Nevertheless, the myth of a fairly recruited *élite* continues to dominate the public mind.

It is not surprising, therefore, that one of the claims made by those who run our great corporations is that they too, through meticulous selection and training programmes, further the aim of equal opportunities. But the facts are against them. Indeed it is the ability of the corporate managers to transmit their special advantages to their children which defines them, decisively, as a class rather than an *élite*.

In the past the main mechanisms through which privilege was transmitted from one generation to another were the inheritance of wealth and the purchase of special forms of education.

Ruling-class training has always provided two sets of qualifications: those that distinguish the ruling group from the rest of the population, in manner, culture, accent, habits of command, etc., and those qualifications of a more formal and specific kind which were recognized *entrées* to *élite* employment. Thus entry to the professions and public service required not simply a high standard of education but proficiency in special subjects—e.g. classics and modern languages—which were either not taught at all or taught with far less thoroughness in non-*élite* schools.

In finance, the land, commerce and industry, formal tests of entry were seldom set or indeed needed. Ruling-class children who embarked on industrial careers would either inherit the family business, buy company directorships or, through the network of business patronage, secure appointment to command positions.

Today, however, the old mechanisms are not working so smoothly. Inheritance has come under increasingly heavy tax. Death duties have reached the level of eighty per cent on great fortunes, and the opportunities of amassing new wealth, though still considerable, have at least been reduced by high taxation. Consequently, even when avoidance and evasion have been allowed for, the transmission of privilege has become, for at least some sections of the ruling class, increasingly difficult.

As a result there has taken place the gradual extension of corporate provision for *élite* education. An increasing number of companies now organize insurance schemes to help pay school fees. The great advantage of such arrangements—to quote the Shell brochure—'as compared with any arrangement you yourself could make with an insurance company is that your employing company will pay you the equivalent of half the annual premiums. The benefit you derive may amount to more than twice your net outlay over the whole period'. Other firms, such as Rolls-Royce and the Midland Bank, prefer to establish closed scholarships for the benefit of employees' children. Others again help the public schools by making substantial contributions to their funds. A large part of Christ's Hospital £500,000 fund, for example, was met by companies which thought it well worth while to support an educational institution which 'endeavours to provide the type of man so much required today for executive positions in commerce and industry'.

The logical conclusion of present trends would be the maintenance by companies of their own schools—as the City Guilds once provided them centuries ago. In fact this has already happened. The 'first public school to be founded since the war' was started 'for industry'. 'A scheme has been worked out under which companies are to be invited to pay one or more annual sums of £225 to the School Governors. Each initial payment of £225 per annum will entitle the payer to nominate a boy for the school entrance tests who, if successful, will receive free education and board up to the value of this payment.'

Not only are the corporations now undertaking the finance of privileged education: they are increasingly reshaping its content to meet the special requirements of a managerial society. The social and attitude training which the public schools have long provided is, in the main, of enduring value in the new society. What needs to be changed is not the outlook of a ruling group but its formal qualifications. For the skills needed in modern industry are significantly different from those required in the old *élite* occupations

—government service and the professions. They require above all understanding and competence in the broad fields of technology and science.

In the last decade a very remarkable change has been accomplished in the curricula of the *élite* schools. The science side is being greatly strengthened, helped by such inducements as the £3,500,000 industry fund created for the purpose. There has never been a time when industry and the *élite* schools have been in closer contact with each other, or more aware of their mutual problems, or more anxious to serve each other. Representatives of the Headmasters' Conference, the grammar schools and the Federation of British Industries meet in regular session. The Public Schools Appointments Board maintains close and continuous contact with business firms.

Those who imagine that the problem of the public schools will disappear because they have been traditionally linked with a ruling group now in decline, or that the expansion of State-financed technical colleges will provide the base for a new and more democratic *élite*, will have to think again. Far from a decline of the public schools, it is reasonable to assume that if present trends continue, there will be a major expansion of private education in the years ahead. Not only are the *élite* schools adapting themselves more quickly than State schools to the needs of the new age: their connections with industry are so strong and intimate that their products are already assured of preferential treatment.

Of course the needs of industry during this period of rapid industrial growth and change are such that they cannot be fully satisfied by management recruitment drawn simply from the *élite* schools. For some time to come recruits will have to be drawn from a wider field. But there is little doubt that the character of the managerial group will be decisively moulded by the private schools and not by the State schools.

But it would be wrong to assume that, once recruited into the managerial ranks, the products of the different kinds of schools will be assured of equal treatment. The favoured entrant moves, to quote the current jargon, by a series of 'knight's moves' over the management board. Formal qualifications, as Wright Mills so convincingly demonstrates in his *Power Elite*, cease to be relevant to appointments to higher positions. The process is one of co-option rather than of selection and the prizes go, given minimum abilities, to men modelled upon the stereotype of those already in power. Since the leadership of British industry today is itself heavily dominated by products of the public schools, class nepotism is likely to remain a dominant factor.

It is indeed the anticipation of these favours together with the promise of managerial rewards that are attracting an ever increasing number of public school leavers into industry. Rugby, for example, in the early post-war years sent something like a third of its school leavers into industry. Last year well over half embarked on industrial careers. Nor is this exceptional, for the Public Schools Appointments Board reports an almost identical increase for the *élite* schools as a whole. Thus while recruitment into the old *élite* occupations—the professions, the Civil Service and foreign service —is at last showing some signs of broadening in favour of children from the working class, management recruitment is narrowing more and more upon children from the upper and middle classes.

Finally it is this close connection between industry and the public schools that has prevented and will prevent any major break in the continuity of our ruling class. In Britain at any rate, the emergence of a new industrial society is not producing a new ruling class but is providing instead a new managerial base for the established order.

Every ruling group must legitimize its control of power. It must win at least the acquiescence of society and, better still, its approval for its use of power. It must present itself as indispensable and demonstrate that its interests and those of the people are welded together.

These tasks are seldom difficult to accomplish in the early phases of a new society. For it is true that the ruling group would never have emerged unless it was able to offer some special service. Like the old entrepreneur, the top manager can today boast that he is indeed indispensable; that in this age of large-scale enterprise, of organized research and corporate planning, his functions of staff work, direction and co-ordination are crucial.

But while the basic case for the managers is in fact strong, their power is immeasurably strengthened both by their sensitivity to public opinion and by their *control* of the mass media of persuasion. It is not just goods that can be sold through advertising but, as the corporate managers have long realized, ideas and attitudes as well. In the paper this morning as I write, an I.C.I. advertisement makes the point. Two workmen are arguing:

'This is the Age of the Common Man, all right!'

'Maybe, but even today I doubt if the worker gets a proper stake in industry.'

'Things are changing, though.'

'Not that I've noticed.'

'Well, quite a number of concerns now have profit-sharing schemes, and some—like I.C.I.'s—also enable their employees to become stockholders.'

'Yes, but these schemes are only smokescreens. The bosses simply depress wages to find the money to pay for them.'

'That's where you're wrong. I.C.I. workers get the wages that have been negotiated on their behalf by seventeen trade unions. Any benefits they receive under the Company's profit-sharing scheme are over and above what they get in their pay envelopes.'

'Yes, but I.C.I. isn't Santa Claus. If the wages don't suffer, something else must—amenities or something.'

'Wrong again, friend. I.C.I.'s policy has led to a steady improvement in the service conditions of its employees, and the profit-sharing scheme is just another example. From now on, the employees are going forward with the stockholders as joint partners in their own efficient and expanding business.'

No one has been asked to buy anything: but a great deal of money has been spent on this and other puffs to make people think well of I.C.I. The inference is clear. Things are pretty good in I.C.I. Under the leadership of Dr Fleck, decent managerial chaps are running things—not a bit like the old capitalists. So why worry, why change?

I.C.I. is not alone in this kind of prestige advertising. All the time similar messages are being transmitted to the public by hundreds of our great corporations. They present, collectively, a picture of a new and dynamic 'Welfare Capitalism' which has grown up alongside the Welfare State—and they argue a case for leaving them alone, for opposing change.

In a sense, it is a tribute to democracy that those who wield power today are more concerned with the problem of consent than any previous ruling group in history. But the fact that consent is considered to be so important should not blind us to their great success in obtaining it.

It is of great significance that, in these last two decades which have seen such an enormous acceleration of the managerial revolution, there has been a noticeable decline in the demand for industrial democracy. The legitimate claim that management requires special skills which ordinary employees do not possess has been successfully confused with the wider assertion that only people with such skills are qualified to govern industry.

For special institutional reasons the trade unions have done little to combat this claim. Indeed they have renounced, formally, the objective of industrial democracy as incompatible with their traditional role. From the idea of democracy there has been a steady retreat to the far more modest objective of joint consultation which neither in theory nor in fact constitutes a challenge to managerial power.

As the drives for industrial democracy have lost impetus, there has taken place in the post-war period an unparalleled growth of management-sponsored corporate welfare: pensions, sickness benefits, holidays with pay, bonuses, training schemes, redundancy payments, etc. Many factors are at work: the desire to attract and retain employees during a prolonged period of acute labour shortage; the ability of the large firms to finance welfare at the expense either of the consumer or of the Inland Revenue; the influence of American management practice and of the Harvard doctrine of 'human relationships in industry'.

But two factors are of special importance. The first, which I call the 'managerial mission' has a deep native root. It grows out of the centuries-old tradition of social responsibility of the British ruling class, out of the High Toryism that Disraeli romanticized but which found substantial expression in rural England, in the armed and civil services and in colonial rule : a tradition, that is, of hierarchy, leadership and discipline, tempered with the ideal of service but wholly paternalistic and anti-democratic in character.

The second factor is the very opposite of the first : it is the factor of conscious manipulation. Here corporate welfare is seen not as an adjunct but as a rival to the Welfare State. Good practices in industry are not introduced for their own sake but to win accept-ance of the *status quo* and to recruit the loyalties of employees to the corporate managers.

One example of this is the sustained effort to extend employee share ownership in industry. The post-war growth of co-partnership schemes has centred on the large managerial firms and most notice-ably in those which have been, or believe themselves to be, threa-tened by nationalization. As a result hundreds of thousands of employees in such firms as I.C.I., Courtaulds, A.P.C., Tate & Lyle, Consett Steel, etc., have been suddenly elevated to the status of shareholders. At the same time great efforts have been made to recruit a new army of small shareholders from the general public. Today, there cannot be less than three million individual share-holders while practically the whole population has a small but widely publicized, indirect holding through insurance companies, trade union funds and superannuation schemes. Before long, if present trends persist, some Labour Chancellor will be heard to say : 'We are all capitalists now.'

These developments do not make a scrap of difference to the distribution of power and wealth in our society. That is not their aim. Indeed it is simply because fragmented share-ownership is being progressively denuded of its rights that management now feels that it can safely extend it. But the widening of ownership gives the illusion, as it is meant to do, that all have a stake in the system, that we are achieving a property-owning democracy.

Meanwhile, the general public is subjected to a continuing bar-rage of propaganda on behalf of the great firms and their control-lers. They serve the nation; they offer careers to talent; they defend us from our enemies; they provide for us in old age; they are raising the standard of living; they are keeping prices down; they are plan-ning for the future. . . . On and on it goes while armies of public relations men, copy writers, journalists and commercial artists, employed to do nothing else, exhaust the vocabulary of self-congratulation and praise.

Love that system!

To those who might otherwise be concerned by the implications of the growth of corporate power, the development of close and intimate ties between industry and the State brings considerable reassurance. For in the new relationship, the State is seen as the dominant partner. Whitehall planners and controlling agencies are seen as the community's countervailing power against the original power of industry. The State, in this view, controls industry, corrects abuses, fits separate and conflicting interests into its own master plan.

It is a pleasing picture, but a false one. For the truth is that the State lacks the personnel, the machinery and the will to exercise effective control. Its relationship with industry is accurately expressed, not in machinery of regulation—of which there is very little—but in the vast network of advisory and consultative committees which at a hundred different points connects business to the State machine. Here there has formed a vast twilight area in which the machinery and personnel of industry and the State blur, mingle and overlap. Here no one tells anyone what to do. But views are exchanged and noted, minds meet and problems of common concern are fully explored.

In practice, these committees are the channels through which industry exerts continuous pressure upon the policy and administration of the State—and they have become an integral and permanent part of our system of government. Industry today is no longer afraid of contact with the State, but on the contrary actively seeks it. For the closer the contact the greater the opportunity of influencing the disposal of the State's resources. It may be the port wine lobby seeking a cut in the excise; or the shipping industry in search of a subsidy; or the N.F.U. after higher guaranteed prices; or the F.B.I. urging reductions in profits tax; or the Institute of Directors asking for lower surtax rates: but all have the common purpose of furthering group interests through manipulating the power of the State.

In this post-war economy, the functions of business at the highest levels become increasingly political while the politician and the administrator become increasingly involved in the conduct of industry. Thus it comes about that business lends government its outstanding personalities; industrialists become Ministers, heads of State agencies, members of State Boards and political leaders, high-ranking officers and senior Civil Servants are recruited to the Boards of great enterprises. The consequential formation of what has been called a 'power *élite*' must be viewed not as a kind of conspiracy, but as a logical consequence of the unification of business with administration and politics.

The complex relationships that result make the very conception of State control elusive, if not meaningless. This was vividly demonstrated during the sterling crisis of last summer. As the Parker Tribunal was later to show, the decision to raise the Bank Rate to seven per cent was not reached through careful analysis in the Treasury but arose from the collective gossip of leading men in high places.

Yet the need for effective planning and control is today more pressing than it has ever been. In the past, in the old world of small-scale private enterprise a case for an uncontrolled economy could at least be made. Leaving aside the appalling social consequences, it could be plausibly argued that competitive profit-seeking in a market economy would lead to rational economic decisions, the most profitable use of resources, to the survival of the fittest, to a balanced and integrated economy. It could even be said, without too many reservations, that within the limits of his purchasing power, the consumer was sovereign.

Today, however, in our new corporate economy no such claims can be made. The profit-seeking remains but the self-regulating mechanism, the 'hidden hand' that unites the private with the public good, no longer functions. In the first place, competition has generally declined. It has been regulated, disciplined and in many instances completely suppressed. Where it survives, its nature and effect have both been radically changed in oligopolistic conditions.

Still more important, monopolistic and quasi-monopolistic control over prices enables the corporations to accumulate out of profits vast sums of new capital—the greater part of the nation's savings. The bulk of new investment resources no longer flows freely, via the shareholder, through the capital market. They are locked up in company reserves. They will be used only for such purposes as the Board Room thinks fit. As the American writer, A. A. Berle, summed it up : 'Not the public opinion of the market place with all the economic world from which to choose, but the directoral opinion of corporate managers as to the line of greatest opportunity within their own concern, now chiefly determines the applications of risk capital.'

This is a decisive change. Admittedly, within their own field of vision the managers will select more rather than less profitable uses —but the field itself is limited. True, examples may be quoted of corporations long established in particular industries suddenly entering entirely new territory where more profitable possibilities have been envisaged. But this is on the whole rare. Far more typical is the giant corporation investing ever more lavishly in its own restricted field—pushed on by the incentives of corporate aggrandizement. To justify such investment through subsequent sales, the consumer has to be subjected to an increasingly frantic and extravagant bombardment of advertising pressures. No passion known to man is too debased, no foible of human nature too trivial to escape the ruthless exploitation of modern advertising. Last year over £500,000,000 were spent in selling goods to the British public. Unilever alone spent £83,000,000. Why? so that, *inter alia*, we should know that 'In the past five years in the United Kingdom there have been four changes in Lux toilet soap, six in Persil, two in Omo and two in Gibbs SR toothpaste'. The horror of it all is that it not only works but the men who conduct these campaigns ultimately come to believe in their own propaganda. Sir Geoffrey Heyworth, Chairman of Unilevers, devoted his 1958 annual address to a defence of the magnitude of Unilever's advertising expenditure. Perhaps the crowning absurdity—there were many passages which competed for the prize—was the defence of free coupon schemes on the grounds that the consumer 'may verify for herself what we mean, for example, when we talk about the whiteness of Persil, the brightness of Omo or the perfume of a toilet soap'.

Perhaps the most conspicuous example of the corporate misuse of resources is the post-war activities of the oil companies. Of the wholly inadequate sums that have been available for Common-wealth and Sterling Area development, probably half have been poured into the Middle East oilfields. Can anyone say, on political, social or moral grounds, that this has been the best use of limited capital resources? Or that any attempt had first been made to assess whether on economic grounds it was better to invest in oil rather than in such alternative sources of power as coal, gas, electricity or atomic power? Is there any justification or rationality in the oil giants' new world plan to spend over the next decade £40,000,000,000 on further expansion—other than the fact that they find it profitable and that, through a world-wide cartel, they can accumulate such a fabulous capital sum by making the consumer pay?

The other side of the coin is, of course, the under-developed sectors of the economy—the industries which for one reason or another can neither accumulate their own nor attract new capital for their needs. The decline of the railways and the coal mines in pre-war Britain is a prominent example; so too was the failure of British capitalism to develop air transport. Viewed in this context the role of nationalization in Britain can be seen as a late attempt to replenish with State capital those sectors of the economy abandoned by private enterprise.

The last and perhaps most serious criticism of the new economy springs from the development outlined in an earlier paragraph— the unification of business and politics. For once the frontiers between economics and politics have been trampled down and the power of the State can be manipulated for sectional ends, the rationality of economic decisions becomes increasingly difficult to assess. If industry A can get a tariff wall erected and industry B cannot, if industry Y wins a subsidy while industry Z has to do without, then profitability loses whatever merit as a test it may have had. It ceases to give a valid record of past decisions or to act as a guide to future ones.

The very conception that a few hundred large corporations, each pursuing its own interests, will somehow lead to the best use of economic resources or solve the very great economic problems we face is today intrinsically absurd. And the actual experience of our post-war economy with its continuing crises, its miserable choice of inflation or stagnation lends the idea no support. I repeat, there-

45

fore, that if the corporate anarchy is to be brought under some kind of order, planning and controls are now indispensable. The current faith that the restoration of competition both within and between countries can provide an adequate corrective is, I believe —except in certain limited areas—misplaced. Competition and market regulation belong to an age that is past.

No one should imagine that the task of bringing order to the economy will be easy to accomplish. With a Tory Government in power neither the will nor the desire to plan exists. The long-standing connections between Tory M.P.s and business enterprise which are today far better organized than ever before both reflect and cement a common outlook on major economic questions. To explore this subject would take me far afield : it will suffice to note that, among the many sponsors of corporate interests, the Institute of Directors, which has become in six years one of the most power-ful organizations in the country, numbers ninety-seven M.P.s among its Fellows. With a membership of over 20,000 directors, including the whole top brass of British industry, there is no reason to dis-agree with these words of its most senior official : 'We have a fine membership but it is not only that. When you think how much capital our members control, and how many men we employ, we are clearly a force to be reckoned with.'

But for any government the tasks of economic control in a cor-porate economy are truly formidable. The need is to create a State power, equipped with appropriate techniques and personnel which will know what to do and which will have the power to do it. It means fighting against vested interests which are highly organized and tenacious and which may on occasion be strongly supported by the trade unions. For one consequence of welfare capitalism is the growth of a kind of tacit syndicalism in the economy. It means, too, fighting against interests with international ramifications and with centres of control that lie outside the territorial authority of the State. The sun may set today on the British Empire, but there are many mammoth corporations on which it never ceases to shine.

It is not difficult to see why Socialists have always disliked the idea of a 'managerial revolution'. If in fact a new ruling group, control-ling the means of production, has grown up inside large-scale private

46

enterprise, what difference would it make if there was a further change from private to public ownership? Would not the new ruling group continue as happily under national as under capitalist ownership? Might not the extension of public ownership actually strengthen and accelerate managerial control?

Of course it can be said that, given other counter-managerial policies, nationalization would exercise a considerable restraint on managerial power. These counter-pressures would have to include a workable system of control, genuine accountability and the substance of industrial democracy. In Britain, however, none of these conditions has been successfully realized. The earlier public corporations—the B.B.C., the London Passenger Transport Board, the Port of London Authority—were of course deliberately designed as autonomous bodies, as far removed as possible from external control. The post-war nationalization measures mark a definite improvement on these earlier models. But the Boards still retained enormous powers over their vast industrial empires, subject only to broad planning controls and to the ministerial power of Board Room appointment.

The Bank of England, whose affairs have recently been floodlit, provides a remarkable example of how little nationalization, as we practise it, can mean. In theory two great changes were accomplished: the ownership of the Bank changed hands and the power of control moved from Threadneedle Street to Whitehall. But since the Bank had paid its private shareholders a fixed dividend for the previous twenty years—and had no intention of raising it—the change of ownership itself made no difference at all to the magnitude or distribution of shareholders' rewards. As for Treasury control, true, the Chancellor of the Exchequer now has the power to issue formal directives to the Bank—but in fact this power has never been exercised: after nationalization, just as much as before it, Bank policy has been 'agreed' between the Chancellor and the Governor.

Beyond these purely formal changes, nothing new has even been attempted. There has seldom been a debate quite so unreal as that which attended the Second Reading of the Bank Nationalization Bill in 1946. The then Conservative Opposition, which normally knows when power interests are threatened, was obviously baffled.

47

Should they oppose, approve or abstain? The late Oliver Stanley, then shadow Chancellor, was forced to conclude: 'We oppose it [the Bill] not because it is a danger but because it is a sham; not because it is going to do harm, but because it is going to do nothing at all.'

Oliver Stanley was right. The administration of the Bank was left under the new régime, exactly as before. The Government does not even decide the Governor's salary: this and the whole internal organization of the Bank falling under its Charter to the Court of Directors. Provided the Bank pays the Treasury a fixed annual sum —in lieu of its pre-nationalization dividend—it is free to use its wealth and authority as it sees fit. How are they used? Does the nationalized Bank finance privilege as the great corporations do? Does it operate schemes for *élite* education for the children of its staff? Does it own property? How and for what ends does it use its power over the City and the Foreign Exchanges?

I do not know the answers to these questions. More important, Parliament does not know either—nor does anyone else who is not on the inside of the Bank's affairs. In the whole twelve years of national ownership, the affairs of the Bank have never even been debated in the House of Commons—until, that is, the publication of the Bank Rate Tribunal's Report. Can one really say, with any degree of confidence, that the nationalized Bank of England is significantly different from the private Bank over which Montagu Norman presided—or from Barclays, the National Provincial or the Westminster today?

It may be objected that the Bank is an exception among nationalized industries—untypical because of its history and its Charter. There is something to this, but there are disquieting signs, if not real evidence, in public corporations generally. In the last few years it has been laid down, as an axiom, that the public sector must in salaries and terms of service compete with the private sector. There is a strong practical argument in support of this doctrine, for if they do not then there is a serious danger that they will lose key personnel. But the implications must be squarely faced. It means first that the norms of managerial behaviour and privilege that are to be found in the private sector are to be accepted in the public sector as well.

It means, too, since the salaries of private enterprise directors are self-determined, an endless pressure towards larger rewards—and greater inequality. Men who have to determine their own worth are seldom ungenerous in their calculations. In the private sector, top positions in the great corporations attract from £20,000 to £50,000 per annum. In the United States, where leading men have never been famous for their modesty, the Presidents of Chrysler, Republic Steel, I.B.M., Distillers and Du Pont receive annual rewards within the range of £100,000 to £200,000 a year, while at the summit the President of General Motors falls just short of £250,000.

But it is not only in managerial rewards that the public sector is increasingly approximating the private. In theory, of course, the two kinds of corporation stand wide apart: those who direct private enterprise are responsible to private shareholders; those who control public enterprise to Ministers and Parliament. But in practice both types of corporations are virtually autonomous, operating as they do under absentee ownership. In size, in organization, in managerial outlook, in treatment of employees, there is indeed little to choose between them. Certainly no distinctive doctrine of management has come out of the public sector. It is these similarities that have made so much of the post-war debate on the merits of nationalization irrelevant and indeed absurd. Contrary to general belief public corporations are no less efficient than private corporations: nor, contrary to minority expectations, are they more so. In similar circumstances their performance is exactly the same. It would need a fine discrimination indeed to judge the overall performance of, say, I.C.I. against the Atomic Energy Authority, or of Associated Electrical Industries against the Central Electricity Authority, or the Ford Motors against B.O.A.C. But then, with so many similarities, why indeed should their performance differ? Of course there are problem industries which fall short of the achievements of these corporations. But they exist—the coal mines in public, cotton in private ownership—in both types of enterprise. The only generalization that one could safely make is that large-scale organization, public or private, is, under twentieth-century conditions, likely to be more efficient than small-scale enterprise.

No, where nationalization matters—and matters enormously—is

that it gets rid of private ownership of industrial property. Even when compensation is paid, as in the United Kingdom, the old shareholders are still denied any claim on the future growth of the enterprise they once owned. The only caveat is that if public ownership is to destroy the basis of property-owning power, there must be enough of it—far more than we have today. But in itself the public corporation offers no challenge to managerial power: it will only do so if additional policies and measures designed to that end are applied.

Are they? Once again we are in the dark. The internal affairs of the public corporations are a closed book—except for what can be gleaned from their Annual Reports or from questions in the House. But since the Reports are written within the corporations themselves and since Ministers make it a rule never to answer the really interesting questions, their value as control mechanisms is obviously limited. Nor indeed will the subject be opened at all until Socialists realize that, with the managers in control, public corporations must be subjected to the same critical scrutiny as private corporations.

That we are some way off this state of enlightenment may be judged by this fabulous exchange between Mr Nabarro and Emanuel Shinwell:

MR NABARRO: I refer to a house known as Mancetter Manor which is stated to be one of the finest examples of half-timbered Manor in Warwickshire and which has been bought by the Board for the Area General Manager. The Chairman of the West Midlands Coal Board told me that it was purchased for £6,750. . . . The gross rateable value was £105 and the Area General Manager was to live there rent free, rates free and gardeners provided. How much of the vast sum of money which annually this House is proposing to grant to the Board for capital investment is being spent on the production of coal and how much on this type of 'fringe' activity which involves the buying of expensive houses? . . .

MR SHINWELL: We ought not to get excited when we learn that an historical Manor house is now to be used by an industrial undertaking under the protection of the State. Far better that these houses should be occupied by people who are expected to do a good day's work, rather than be occupied by a decadent aristocracy.

Far better indeed!

At the beginning, I wrote that I did not believe that we were moving towards a Socialist society. I meant by that that I could find little evidence of greater equality in the distribution of incomes, wealth and opportunities and none at all in the distribution of power. I meant further that I could not detect any significant shift in the values of our society—no decline in acquisitiveness, no increase in the awareness that we are involved in and must help each other. The title of a recent novel, *Room at the Top*, aptly expresses both the dominant obsession and the compelling myth of our time. But the truth is that there never has been and never will be room at the top for the great mass of mankind. Today, the ladders of the 'opportunity state' are just as much an illusion as were thrift and hard work in the age of Samuel Smiles. Clearly in spite of all the changes of the past twenty years, ours remains a class society. The institutions which support it flourish and human relationships continue to be governed by wealth, power and social background. There is no doubt in my mind that, as Socialists have long believed, the ownership and control of industrial property still provide the material foundations upon which our class structure is built. Yet, in spite of war-socialism and the Attlee Government, in spite of nationalization, death duties and high taxation, the class structure seems as strong as it ever was.

Why? I would answer: partly because the property base is immensely strong, but partly too because the policies pursued have led less to the dispersal or redistribution of property than to its concentration and reorganization under corporate control. At the top, the men of great property have been joined and partly replaced by the controllers of corporate wealth. In so far as the old base of the class society has been weakened by the reduction of great personal fortunes, a new base has been created through the growth and use of corporate funds. The peaceful revolution of post-war Britain turns out to be no more than a managerial semi-revolution.

When I look ahead, the task of eliminating great private fortunes does not seem particularly difficult. I do not mean by that that there would be any tame surrender or that the attempt would not alter the climate of British politics. But I believe that we would succeed. For public opinion is becoming aware of the truth that, in the modern corporation, private ownership has lost its function—and

therefore the justification for its reward. Society is no longer dependent upon the property owner either for its supply of savings or
for the running of business enterprise. As a class, the corporate
shareholders have become like the absentee landlords of nineteenth-
century Ireland, or the royalty owners of our pre-war coal fields,
completely parasitical.

One point needs to be clarified. The assertion that ownership has
lost its function is, I find, sometimes confused with the quite
different statement that ownership no longer matters. This can only
arise from a failure to distinguish between the economic and social
roles of private property. If this essay had been about the old
rather than the emergent society it would not have been difficult
to show how tremendously important unequally held property
ownership is in shaping our society. Indeed there will be no possibility of developing towards a classless society until the private
ownership of wealth is radically reduced. This is one of the major
reasons why the corporations should be brought into public ownership. But this involves no serious economic problem. To detach the
private shareholder from the corporation is not like amputating a
limb but like shaking a dead leaf from a tree. All that is needed,
therefore, is resolution and courage.

But the managerial base of our society is inherently stronger, for
the managers, unlike the shareholders, perform functions that are
indispensable to the enterprise. Yet—and it is essential to recognize
this—the managerial control of industrial property is quite enough
in itself to sustain a class society. This is certainly true of Britain
where old class institutions are strongly entrenched and where the
corporate managers are themselves largely recruited from the
property-owning class. But even if a ruling class did not already
exist, even if it had been destroyed as in the Soviet Union and
Yugoslavia, the power of corporate control would, if left unchecked, certainly lead to the emergence of a 'power *élite*' and in
the course of time to a 'new class'. The tardy and incomplete recognition of this truth has been, I believe, the main intellectual failure
of contemporary Socialism. For if Socialists have been right to
assume that private ownership of industrial property is the key to
a capitalist society, they have been wrong in assuming that public
ownership leads necessarily to a classless society. It does not. The

power of industrial property remains, under public no less than private ownership, and the shape that it gives to society depends upon who controls it and the purposes for which it is used. It is not a natural pessimism but history and the evidence of our times that lead me to believe that those who control the community's wealth, whatever the legal forms of ownership may be, will use it to establish privileged positions and high rewards for themselves and to hand on such advantages as they can to their heirs. Where democratic counter-pressures are lacking, a 'new class' indeed seems unavoidable.

But the problems that this raises, though difficult, are not insuperable. If we develop and extend our democracy, we *can* make the corporate economy serve the community's needs; we *can* prevent managerial control leading to an excessive accumulation of advantages. We *can*, too, distribute decision-making power throughout industry and society. What stands in the way is not so much lack of techniques—although these are important—nor the inherent difficulties—and at times it does seem rather like separating a magnet from its field of force—but at root lack of will to further change. For the managerial society is not without its attractions. At least it is an advance on the past. It is more hygienic, more discreet, more efficient. It promises to supply us with an endless stream of new toys. If we lowered our sights sufficiently, might it not be possible to come to terms?

I know the answer I would give. I do not want a society in which an *élite*, viewing the world through Board Room windows, makes the big decisions, collects the big rewards, while the mass of men deprived of power and responsibility dig their gardens or watch the telly.

I want instead a society which shapes its institutions so that men may become self-determining, their own masters. For we are in the end what society allows us to be: adults or children, masters or men, apathetic or involved. Humanity can only develop if we have faith in its innate capacity, if we refuse to believe that men are what they are because they can be no different. This is to me the starting point of democratic Socialism and the basic case for social change.

There is much that needs to be done. But there is today, with the

53

vast enlargement of our capacity to create wealth, no reason to falter. For the first time in history a 'society of equals' has ceased to be a Utopian dream, is materially possible. It is up to us to achieve it.

BRIAN ABEL-SMITH

Whose welfare state?

W HY ARE THE BRITISH middle classes
such hypocrites in their attitude to the Welfare State? Why do they
want to emasculate the social services, from which they derive so
much benefit, in order to punish the better-off sections of the working classes? Why do they pretend to others—and to themselves—
that they get no advantage from the social services?

They seem convinced that they are giving social services to the
working classes who receive and do not pay. They are quite prepared to help the very poor. But they resent giving to people who
seem to be as well off as they are, and they object to providing
standards of services which are in line with their own standard of
life—nourishing cottage pie but not roast chicken. They feel that
too much is being given to too many at too high a standard, and
they are being forced to foot the whole bill. This leads to class
bitterness as all the ills of the middle classes and of the country
at large get blamed on the Welfare State—inflation, economic
stagnation and the drain on the gold and dollar reserves. This leads
to more demands to cut the Welfare State.

But *whose* Welfare State? Who pays for what? What *are* the
standards of welfare and security that are received by different
sections of the population? It may seem at first sight that these
are silly questions to ask. But after some years of watching, reading and thinking, I have come to the conclusion that these are the
critical questions.

It is the practice of critics of the public social services to call the
changes made during and after the war 'the creation of the Welfare
State'. I am going to suggest that the major beneficiaries of these
changes have been the middle classes, that the middling income
groups get more from the State than the lower income groups, that
taxation often hits the poor harder than the well-to-do, and in

general that the middle classes receive good standards of welfare while working people receive a Spartan minimum.

My working life falls into three parts. I help with the administration of the social services. I teach people who are going to work in the social services. And finally, perhaps the most creative part of my life, I study and write about the social services. This, I believe, is what a university teacher should do. There is a danger, even in a democracy, that apart from the occasional Royal Commission the only source of detailed information on social or financial questions will be the Civil Service. There is a danger, too, that government will release only the information that vindicates its policies. It is in my view the duty of the universities to hunt out and publish whatever a government may wish to conceal. I try to be a continuous but fair critic of the 'Establishment view'.

Many years may be needed to collect and document all the facts needed to prove a particular hypothesis. And classical scholars can safely wait to learn the exact date and authorship of the *Iliad*. But society cannot always wait for the results of social research. So here I want to do what the classical scholar need never do—suggest an interpretation of facts which I have not finished collecting and point out conclusions which I believe should follow if my interpretation is right.

Before the war, there were fairly well-developed social services, and from most of them the working classes were the main beneficiaries. With some exceptions, people with incomes under £5 per week were in the State social security system. In unemployment a single man got 20s. a week, in sickness 18s. a week and in old age 10s. a week. Now all employed persons rich and poor can get 50s. Prices have multiplied by about two and three-quarters, the earnings of the average worker have multiplied by about four. So the single working man in sickness and unemployment had a better deal pre-war than he does today.

The working classes could also get free education and health services before the war. The contributor to National Health Insurance had the services of a panel doctor and anyone who was poor could go to a voluntary or local authority hospital without any payment. Secondary education was available subject to a means test and was thus provided free for those with low incomes. Middle-class people, who bought their own social services, often paid more than the cost. Medical fees in particular were deliberately scaled to take more from the rich than the poor.

Of course there were geographical gaps in, and distasteful conditions attached to, the social services, but by and large they were available to the poor. The main effect of the post-war development of the social services, the 'creation of the Welfare State', has been to provide free social services to the middle classes. They are now entitled to use the free health services, to send their children to grammar schools without charge, to get the same State pension as everybody else. Mr Griffiths went even further: he allowed middle-class people to draw full pensions after only ten years of contribution, while some manual workers have been paying insurance contributions for forty-seven years. Thus the major beneficiaries of the post-war changes in the social services have been the middle classes.

Don't imagine that professional people don't take advantage of their rights in the Welfare State. They are entitled to do so, and their participation has undoubtedly had a healthy effect in making us scrutinize the standard of service provided. I live in Westminster and friends of mine who are actors or who have recently been barristers call in on their way to draw their unemployment benefit. Some have quite large unearned incomes but they have paid for their insurance like everybody else, and they are not ashamed of taking advantage of what they have paid for. On the South Coast you will find bank managers, who are compulsorily retired at sixty, drawing their tax-free unemployment benefit while the Labour Exchange tries to find them jobs—as bank managers. In the case of health and primary education all but about four per cent of the population use the State services. And quite a number of parents who send their children to private schools send them on to an Exchequer-assisted university; and the cost to the State of three years of university education can be more than the cost of keeping a child at a State school from the age of five to fifteen. And even those parents who think they are paying for their children to attend a university are not paying the full cost: fees for university education only represent a small part of the cost of running them—probably not much more than one-fifth.

Not only does nearly everybody use the Welfare State but the wealthier user often gets more from it than the poorer user. A recent study by John Vaizey has shown that the average parent with an income of £500–£2,000 in 1952 got about eighty per cent more from the education service than the average parent with an income under £500. This is because their children are more likely to be selected for the more expensive secondary schools and are more likely to stay on after the compulsory school-leaving age. And in the case of the health services, it has been noted that the middle classes go to the doctor and dentist more than the working classes, ask for more expensive drugs, and find their way into the more expensive hospitals—particularly the teaching hospitals.

Who pays for the social services? It is usually assumed that the tax system is progressive—that the richer pay a greater part of their incomes in taxation than the poorer. This simple notion comes partly from thinking that income tax and surtax are the only taxes and forgetting that taxes are also collected indirectly by increasing the prices of goods in the shops. Half the revenue is collected this way and half of the indirect taxes come from alcohol and tobacco. For people earning less than £12 a week, tobacco and alcohol taxes may amount to almost three-quarters of their total tax payments, though of course they spend less on tobacco and alcohol than people who earn more.

It seems likely that those whose whole earnings are subject to tax before payment and who earn over £40 a week pay a higher proportion of their incomes in taxes than those who earn less. But among the middling to low incomes this is much less certain. Indeed, if we restrict ourselves to people with family responsibilities it seems likely that within the group taxation falls more heavily on the worse-off than the better-off. This is because family responsibilities lead to special high exemption limits from income tax. Thus a man with a wife and three children can earn over £15 a week without paying a penny of income tax. Let us compare the position of an agricultural worker earning £7 a week with that of a clerk earning £15 a week. What taxes do they pay? Each pays 9s. 11d. in National Insurance. Tobacco tax must be the largest other item. In an inquiry made in 1953–54, the average man with a wife and three children earning £7 a week said he spent about 14s.

a week on tobacco while a similar man earning £15 per week admitted to spending about 18s. per week on tobacco. Then there are rates, taxes on alcohol and other goods. I would guess that the agricultural worker would pay about 25s. in taxes of all kinds and the clerk about 40s., and 25s. is eighteen per cent of an income of £7 and 40s. is thirteen per cent of an income of £15. No one knows the answer for certain, but I am prepared to bet that the burden of taxation is higher on the agricultural worker than the clerk.

Let me therefore sum up the argument so far. First, the post-war changes in the social services did not consist in lavishing gifts upon the working classes. The major beneficiaries of these changes were the middle-income groups. Secondly, when one remembers that these groups probably make more use of the nationally financed social services than the lower income groups, and also that the tax system does not always hit the rich harder than the poor, it becomes far from easy to say who is helping whom. If the Welfare State were abolished (whatever that means) and all taxes reduced proportionately, many well-to-do people would be worse off.

A few months ago I was in a bus going down Regent Street sitting behind two expensively dressed middle-aged women. One was complaining that the painters had not turned up that morning. 'People have too much done for them these days. They don't do a full day's work.' Later the conversation drifted to future engagements. 'Yes, we will be at Ascot, Charles wouldn't miss it for anything.'

Not only do the middle classes do well out of the public social services but in addition they participate with the higher-income groups in special benefits from their employment—benefits which are never counted in the total bill for national welfare. Indeed, higher executives in industry, senior Civil Servants, and many others, can pour scorn upon many of the public social services because they get excellent welfare benefits from their occupation. They are entitled to full pay in sickness, and even a guaranteed annual wage. It is not called sickness benefit, but sick pay. It is not called unemployment benefit, but a contract of service, and in practice some contracts last until superannuation ceases. Who can sack, for sheer incompetence, a university professor, a headmaster, a matron, a medical superintendent? For immorality or embezzlement, perhaps, but not for incompetence. Can it really be true that the quality of their work never slips throughout twenty or thirty years of service? I don't want to suggest that people should lose pay when they are past their prime or even when an appointments committee has made a mistake. 'We must all carry our passengers'; how often have you heard it said? But we must consider, too, the thousands of pupils or patients who are not getting the best.

The contract of service is not the only welfare guarantee given to the professional man. There is also an incremental salary scale —an automatic rise of anything from £25 to £100 each year without any test of merit. The manual worker seldom gets this kindly treatment. When *he* asks for a rise each year, it is called an irresponsible wage demand. His rise, we read, should be related to productivity. And when the time comes when he can't do the better paid work, he is found a lighter job with a lighter pay packet. A business can carry its share of sleeping directors, but if a manual worker has to drop £2 a week because he is not as fit as he was, there is nothing for it. The cost accountants say so.

Look at the hierarchy of privileges that are built into our wage and salary structures. Look at the sickness rights, the periods of notice, the means of challenging dismissal. Who needs special privileges? The manager and administrator who get exhausted by their talking, travelling and dictating, who carry their responsibilities twenty-four hours a day, who get ulcers and coronaries from tension and worry (or possibly, as some doctors say, from eating too much butter and salt)? Or the coal miner who works in damp and dust below the daylight, who shifts twenty-four tons a day, who contracts silicosis and risks death by suffocation? What about the dustmen, the sewer men, the quarry men, the bricklayers in January, the road drillers in July, and the steel workers with their swinging cauldrons of molten metal, and their white-hot speeding sheets and wires and tubes? Who has the energy to dig the garden after a day's work?

Industry has its own Welfare State. There are costly rights and privileges provided mainly for the salaried worker. How does it compare with the benefits provided by the State social security system? A manual worker can expect not full pay in sickness but 80s. per week if he is married and 50s. per week if he is single. The average man today earns £12 a week. So a married man gets a third of average male earnings, the single man gets less than a quarter. There is no lavishness here. Indeed the general level of British benefits is lower than those of most of Western Europe. Who will be induced not to work by the prospect of 50s. or 80s. a week? After all, 50s. a week is stark poverty. Remember, too, the complicated rules and regulations designed to prevent the abuse of National Insurance. Did you know that unemployment benefit is not paid for six weeks to a man who is sacked for misconduct? Did you know there were Ministry inspectors who visit the sick at home? What steps does a private firm take to police its full-pay sickness scheme?

I once said all this to a mixed group at an adult education class. One Civil Servant was most indignant. He did not say outright that he could be trusted while other people couldn't. There were too many manual workers present for that. Instead he pointed out that he paid for all his privileges in lower pay. Civil Servants were pooling their risks and spreading their remuneration over the life span to cover sickness and old age. He was quite right about the spreading. But this is exactly what a State social security system is doing. Don't imagine the manual worker doesn't pay for his insurance benefits. To be exact, the present national contribution taking the employer's and employee's part together (without any Exchequer assistance) will pay for two and a half per cent more than the cost of all benefits.

I begrudge no one his sick pay, his pension, his contract of service, his holiday, his Wembley or his Ascot. All I ask is that we are honest about it. It is nonsense to regard National Insurance as a millstone round the economy's neck and occupational privileges as emblems of the virtues of the good employer—to regard the former as the destroyer of incentives and the latter as the promoter of loyal service. These are both social security services. In the last ten years there has been hardly any change in the scope or purchasing power of National Insurance benefits, but sick pay and pensions have been extending rapidly. If security payments have been straining the economy, blame industry not the State.

Not only do the middle classes get more than their share of the public social services, draw special extra benefits from their occupation, but in addition there are the hidden social services provided by tax concessions in the income tax. Working people pay most of their taxes in the indirect way—by buying taxed goods. There are no special concessions on these taxes. Middle-class people pay most of their taxes in income tax but they can claim for children, for dependent relatives, for housekeepers, for divorced wives, for old age, for mortgage payments, for life assurance and other expenditure.

The middle classes are becoming very conscious of the value of all these tax allowances, but they never think of them as social services. This hit me very forcibly when I heard a rich young wife chattering gaily over her tomato juice at a cocktail party. 'Yes it has planned out quite well. The baby is due in March and my husband says we will be able to save nearly £100 in income tax. . . . No, we won't bother with the family allowance. It all goes in income tax anyway. They give with one hand and take away with the other. My husband has worked it out. By the time you pay for the petrol it is not worth going down to the post office to collect it. And anyway I don't think it's right. My Mrs Jones says she has seen the young women down her way drawing their allowances and going straight to the tobacconist's next door.'

How does the family allowance compare with the child allowance in the income tax? Family allowances cost the State about £120,000,000; child allowances cost £320,000,000. Family allowances are available for the second and later children, tax allowances for all children. The highest benefit obtainable from a family allowance is £26 per year; the highest benefit from a tax allowance is £135 per year. The family allowance takes no account of the age of the child; the tax allowance is graded by age. The family allowance must end at age eighteen; the tax allowance can continue throughout university education. The family allowance starts from the birth of the child; the tax allowance starts at the beginning of the year in which the child is born.

Why do we have a tax allowance for children? It is given to *compensate* richer parents for the sacrifices they have had to bear in bringing up children. It is assumed that the richer parent would make some sacrifices even if the allowance was not paid. Its purpose is to enable the richer parent to get back some part of the standard of living which would otherwise be lost. It is *meant* to be spent on all those niceties that would otherwise have to be sacrificed—on motor-cars and concerts, and holidays abroad—in short on all those things which are needed to maintain the middle-class way of life. Is it impossible to believe that working people would sacrifice their standard of living to look after their children? Why shouldn't people who have to pay their taxes the indirect way get an allowance for their children?

Most people today say they believe in equal opportunity (not equality—equal opportunity). This means in practice that the State should help each child on its merits—for example, that the educational system should provide for the aptitudes and abilities of each child. The present system of tax allowances for children contradicts this principle. It actively assists the richer parents to provide their children with a better start than poorer parents. Of course the well-to-do will be able to give their children advantages. Why shouldn't they? But it is quite a different matter for the State to help them to do so. Indeed perhaps the State ought to try and counterbalance the help given to the richer parent by providing larger financial aid to the poorer parent. But we can't talk about equal opportunity and support tax allowances.

When we follow the logic of the argument, the conclusion is irresistible. The middle classes get the lion's share of the public social services, the elephant's share of occupational welfare privileges, and in addition can claim generous allowances to reduce their tax liability. Who has a Welfare State?

I will never forget my first visit to a mental hospital. Through the iron gates I could see the eerie, century-old building clad in fire escapes, the decrepit old summer-houses marking out the 'airing courts', the geraniums, the flagpole and the dishevelled old patient clipping at the hedge. I found a dormitory with eighty beds in four rows with about nine inches between the beds and eighteen inches between the rows—no lockers, no wardrobes, no chests of drawers, no bed lights—no furniture at all except eighty beds with stained white cotton bed covers in a room which hadn't been painted for thirty years. There was a communal bathroom—a row of baths on a cracked tiled floor, no curtains, no taps on the baths, the only decoration a discoloured notice framed on the wall headed 'bathing instructions'. And what about the sanitary annexes—a row of six cracked basins set into a dirty black slab with running cold water for seventy patients. What was this like first thing in the morning? What about the four lavatories with wooden partitions and low wooden doors for easy observation—so ingrained with faeces that no amount of disinfectant could hide the smell. There are in Britain today wards which haven't been papered or painted in this century. There are ward kitchens without refrigerators, ovens or hotplates. There are sluices without bedpan washers. There are patients being fed at a cost of 14s. 10d. a week. And one British person in forty dies in a mental hospital.

I know a corrugated iron hut put up over sixty years ago that serves as the home (dormitory and day room) for sixty mentally deficient children—many physically deformed, some mentally disturbed, nearly all incontinent. There are four W.C.s, three washbasins, and two baths. Years of urine and faeces have seeped into the wooden floors and radiator grilles. It is usual for new admissions to get dysentery until they become immune. The Minister of Health has cut the hospital services by £6,000,000 this current year.

So much for the worst. There have been remarkable improvements in some hospitals since 1948, but the average is still low. I would say that the majority of mental patients have no proper place to put their possessions, sanitary facilities that would disgrace a barracks, and the sad environment of brown tiles and stained furniture. And nearly half the hospital patients in this country are in mental hospitals and mental deficiency institutions. There are still some reactionary managements (I have been told that horsehair mattresses are good enough for patients and I have seen institutional green paint renewed 'because it lasts') but by and large the real lack is money. Nevertheless, Mr Nicholson, the chairman of the Select Commitee on Estimates told the chairman of a mental hospital on 12th March, 1957, that 'this Sub-Committee would like to hear that you are always trying to save money and return as much as possible'.

The mental hospitals are not the only shocking institutions in the Welfare State. Many of the chronic hospitals are a disgrace.

You can't judge hospitals from television programmes. For instance only one patient in twenty is in a teaching hospital. There are ramshackle schools without any sanitary facilities. There are still large children's homes which cannot provide anything that approaches a normal home life. There are makeshift out-patient departments with appalling accommodation for both patients and staff. And four out of five old people in L.C.C. welfare accommodation are living in the old workhouses. Go and see them sitting in those long bare rooms, staring at the radiator, waiting to die.

Of course there has been progress in the last ten years. All over the country there are new schools. But little more has been done than to provide room for the large number of children born after the war. Few of the grim charity relics of the nineteenth century have been replaced. How many bungalows for old people have been built? Aren't they just an oddity which the mayor takes foreign visitors to see? If you search carefully you might be able to find an occasional new out-patient department. Perhaps your local M.P. has bullied the Minister of Health to give priority to your area even though the need wasn't half as great as in other places.

Isn't it possible for the buildings of the Welfare State to keep pace with the buildings that house private enterprise? All around us we see palatial prestige offices, new shops, new factories—putting to shame the grubby old institutions of welfare. The south bank of the Thames is to have a new Shell skyscraper only about thirty years after the north bank Shell building. Bowaters is to tower above the new Knightsbridge entrance to the Park. I read in *The Times* of 12th May, 1958, that a bank has opened a new branch in Piccadilly Circus. 'The interior decoration incorporates rea marble quarried in Oran, ebony black granite from Sweden, Italian glass mosaic, delabole grey and Italian slate and afromoria, and linoleum patterned with the bank's crest.' But less than £20,000,000 is to be spent this year on hospital building all over Britain. At this rate it is going to take two hundred years to rebuild the hospitals. There will be time for six new Shell buildings. And there will be no marble for the hospitals—not even glass mosaics. Use them to attract casual customers to the bank. Don't waste them on worried mothers waiting all morning in the out-patients department of the hospital.

If we can't have better social values, then at least we should be

able to have sound economic sense in the Welfare State. Think of
the amount of money that is wasted in old buildings. There are vast
opportunities for saving money by spending money. There are
greedy sixty-year-old boilers nursed by three different shifts of
stokers. What about some more automatic oil-fired equipment?
There are hospital laundries too small to take modern labour-saving
machines. What about some new ones? And what about designing
uniforms to suit the laundries instead of laundries to suit the
uniforms? Surely something just as smart could be devised? And
think of the cost of cleaning those decrepit old buildings. There
are many investments in the hospitals which could pay for themselves within five years. No modern business would dream of working with the Welfare State's equipment.

There is no room for manœuvre with a tight budget. In the
mental services, in the services for the physically sick, in the welfare services for the aged, even in services for children and criminals,
it is recognized that more effective home services and earlier discoveries of cases could substantially reduce the need for institutional care. Such changes might even pay. But there is next to no
government money used to try this out on an experimental basis.
By industrial standards, operational research is sadly lacking. What
firm would spend nearly £700,000,000 but begrudge a few thousands to see if it is wisely spent? This is what is happening in the
National Health Service.

The buildings and furnishings are not the only gaps in the fabric
of the Welfare State. There is a shortage of doctors in those special-
ties which would not attract the type of young man who wrote
those angry articles in the *Observer* and went back to South Africa.
There is a shortage of nurses, particularly in the mental hospitals
where a substantial proportion of the work is done by foreigners,
some of whom do not even speak English. There is a shortage of
teachers, particularly of science teachers. There is an acute shortage
of dentists, probation officers, health visitors, radiographers, and
every type of qualified social worker. One reason for all this is that,
with the notable exceptions of doctors and dentists, our society
does not value highly in terms of cash the services of those who
work in the Welfare State.

Nor is this all. Except when doctors are authorizing expenditures.

the public services are subjected to a petty meanness which is noticeably absent in private industry. How does waiting time in the shops compare with that in the local housing office, the employment exchange and at the hospital? Why have so many Civil Servants to work in such disgraceful offices? Why have hospitals so few shorthand typists that they can't always dispatch a letter to your doctor on the day you leave hospital, while any reputable business can reply by return of post? Your financial affairs are discussed in the privacy of the bank manager's office. But how often have people had to explain the most intimate details of their private lives to the official at the local Pensions Office, the Labour Exchange, the housing office, the welfare office or the tax office at an open wooden counter with an impatient queue behind overhearing every word? No housewife alive in Britain today can be unaware of the claimed merits of 'Tide'—how to buy it and when to buy it, how to use it and how not to use it. But how many housewives know how to change their doctor, how to summon the National Assistance Board Officer, or what welfare services are available and how to get them? Why is the customer always right and the citizen usually wrong? Is it because Civil Servants are corrupted by power? Or is it because their case load is so heavy and their training so narrow that they just aren't always polite?

Chains of auditors, gaggles of politicians and circuses of busybodies are scrutinizing the expenditure of the public services. But who investigates what private industry spends on advertising, on quality control, and public relations? Why can't we live down the legacy of Mr Gladstone, the Poor Law and the Geddes axe? Can't we make public services serve the public?

Let me make it quite clear that I don't want to drag anyone down. Rather I want to raise the standards of welfare for working people and for the minority groups in every social class—the mentally ill, the disabled, the infirm, the aged and the mental deficients and the millions who live in the mean streets of our industrial cities. I want to see working people being treated in the same way as the middle classes treat themselves. More money must be spent on welfare.

Opposition to welfare expenditures comes from three deeply rooted prejudices. The first is drawn from economic theory—that the consumer wants most what he chooses in a free market. The

second comes from our legacy of thinking about State intervention
—the belief that the State must do no more than provide 'a minimum of civilized life'. The third is the taxation taboo—that high
taxation will ruin the economy. I am going to say a bit about
each.

Free choice works admirably for a housewife buying vegetables.
There is the cauliflower. There is the cabbage. Take your choice,
dearie. But can you really conclude anything from the choice between a cabbage and a one-in-a-million chance of contracting polio,
between a cauliflower today and a cauliflower in the year 2000?
How many people know the exact chances of getting ill, of surviving to old age, of breeding a backward child? If they don't know,
what conclusions can you draw from the fact that people don't
choose to save or pre-insure? When there is delay or risk, free
choice proves nothing.

With a few pathological exceptions, people are optimists: they
would never venture on the public highway if they weren't. They
overestimate the chances of anything nice—like winning the football pools—and underestimate the chances of anything nasty—like
having a mentally deficient child, being injured at work, or going
senile. But when bad luck comes, they will mortgage anything to
get by. After all, it's a battle for survival.

There are exceptions to the free-choice principle which are
already sanctioned by public opinion. While interference by the
State is suspect, interference by the employer is given a position of
special moral approbation. It is public-spirited for an employer to
tax the consumer, the shareholder or his own workpeople to provide sick pay, a pension scheme, a subsidized canteen, playing
fields, science laboratories for fee-paying schools, or scholarships
for 'adventurous children'. How many salaried people could find a
job which *didn't* offer a pension?

If we abandon the market-choice criterion, how do we decide
what to spend on welfare? All I can suggest is a very homely way.
Take a cross-section of population, show them the standards in the
Welfare State and then ask them the following questions. Would
you let your mother go into this home? If your husband had a
nervous breakdown, would you like him to live in this mental
hospital? Would you let a child of yours go into this institution

if you couldn't look after it? If you lost your home, would you like to live here while you looked for another? And finally, if you don't like the look of the Welfare State, now you have seen it, would you be prepared to pay a few more shillings a week to have it put right?

I need say little more here about the assumption that State intervention should only provide a minimum of civilized life—the legacy of mutton-eating Beatrice Webb and the Poor Law. This is just hypocrisy when the employer is intervening to do exactly the opposite for his salaried employees. The subsistence minimum was an excellent target when the State was hardly doing anything at all, but it makes no sense in a community which is getting rich at the rate of the last ten years. With rising standards of life, a belief in a subsistence minimum is a belief in ever increasing inequality and class distinction. Make no mistake about that.

We are left, then, with the taxation taboo. Let me quote from Paul Bareau speaking in a broadcast on 20th March, 1958. 'If the growth in the social services means higher and higher taxes, it will mean that ultimately damage may be done to trade, to industry in this country.' What evidence is there of this? How do we account for the fact that in the early post-war years, when taxation was at its peacetime highest, industry was booming and the country was getting richer very quickly? How do we account for the facts that four times more married women are at work than before the war, that the average man is working much the same hours as before the war, that in recent years effort has been directed at restraining investment rather than stimulating it? Are these just the effects of full employment? What signs are there that high taxation has ever damaged economic growth? It is hard to think of any widely held belief which has been subjected to less empirical investigation. How often does one find people taking up the position that the rich work less when they are made poorer, and the poor work less when they are made richer?

Of course taxation is unpopular, of course we would all like to have our cake and eat it, but what evidence have we that taxation does any other damage than to weaken the moral stamina of the middle classes? How many people who talk about the abuse of the Welfare State abuse the tax system themselves? There are two noble professions at hand to assist in tax fiddling, but no profession is yet established which will tell you how to get the best out of the Welfare State.

A few weeks ago, a middle-aged lady with the trunk of her body in a plaster cast made her way in pain to the local welfare office and told her story within earshot of seven people. She was being evicted from her one-roomed flat. Could they find her somewhere else to live? All she wanted was one private room on the ground floor. All they could offer was a place in a welfare home. She burst into tears. 'I am not finished yet. I don't want to go into an institution.' But this was all the Welfare State could offer: and a place in the welfare home would cost the State £5 per week, while a suitable room, if it could be found, would cost the State very much less. But there was no choice.

Let us face the fact that there are people with special needs and see that these needs are met as if they were our own. Remember that economic needs are not necessarily the most important—there are educational needs, medical needs and social needs. Ascertainment of need is partly a professional matter. What sort of education does this child need? What sort of medical care does this patient need? But professional ascertainment only goes half the way. We must never forget to ask the clients their preference. How do they wish their needs to be met?

Paradoxically, concern about limiting free choice in the consumer market has been one underlying reason for restricting choice for the client of the social services. By attempting to run services on the cheap, we have been forced to ration, sometimes arbitrarily, the little that is available. For example, selection at eleven-plus for secondary schools arises in part because we are not willing to provide enough education to allow the child or parent to do much choosing. But there are three other reasons why people have decisions taken for them. There is the Poor Law tradition which taught us that people in need were second-class citizens. There is the long tradition of personal authoritarianism behind the voluntary charity movement. And last but not least, there is the tradition of personal arrogance of some professional groups—particularly the poor man's lawyer and the honorary consultant. If the social services are to serve, people must not be packed into an institution or certified simply because it is customary or cheaper or easier.

If we were really prepared to put our hands in our pockets and apply these principles, what would we do? Let me give just an outline. We would provide for all the type of social security the middle classes expect and usually get—that means a high level of wage-related benefits in sickness, unemployment and old age. We would provide family allowances of at least £1 a week for *all* children. We would rebuild the shocking schools, provide proper maintenance grants at the secondary-school level with a generous means test or perhaps no means test at all. We would rebuild hospitals on modern lines—vast out-patient departments (or health centres) with a few beds tucked away in the corners. We would close the mental deficiency colonies, and build new villas with small wards. How many could be looked after by quasi-housemothers in units of eight just like good local authorities are doing for children deprived of a normal home life? How many could be looked after at home if there were proper occupational centres and domiciliary services? We would plough up the sinister old mental hospitals and build small ones in or near the towns. We would pull down most of the institutions for old people and provide them with suitable housing. All this would be backed up by a *full* home-care service for the mentally ill, the physically ill, and those in social need. And to make sense of home care, we would have to make a far more determined assault on all our dirty slum houses without baths, lavatories or adequate water supply. We would provide a full range of occupations at home and elsewhere for the disabled, the aged, and the sick. We would discharge prisoners into the psychiatric hospitals and try and cure them. The criminal law would become a social service and stop being so bloody majestic.

How is the citizen going to know what services are available and how to use them? How is the citizen to get redress of grievance if he isn't properly treated? It is not enough to stick up closely printed notices outside the post office and appoint a battery of advisory committees, consumers' councils, and complaints tribunals. What we need is a citizens' office in every town run on public money by a public Board independent of every Government department except the Treasury. The office would employ specially trained staff, not enthusiastic amateurs. It would have the duty not just to provide information about services but to put the person actually in touch with them. It would have the duty not just to receive complaints but to forward them to the appropriate authority and *represent* the complainant from then onwards. If this were done we might have real democracy and not just a façade behind which caucuses rule.

Here is the outline of a programme for fifty years which would have to be amended as it went along. Until more money is put up for social research no one can be sure of the right answers. And I don't pretend that there aren't vast problems involved in implementing it. First, there would have to be many more trained people to operate the services. Indeed much of it depends upon more and better secondary education, particularly for women. Secondly, there would be the problem of who would run it. Will any Government have the courage to carry out the drastic reform of local government functions and finance which would be essential to any bold programme? Or will local authorities have to be by-passed by more *ad hoc* authorities? And what about the professions? Who is going to keep their feet on the ground?

Where is the money to come from? I am not going to by-pass this one with the usual line about plugging the holes in the tax system. In general it is my belief that if the British people knew the truth about the social services they would pay the bill. So I am not afraid of asking them to do so—be it by a complete recasting of contributions to the social security system on a proportional basis or by other means. Secondly, there needs to be a drastic review of tax concessions to income tax which have been providing indirect social services for the better-off for years before any proper social services were provided for anyone else. In particular there is the tax treatment of pension plans, dependants and children. With a high level of tax-free family allowances I can see no justification at all for tax allowances for children (that would save £320,000,000 to be spent on higher family allowances). Thirdly, I want a higher national income instead of the present stagnation.

I wouldn't be human if I didn't wonder how the reviewers will treat this essay, or for that matter what my academic colleagues will say when I am not there (why shouldn't I bring my bias out into the open?). Some will ignore it, others will discuss one point and give a completely false impression of what I have written. Others will disagree and say so, and that is quite fair. But most insidious of all is the review which gives the impression of being fair, plays up to the reader's instinctive complacency, and then restates the Establishment view without attempting to get to grips with the argument. Let me inoculate you against it.

Mr Abel-Smith has chosen the current economic crisis, when the future of the pound is still in the balance, to argue the case for spending more not less on the Welfare State. What have been described elsewhere as his 'revelations on the state of the social services' add little to existing knowledge. The condition of the mental hospitals has long caused concern in official circles and a few years ago the Minister of Health allocated £1,000,000 for new developments in this important field. Nor are the remedies which he suggests wholly new. They follow the broad lines of the reports of recent committees and of the Royal Commission on Mental Health.

Mr Abel-Smith has done us a service by drawing attention once more to the fields where standards are low and indicating the lines upon which policies may need to be developed. He is, however, on less firm ground in recommending precipitate action. What he fails to appreciate is that action in this field as elsewhere must await improvement in the general financial situation and particularly in the balance of payments. Our prosperity depends upon a sound economy and any further expenditure on the Welfare State will do more harm than good to the cause he has at heart.

Whose prosperity? Whose Welfare State?

Culture is ordinary

THE BUS-STOP was outside the cathedral.
I had been looking at the Mappa Mundi, with its rivers out of
Paradise, and at the chained library, where a party of clergymen
had got in easily, but where I had waited an hour and cajoled a
verger before I even saw the chains. Now, across the street, a
cinema advertised the *Six-Five Special* and a cartoon version of
Gulliver's Travels. The bus arrived, with a driver and conductress
deeply absorbed in each other. We went out of the city, over the
old bridge, and on through the orchards and the green meadows
and the fields red under the plough. Ahead were the Black Mountains, and we climbed among them, watching the steep fields end
at the grey walls, beyond which the bracken and heather and whin
had not yet been driven back. To the east, along the ridge, stood
the line of grey Norman castles; to the west, the fortress wall of
the mountains. Then, as we still climbed, the rock changed under
us. Here, now, was limestone, and the line of the early iron work-
ings along the scarp. The farming valleys, with their scattered white
houses, fell away behind. Ahead of us were the narrower valleys:
the steel rolling-mill, the gasworks, the grey terraces, the pitheads.
The bus stopped, and the driver and conductress got out, still
absorbed. They had done this journey so often, and seen all its
stages. It is a journey, in fact, that in one form or another we have
all made.

I was born and grew up halfway along that bus journey. Where
I lived is still a farming valley, though the road through it is being
widened and straightened, to carry the heavy lorries to the north.
Not far away, my grandfather, and so back through the generations, worked as a farm labourer until he was turned out of his
cottage and, in his fifties, became a roadman. His sons went at
thirteen or fourteen on to the farms; his daughters into service.
My father, his third son, left the farm at fifteen to be a boy porter

on the railway, and later became a signalman, working in a box in this valley until he died. I went up the road to the village school, where a curtain divided the two classes—Second to eight or nine, First to fourteen. At eleven I went to the local grammar school, and later to Cambridge.

Culture is ordinary: that is where we must start. To grow up in that country was to see the shape of a culture, and its modes of change. I could stand on the mountains and look north to the farms and the cathedral, or south to the smoke and the flare of the blast furnace making a second sunset. To grow up in that family was to see the shaping of minds: the learning of new skills, the shifting of relationships, the emergence of different language and ideas. My grandfather, a big hard labourer, wept while he spoke, finely and excitedly, at the parish meeting, of being turned out of his cottage. My father, not long before he died, spoke quietly and happily of when he had started a trade union branch and a Labour Party group in the village, and, without bitterness, of the 'kept men' of the new politics. I speak a different idiom, but I think of these same things.

Culture is ordinary: that is the first fact. Every human society has its own shape, its own purposes, its own meanings. Every human society expresses these, in institutions, and in arts and learning. The making of a society is the finding of common meanings and directions, and its growth is an active debate and amendment, under the pressures of experience, contact, and discovery, writing themselves into the land. The growing society is there, yet it is also made and remade in every individual mind. The making of a mind is, first, the slow learning of shapes, purposes, and meanings, so that work, observation and communication are possible. Then, second, but equal in importance, is the testing of these in experience, the making of new observations, comparisons, and meanings. A culture has two aspects: the known meanings and directions, which its members are trained to; the new observations and meanings, which are offered and tested. These are the ordinary processes of human societies and human minds, and we see through them the nature of a culture: that it is always both traditional and creative; that it is both the most ordinary common meanings and the finest individual meanings. We use the word culture in these two senses: to mean a whole way of life—the common meanings; to mean the arts and learning—the special processes of discovery and creative effort. Some writers reserve the word for one or other of these senses; I insist on both, and on the significance of their conjunction. The questions I ask about our culture are questions about our general and common purposes, yet also questions about deep personal meanings. Culture is ordinary, in every society and in every mind.

Now there are two senses of culture—two colours attached to it—that I know about but refuse to learn. The first I discovered at Cambridge, in a teashop. I was not, by the way, oppressed by Cambridge. I was not cast down by old buildings, for I had come from a country with twenty centuries of history written visibly into the earth: I liked walking through a Tudor court, but it did not make me feel raw. I was not amazed by the existence of a place of learning; I had always known the cathedral, and the bookcases I now sit to work at in Oxford are of the same design as those in the chained library. Nor was learning, in my family, some strange eccentricity; I was not, on a scholarship in Cambridge, a new kind of animal up a brand-new ladder. Learning was ordinary; we learned where we could. Always, from those scattered white houses, it had made sense to go out and become a scholar or a poet or a teacher. Yet few of us could be spared from the immediate work; a price had been set on this kind of learning, and it was more, much more, than we could individually pay. Now, when we could pay in common, it was a good, ordinary life.

I was not oppressed by the university, but the teashop, acting as if it were one of the older and more respectable departments, was a different matter. Here was culture, not in any sense I knew, but in a special sense: the outward and emphatically visible sign of a special kind of people, cultivated people. They were not, the great majority of them, particularly learned; they practised few arts; but they had it, and they showed you they had it. They are still there, I suppose, still showing it, though even they must be hearing the rude noises from outside, from a few scholars and writers they call—how comforting a label is!—angry young men. As a matter of fact there is no need to be rude. It is simply that if that is culture, we don't want it; we have seen other people living.

But of course it is not culture, and those of my colleagues who, hating the teashop, make culture, on its account, a dirty word, are mistaken. If the people in the teashop go on insisting that culture is their trivial differences of behaviour, their trivial variations of speech habit, we cannot stop them, but we can ignore them. They are not that important, to take culture from where it belongs.

Yet, probably also disliking the teashop, there were writers I read then, who went into the same category in my mind. When I now read a book such as Clive Bell's *Civilisation*, I experience not so much disagreement as stupor. What kind of life can it be, I wonder, to produce this extraordinary fussiness, this extraordinary decision to call certain things culture and then separate them, as with a park wall, from ordinary people and ordinary work? At home we met and made music, listened to it, recited and listened to poems, valued fine language. I have heard better music and better poems since; there is the world to draw on. But I know, from the most ordinary experience, that the interest is there, the capacity is there. Of course, farther along that bus journey, the old social organization in which these things had their place has been broken. People have been driven and concentrated into new kinds of work, new kinds of relationship; work, by the way, which built the park walls, and the houses inside them, and which is now at last bringing, to the unanimous disgust of the teashop, clean and decent and furnished living to the people themselves. Culture is ordinary: through every change let us hold fast to that.

The other sense, or colour, that I refuse to learn, is very different. Only two English words rhyme with culture, and these, as it happens, are sepulture and vulture. We don't yet call museums or galleries or even universities culture-sepultures, but I hear a lot, lately, about culture-vultures (man must rhyme), and I hear also, in the same North Atlantic argot, of do-gooders and highbrows and superior prigs. Now I don't like the teashop, but I don't like this drinking-hole either. I know there are people who are humourless about the arts and learning, and I know there is a difference between goodness and sanctimony. But the growing implications of this spreading argot—the true cant of a new kind of rogue—

I reject absolutely. For, honestly, how can anyone use a word like 'do-gooder' with this new, offbeat complacency? How can anyone wither himself to a state where he must use these new flip words for any attachment to learning or the arts? It is plain that what may have started as a feeling about hypocrisy, or about pretentiousness (in itself a two-edged word), is becoming a guilt-ridden tic at the mention of any serious standards whatever. And the word 'culture' has been heavily compromised by this conditioning: Goering reached for his gun; many reach for their cheque-books; a growing number, now, reach for the latest bit of argot.

'Good' has been drained of much of its meaning, in these circles, by the exclusion of its ethical content and emphasis on a purely technical standard; to do a good job is better than to be a do-gooder. But do we need reminding that any crook can, in his own terms, do a good job? The smooth reassurance of technical efficiency is no substitute for the whole positive human reference. Yet men who once made this reference, men who were or wanted to be writers or scholars, are now, with every appearance of satisfaction, advertising men, publicity boys, names in the strip newspapers. These men were given skills, given attachments, which are now in the service of the most brazen money-grabbing exploitation of the inexperience of ordinary people. And it is these men—this new, dangerous class—who have invented and disseminated the argot, in an attempt to influence ordinary people—who because they do real work have real standards in the fields they know—against real standards in the fields these men knew and have abandoned. The old cheapjack is still there in the market, with the country boys' half-crowns on his reputed packets of gold rings or watches. He thinks of his victims as a slow, ignorant crowd, but they live, and farm, while he coughs behind his portable stall. The new cheapjack is in offices with contemporary *décor*, using scraps of linguistics psychology and sociology to influence what he thinks of as the mass-mind. He too, however, will have to pick up and move on, and meanwhile we are not to be influenced by his argot; we can simply refuse to learn it. Culture is ordinary. An interest in learning or the arts is simple, pleasant and natural. A desire to know what is best, and to do what is good, is the whole positive nature of man. We are not to be scared from these things by noises.

There are many versions of what is wrong with our culture. So far I have tried only to clear away the detritus which makes it difficult for us to think seriously about it at all. When I got to Cambridge, I encountered two serious influences, which have left a very deep impression on my mind. The first was Marxism; the second the teaching of Leavis. Through all subsequent disagreement I retain my respect for both.

The Marxists said many things, but those that mattered were three. First, they said that a culture must be finally interpreted in relation to its underlying system of production. I have argued this theoretically elsewhere—it is a more difficult idea than it looks—but I still accept its emphasis. Everything I had seen, growing up in that border country, had led me towards such an emphasis: a culture is a whole way of life, and the arts are part of a social organization which economic change clearly radically affects. I did not have to be taught dissatisfaction with the existing economic system, but the subsequent questions about our culture were, in these terms, vague. It was said that it was a class-dominated culture, deliberately restricting a common human inheritance to a small class, while leaving the masses ignorant. The fact of restriction I accepted—it is still very obvious that only the *deserving* poor get much educational opportunity, and I was in no mood, as I walked about Cambridge, to feel glad that I had been thought deserving; I was no better and no worse than the people I came from. On the other hand, just because of this, I got angry at my friends' talk about the ignorant masses: one kind of Communist has always talked like this, and has got his answer, at Poznan and Budapest, as the imperialists, making the same assumption, were answered in India, in Indo-China, in Africa. There is an English bourgeois culture, with its powerful educational, literary and social institutions, in close contact with the actual centres of power. To say that most working people are excluded from these is self-evident, though the doors, under sustained pressure, are slowly opening. But to go on to say that working people are excluded from English culture is nonsense; they have their own growing institutions, and much of the strictly bourgeois culture they would in any case not want. A great part of the English way of life, and of its arts and learning, is not bourgeois in any discoverable sense. There are institutions, and common meanings, which are in no sense the sole product of the commercial middle class; and there are art and learning, a common English inheritance, produced by many kinds of men, including many who hated the very class and system which now take pride in consuming it. The bourgeoisie has given us much, including a narrow but real system of morality, that is at least better than its court predecessors. The leisure which the bourgeoisie attained has given us much of cultural value. But this is not to say that contemporary culture is bourgeois culture: a mistake that everyone, from Conservatives to Marxists, seems to make. There is a distinct working-class way of life, which I for one value—not only because I was bred in it, for I now, in certain respects, live differently. I think this way of life, with its emphases of neighbour-hood, mutual obligation, and common betterment, as expressed in the great working-class political and industrial institutions, is in fact the best basis for any future English society. As for the arts and learning, they are in a real sense a national inheritance, which is, or should be, available to everyone. So when the Marxists say that we live in a dying culture, and that the masses are ignorant, I have to ask them, as I asked them then, where on earth they have lived. A dying culture, and ignorant masses, are not what I have known and see.

What I had got from the Marxists then, so far, was a relationship between culture and production, and the observation that educa-tion was restricted. The other things I rejected, as I rejected also their third point, that since culture and production are related, the advocacy of a different system of production is in some way a cultural directive, indicating not only a way of life but new arts and learning. I did some writing while I was, for eighteen months, a member of the Communist Party, and I found out in trivial ways what other writers, here and in Europe, have found out more gravely: the practical consequences of this kind of theoretical error. In this respect, I saw the future, and it didn't work. The Marxist interpretation of culture can never be accepted while it retains, as it need not retain, this directive element, this insistence that if you honestly want Socialism you must write, think, learn in certain prescribed ways. A culture is common meanings, the product of a whole people, and offered individual meanings, the product of a man's whole committed personal and social experience. It is stupid and arrogant to suppose that any of these meanings can in any way be prescribed; they are made by living, made and remade, in ways we cannot know in advance. To try to jump the future, to pretend that in some way you *are* the future, is strictly insane. Prediction is another matter, an offered meaning, but the only thing we can say about culture in an England that has socialized its means of production is that all the channels of expression and communication should be cleared and open, so that the whole actual life, that we cannot know in advance, that we can know only in part even while it is being lived, may be brought to consciousness and meaning.

Leavis has never liked Marxists, which is in one way a pity, for they know more than he does about modern English society, and about its immediate history. He, on the other hand, knows more than any Marxist I have met about the real relations between art and experience. We have all learned from him in this, and we have also learned his version of what is wrong with English culture. The diagnosis is radical, and is rapidly becoming orthodox. There was an old, mainly agricultural England, with a traditional culture of great value. This has been replaced by a modern, organized, industrial State, whose characteristic institutions deliberately cheapen our natural human responses, making art and literature into desperate survivors and witnesses, while a new mechanized vulgarity sweeps into the centres of power. The only defence is in education, which will at least keep certain things alive, and which will also, at least in a minority, develop ways of thinking and feeling which are competent to understand what is happening and to maintain the finest individual values. I need not add how widespread this diagnosis has become, though little enough acknowledgment is still made to Leavis himself. For my own part, I was deeply impressed by it; deeply enough for my ultimate rejection of it to be a personal crisis lasting several years.

For, obviously, it seemed to fit a good deal of my experience. It did not tell me that my father and grandfather were ignorant wage-slaves; it did not tell me that the smart, busy, commercial culture (which I had come to as a stranger, so much so that for years I had violent headaches whenever I passed through London and saw underground advertisements and evening newspapers) was the thing I had to catch up with. I even made a fool of myself, or was made to think so, when after a lecture in which the usual point was made that 'neighbour' now does not mean what it did to Shakespeare, I said—imagine!—that to me it did. (When my father was dying, this year, one man came in and dug his garden; another loaded and delivered a lorry of sleepers for firewood; another came and chopped the sleepers into blocks; another—I don't know who, it was never said—left a sack of potatoes at the back door; a woman came in and took away a basket of washing.) But even this was explicable: I came from a bit of the old society, but my future was Surbiton (it took me years to find Surbiton, and have a good look at it, but it's served a good many as a symbol—without having lived there I couldn't say whether rightly). So there I was, and it all seemed to fit.

Yet not all. Once I got away, and thought about it, it didn't really fit properly. For one thing I knew this: at home we were glad of the Industrial Revolution, and of its consequent social and political changes. True, we lived in a very beautiful farming valley, and the valleys beyond the limestone we could all see were ugly. But there was one gift that was overriding, one gift which at any price we would take, the gift of power that is everything to men who have worked with their hands. It was slow in coming to us, in all its effects, but steam power, the petrol engine, electricity, these and their host of products in commodities and services, we took as quickly as we could get them, and were glad. I have seen all these things being used, and I have seen the things they replaced. I will not listen with patience to any acid listing of them—you know the sneer you can get into plumbing, baby Austins, aspirin, contraceptives, canned food. But I say to these Pharisees: dirty water, an earth bucket, a four-mile walk each way to work, headaches, broken women, hunger and monotony of diet. The working people, in town and country alike, will not listen (and I support them) to any account of our society which supposes that these things are not progress: not just mechanical, external progress either, but a real service of life. Moreover, in the new conditions, there was more real freedom to dispose of our lives, more real personal grasp where it mattered, more real say. Any account of our culture which explicitly or implicitly denies the value of an industrial society is really irrelevant; not in a million years would you make us give up this power.

So then the social basis of the case was unacceptable, but could one, trying to be a writer, a scholar, a teacher, ignore the indictment of the new cultural vulgarity? For the plumbing and the tractors and the medicines could one ignore the strip newspapers, the multiplying cheapjacks, the raucous triviality? As a matter of priorities, yes, if necessary; but was the cheapening of response really a consequence of the cheapening of power? It looks like it, I know, but is this really as much as one can say? I believe the central problem of our society, in the coming half-century, is the use of our new resources to make a good common culture; the means to a good, abundant economy we already understand. I think the good common culture can be made, but before we can be serious about this, we must rid ourselves of a legacy from our most useful critics; a legacy of two false equations, one false analogy, and one false proposition.

The false proposition is easily disposed of. It is a fact that the new power brought ugliness: the coal brought dirt, the factory brought overcrowding, communications brought a mess of wires. But the proposition that ugliness is a price we pay, or refuse to pay, for economic power need no longer be true. New sources of power, new methods of production, improved systems of transport and communication can, quite practically, make England clean and pleasant again, and with much more power, not less. Any new ugliness is the product of stupidity, indifference, or simply inco-ordination; these things will be easier to deal with than when power was necessarily noisy, dirty, and disfiguring.

The false equations are more difficult. One is the equation between popular education and the new commercial culture: the latter proceeding inevitably from the former. Let the masses in, it is said, and this is what you inevitably get. Now the question is obviously difficult, but I can't accept this equation, for two reasons. The first is a matter of faith: I don't believe that the ordinary people in fact resemble the normal description of the masses, low and trivial in taste and habit. I put it another way: that there are in fact no masses, but only ways of seeing people as masses. With the coming of industrialism, much of the old social organization broke down and it became a matter of difficult personal experience that we were constantly seeing people we did not know, and it was tempting to mass them, as 'the others', in our minds. Again, people were physically massed, in the industrial towns, and a new class structure (the names of our social classes, and the word 'class' itself in this sense, date only from the Industrial Revolution) was practically imposed. The improvement in communications, in particular the development of new forms of multiple transmission of news and entertainment, created unbridgeable divisions between transmitter and audience, which again led to the audience being interpreted as an unknown mass. Masses became a new word for mob: the others, the unknown, the unwashed, the crowd beyond one. As a way of knowing other people, this formula is obviously ridiculous, but, in the new conditions, it seemed an effective formula—the only one possible. Certainly it was the formula that was used by those whose money gave them access to the new communication techniques; the lowness of taste and habit, which human beings assign very easily to other human beings, was assumed, as a bridge. The new culture was built on this formula, and if I reject the formula, if I insist that this lowness is not inherent in ordinary people, you can brush my insistence aside, but I shall go on holding to it. A different formula, I know from experience, gets a radically different response.

My second reason is historical: I deny, and can prove my denial, that popular education and commercial culture are cause and effect. I have shown elsewhere that the myth of 1870—the Education Act which is said to have produced, as its children grew up, a new cheap and nasty press—is indeed myth. There was more than enough literacy, long before 1870, to support a cheap press, and in fact there were cheap and really bad newspapers selling in great quantities before the 1870 Act was heard of. The bad new commercial culture came out of the social chaos of industrialism, and out of the success, in this chaos, of the 'masses' formula, not out of popular education. Northcliffe did few worse things than start this myth, for while the connection between bad culture and the social chaos of industrialism is significant, the connection between it and popular education is vicious. The Northcliffe

Revolution, by the way, was a radical change in the financial structure of the press, basing it on a new kind of revenue—the new mass advertising of the 1890's—rather than the making of a cheap popular press, in which he had been widely and successfully preceded. But I tire of making these points. Everyone prefers to believe Northcliffe. Yet does nobody, even a Royal Commission, read the most ordinarily accessible newspaper history? When people do read the history, the false equation between popular education and commercial culture will disappear for ever. Popular education came out of the other camp, and has had quite opposite effects.

The second false equation is this: that the observable badness of so much widely distributed popular culture is a true guide to the state of mind and feeling, the essential quality of living of its consumers. Too many good men have said this for me to treat it lightly, but I still, on evidence, can't accept it. It is easy to assemble, from print and cinema and television, a terrifying and fantastic congress of cheap feelings and moronic arguments. It is easy to go on from this and assume this deeply degrading version of the actual lives of our contemporaries. Yet do we find this confirmed, when we meet people? This is where 'masses' comes in again, of course: the people *we* meet aren't vulgar, but God, think of Bootle and Surbiton and Aston! I haven't lived in any of those places; have you? But a few weeks ago I was in a house with a commercial traveller, a lorry-driver, a bricklayer, a shopgirl, a fitter, a signalman, a nylon operative, a domestic help (perhaps, dear, she is your very own treasure). I hate describing these people like this, for in fact they were my family and family friends. Now they read, they watch, this work we are talking about; some of them quite critically, others with a good deal of pleasure. Very well, I read different things, watch different entertainments, and I am quite sure why they are better. But could I sit down in that house and make this equation we are offered? Not, you understand, that shame was stopping me; I've learned, thank you, how to behave. But talking to my family, to my friends, talking, as we were, about our own lives, about people, about feelings, could I in fact find this lack of quality we are discussing? I'll be honest—I looked; my training has done that for me. I can only say that I found as much natural fineness of feeling, as much quick discrimination, as much clear grasp of ideas within the range of experience as I have found anywhere. I don't altogether understand this, though I am not really surprised. Clearly there is something in the psychology of print and image that none of us has yet quite grasped. For the equation looks sensible, yet when you test it, in experience—and there's nowhere else you can test it—it's wrong. I can understand the protection of critical and intelligent reading: my father, for instance, a satisfied reader of the *Daily Herald*, got simply from reading the company reports a clear idea, based on names, of the rapid development of combine and interlocking ownership in British industry, which I had had made easy for me in two or three academic essays; and he had gone on to set these facts against the opinions in a number of articles in the paper on industrial ownership. That I understand; that is simply intelligence, however partly trained. But there is still this other surprising fact: that people whose quality of personal living is high are apparently satisfied by a low quality of printed feeling and opinion. Many of them still live, it is true, in a surprisingly enclosed personal world, much more so than mine, and some of their personal observations are the finer for it. Perhaps this is enough to explain it, but in any case, I submit, we need a new equation, to fit the observable facts.

Now the false analogy, that we must also reject. This is known, in discussions of culture, as a 'kind of Gresham's Law'. Just as bad money will drive out good, so bad culture will drive out good, and this, it is said, has in fact been happening. If you can't see, straight away, the defect of the analogy, your answer, equally effective, will have to be historical. For in fact, of course, it has not been happening. There is more, much more bad culture about; it is easier, now, to distribute it, and there is more leisure to receive it. But test this in any field you like, and see if this has been accompanied by a shrinking consumption of things we can all agree to be good. The editions of good literature are very much larger than they were; the listeners to good music are much more numerous than they were; the number of people who look at good visual art is larger than it has ever been. If bad newspapers drive out good newspapers, by a kind of Gresham's Law, why is it that, allowing for the rise in population, *The Times* sells nearly three times as many copies as in the days of its virtual monopoly of the press, in 1850? It is the law I am questioning, not the seriousness of the facts as a whole. Instead of a kind of Gresham's Law, keeping people awake at nights with the now orthodox putropian nightmare, let us put it another way, to fit the actual facts: we live in an expanding culture, and all the elements in this culture are themselves expanding. If we start from this, we can then ask real questions: about relative rates of expansion; about the social and economic problems raised by these; about the social and economic answers. I am working now on a book to follow my *Culture and Society*, trying to interpret, historically and theoretically, the nature and conditions of an expanding culture of our kind. I could not have begun this work if I had not learned from the Marxists and from Leavis; I cannot complete it unless I radically amend some of the ideas which they and others have left us.

I give myself three wishes, one for each of the swans I have just been watching on the lake. I ask for things that are part of the ethos of our working-class movement. I ask that we may be strong and human enough to realize them. And I ask, naturally, in my own fields of interest.

I wish, first, that we should recognize that education is ordinary: that it is, before everything else, the process of giving to the ordinary members of a society its full common meanings, and the skills that will enable them to amend these meanings, in the light of their personal and common experience. If we start from that, we can get rid of the remaining restrictions, and make the necessary changes. I do not mean only money restrictions, though these, of course, are ridiculous and must go. I mean also restrictions in the mind: the insistence, for example, that there is a hard maximum number—a fraction of the population as a whole—capable of really profiting by a university education, or a grammar school education, or by any full course of liberal studies. We are told that this is not a question of what we might personally prefer, but of the hard cold facts of human intelligence, as shown by biology and psychology. But let us be frank about this: are biology and psychology different in the USA and USSR (each committed to expansion, and not to any class rigidities), where much larger numbers, much larger fractions, pass through comparable stages of

87

education? Or were the English merely behind in the queue for intelligence? I believe, myself, that our educational system, with its golden fractions, is too like our social system—a top layer of leaders, a middle layer of supervisors, a large bottom layer of operatives—to be coincidence. I cannot accept that education is a training for jobs, or for making useful citizens (that is, fitting into this system). It is a society's confirmation of its common meanings, and of the human skills for their amendment. Jobs follow from this confirmation: the purpose, and then the working skill. We are moving into an economy where we shall need many more highly trained specialists. For this precise reason, I ask for a common education that will give our society its cohesion, and prevent it disintegrating into a series of specialist departments, the nation become a firm.

But I do not mean only the reorganization of entry into particular kinds of education, though I welcome and watch the experiments in this. I mean also the rethinking of content, which is even more important. I have the honour to work for an organization through which, quite practically, working men amended the English university curriculum. It is now as it was then: the defect is not what is in, but what is out. It will be a test of our cultural seriousness whether we can, in the coming generation, redesign our syllabuses to a point of full human relevance and control. I should like to see a group working on this, and offering its conclusions. For we need not fear change; oldness may or may not be relevant. I come from an old place; if a man tells me that his family came over with the Normans, I say 'Yes, how interesting; and are you liking it here?' Oldness is relative, and many 'immemorial' English traditions were invented, just like that, in the nineteenth century. What that vital century did for its own needs, we can do for ours; we can make, in our turn, a true twentieth-century syllabus. And by this I do not mean simply more technology; I mean a full liberal education for everyone in our society, and then full specialist training to earn our living in terms of what we want to make of our lives. Our specialisms will be finer if they have grown from a common culture, rather than being a distinction from it. And we must at all costs avoid the polarization of our culture, of which there are growing signs. High literacy is expanding, in direct relation to exceptional educational opportunities, and the gap between this and common literacy may widen, to the great damage of both, and with great consequent tension. We must emphasize, not the ladder but the common highway, for every man's ignorance diminishes me, and every man's skill is a common gain of breath.

My second wish is complementary: for more and more active public provision for the arts and for adult learning. We now spend £20,000,000 annually on all our libraries, museums, galleries, orchestras, on the Arts Council, and on all forms of adult education. At the same time we spend £365,000,000 annually on advertising. When these figures are reversed, we can claim some sense of proportion and value. And until they are reversed, let there be no sermons, from the Establishment, about materialism: this is their way of life, let them look at it. (But there is no shame in them: for years, with their own children away at school, they have lectured working-class mothers on the virtues of family life; this is a similar case.)

I ask for increased provision on three conditions. It is not to be a disguised way of keeping up consumption, but a thing done for its own sake. A Minister in the last Labour Government said that we didn't want any geniuses in the film industry; he wanted, presumably, just to keep the turnstiles clicking. The short answer to this is that we don't want any Wardour Street thinkers in the leadership of the Labour Party. We want leaders of a society, not repair-workers on this kind of cultural economy.

The second condition is that while we must obviously preserve and extend the great national institutions, we must do something to reverse the concentration of this part of our culture. We should welcome, encourage and foster the tendencies to regional re-creation that are showing themselves, for culture is ordinary, you should not have to go to London to find it.

The third condition is controversial. We should not seek to extend a ready-made culture to the benighted masses. We should accept, frankly, that if we extend our culture we shall change it: some that is offered will be rejected, other parts will be radically criticized. And this is as it should be, for our arts, now, are in no condition to go down to eternity unchallenged. There is much fine work; there is also shoddy work, and work based on values that will find no acceptance if they ever come out into the full light of England. To take our arts to new audiences is to be quite certain that in many respects those arts will be changed. I, for one, do not fear this. I would not expect the working people of England to support works which, after proper and patient preparation, they could not accept. The real growth will be slow and uneven, but State provision, frankly, should be a growth in this direction, and not a means of diverting public money to the preservation of a fixed and finished partial culture. At the same time, if we understand cultural growth, we shall know that it is a continual offering for common acceptance; that we should not, therefore, try to determine in advance what should be offered, but clear the channels and let all the offerings be made, taking care to give the difficult full space, the original full time, so that it is a real growth, and not just a wider confirmation of old rules.

Now, of course, we shall hear the old cry that things shouldn't be supported at a loss. Once again, this is a nation, not a firm. Parliament itself runs at a loss, because we need it, and if it would be better at a greater loss, I and others would willingly pay. But why, says Sir George Mammon, should *I* support a lot of doubtful artists? Why, says Mrs Mink, should I pay good money to educate, at *my* expense, a lot of irresponsible and ungrateful State scholars? The answer, dear sir, dear madam, is that *you* don't. On your own —learn your size—you could do practically nothing. We are talking about a method of common payment, for common services; we too shall be paying.

My third wish is in a related field: the field now dominated by the institutions of 'mass culture'. Often, it is the people at the head of these institutions who complain of running things at a loss. But the great popular newspapers, as newspapers, run at a loss. The independent television companies are planned to run at a loss. I don't mean temporary subsidies, but the whole basis of financing such institutions. The newspapers run at a heavy loss, which they make up with money from advertising—that is to say a particular use of part of the product of our common industry. To run at a loss, and then cover yourself with this kind of income, is of the essence of this kind of cultural institution, and this is entirely characteristic of our kind of capitalist society. The whole powerful array of mass cultural institutions has one keystone: money from advertising. Let them stop being complacent about other cultural institutions which run at a smaller loss, and meet it out of another part of the common product.

But what is it then that I wish? To pull out this keystone? No, not just like that. I point out merely that the organization of our present mass culture is so closely involved with the organization of capitalist society that the future of one cannot be considered except in terms of the future of the other. I think much of contemporary advertising is necessary only in terms of the kind of economy we now have: a stimulation of consumption in the direction of particular products and firms, often by irrelevant devices, rather than real advertising, which is an ordinary form of public notice. In a Socialist economy, which I and others want, the whole of this pseudo-advertising would be irrelevant. But then what? My wish is that we may solve the problems that would then arise, where necessary things like newspapers would be running at something like their real loss, without either pricing them out of ordinary means, or exposing them to the dangers of control and standardization (for we want a more free and more varied press, not one less so). It is going to be very difficult, but I do not believe we are so uninventive as to be left showing each other a pair of grim alternatives: either the continuance of this crazy peddling, in which news and opinion are inextricably involved with the shouts of the market, bringing in their train the new slavery and prostitution of the selling of personalities; or else a dull, monolithic, controlled system, in which news and opinion are in the gift of a ruling party. We should be thinking, now, about ways of paying for our common services which will guarantee proper freedom to those who actually provide the service, while protecting them and us against a domineering minority whether political or financial. I think there are ways, if we really believe in democracy.

But that is the final question: how many of us really believe in it? The capitalists don't; they are consolidating a power which can survive parliamentary changes. Many Labour planners don't; they interpret it as a society run by experts for an abstraction called the public interest. The people in the teashop don't; they are quite sure it is not going to be nice. And the others, the new dissenters?

Nothing has done more to sour the democratic idea, among its natural supporters, and to drive them back into an angry self-exile, than the plain, overwhelming cultural issues: the apparent division of our culture into, on the one hand, a remote and self-gracious sophistication, on the other hand, a doped mass. So who then believes in democracy? The answer is really quite simple: the millions in England who still haven't got it, where they work and feel. There, as always, is the transforming energy, and the business of the Socialist intellectual is what it always was: to attack the clamps on that energy—in industrial relations, public administration, education, for a start; and to work in his own field on ways in which that energy, as released, can be concentrated and fertile. The technical means are difficult enough, but the biggest difficulty is in accepting, deep in our minds, the values on which they depend: that the ordinary people should govern; that culture and education are ordinary; that there are no masses to save, to capture, or to direct, but rather this crowded people in the course of an extraordinarily rapid and confusing expansion of their lives. A writer's job is with individual meanings, and with making these meanings common. I find these meanings in the expansion, there along the journey where the necessary changes are writing themselves into the land, and where the language changes but the voice is the same.

PETER TOWNSEND

A society for people

During the war I lived in London. For a youngster there was much excitement. As soon as the barrage balloons began to perch on their wires I started building an air-raid shelter in the garden, and it was not long before I took my turn as a fire-watcher and learned how to handle a stirrup-pump. When the London docks were first bombed I cycled for miles through the East End to see what had happened. I remember many days spent in improvised classrooms in the school crypt and nights curled up on a mattress under an iron bedstead, or huddled at the foot of the basement stairs with my mother and grandmother and the other tenants in our large, gloomy Victorian house. There was less reserve between neighbours and everyone seemed to be in and out of one another's houses, papering over pin-pricks of light in blackened windows, claiming access to stairways and roofs, keeping meaningless records of alerts and all-clears, drinking cups of tea at all hours and, increasingly as time went on, arguing about the kind of society they wanted after the war.

I was not old enough to take much of an interest in proposals for social change but I was aware of the lowering of social barriers and of the popular support for social reform. This had a profound influence on me and, so it seems now, on many others of my generation. At the start of the war my mother was on tour in Blackpool and some evacuees from Liverpool were lodged temporarily in our boarding-house. A poorly-dressed woman with leaden eyes climbed off the bus with a tearful baby and, without a thought for the landlady and two sharp-nosed women guests, undid her blouse and pulled out one of her breasts to comfort the child. I remember how shocked the three women were by her unselfconscious behaviour and, more important, how shocked they and many others were too by the poverty of the evacuees. In the early part of the war the upheavals of evacuation caused many people to

93

understand for the first time how the other half lived, and what the years of unemployment had wrought. Here were two nations confronted.

The rich were chastened by this sudden revelation of social misery and the young wanted to put an end to it. Involvement in the problems of others, and a respect for them, as well as mere patriotism, made people prepared to accept sacrifices. National assistance was liberalized, welfare foods and all kinds of benefits for mothers were introduced, stiff taxation was accepted and the most envied rationing system of the war raised the living standards of the poor. Experts who had been arguing seriously whether the number of 'unemployables' in the population was half a million or one million were shamed into silence. Other experts who had predicted widespread war neurosis and panic to get out of the cities were humbled by the calm and steadiness of the people. Infant and child mortality fell sharply, morbidity was amazingly low and, despite the apparent rigours of rationing, the submarine blockade, the bombing and everything else, a near-miracle occurred—there was in 1942 a greater sense of national well-being than in any year of the thirties.

Although social objectives which had been sought from one Royal Commission to another were now secured within weeks and months few people were satisfied. The guilt of the thirties had to be erased. The Beveridge Report successfully competed with the battles in Russia and North Africa for the front pages of the daily press. A Coalition Government produced the first White Paper on a National Health Service, more remarkable, in some respects, than the plan finally agreed; *The Times* even complained in the middle of the war that the Government was dragging its feet in putting forward proposals for social reform; and a Tory who had been one of the Foreign Office spokesmen in Parliament at the time of Munich actually piloted through the Education Act of 1944. These were measures of the agreement that existed. A new post-war society seemed ready to emerge.

The details of the plan seemed not to matter. The will was there and that was enough. The public was determined that there must be no return to pre-war conditions and sought a Government which could maintain the momentum of social change. Those people who believed Winston Churchill's charges in his ill-phrased 'Gestapo' speeches, like the two old women in our street who bolted their doors for four whole days after the 1945 election, belonged to another world.

Looking back now at the popular feeling generated by the events of the war years it is difficult to understand how anyone could have been surprised by the Labour Party's victory. A transformation had taken place. In the Britain of 1945 it seems possible to detect the two human impulses which, as I understand it, are necessary to any Socialist society. Tracing what has happened to these two provides, in a sense, the theme of this essay. There was an attitude of trust, tolerance, generosity, goodwill—call it what you like—towards others; a pervasive faith in human nature. Then there was a prevailing mood of self-denial, a readiness to share the good things in life and to see that others got the same privileges as oneself; an urge to give everyone, including the poor, the sick, the old and the handicapped, the chance of having certain elementary rights or freedoms so that they could achieve individual self-respect. Am I wrong in supposing that these were the really important attitudes struck by society then, despite the effects of a long war? After all, millions of people were thankful to be safely home once more, and their memories were still fresh with the sufferings of the victims of the war.

Perhaps I exaggerate. Perhaps I am being sentimental about the carry-over of a popular mood from the period of the blitz. Or maybe I am simply recollecting some of the ideals of adolescence, fed on such unforgettable books as Richard Hillary's *The Last Enemy*. Whatever the truth, many others, now in their late twenties and thirties, felt much the same. From war-time experiences of evacuation, sleeping in shelters, civil defence, farming and forestry camps during school holidays and finally service in the armed forces, many of us gained a sense of fair shares, of common effort, of mixing with people of different class and of planning for the future which came at the most impressionable age and which could at times be intoxicating.

At first all seemed to go well. In the early years after the war a daunting programme of legislation was undertaken which seemed to match popular feeling. By the middle of 1948 national insurance,

95

industrial injuries and assistance benefits, as well as family allowances, were being paid and the Health Service had started. There were new charters for the care of children, the sick and the old. For a nation struggling with the economic consequences of the war the programme was little short of breathtaking. But instead of gaining a sense of purpose and of confidence as the war-time plans began to take recognizable shape the Labour Government hesitated more and more; doubts crept into the discussions of social policy and the first flush of post-war enthusiasm began to wane. Concessions were made to pressure-groups by men uncertain of their direction. There was no steadying voice to remind the Government of its objectives, to say that more was required than the institutional framework for a new society (even supposing it was the right framework), or to say that it takes more than Acts of Parliament, however well-intentioned, to establish trust and equality. The staff who had worked the Poor Law, to take one example, could not be changed overnight. A long process of education, and education by example, was required.

By 1950 the momentum following the war was spent and the Labour Party's victory at the polls was a hollow one, the succeeding year before the defeat of 1951 being one of the most painful and degrading in recent political history. It is true that the Government was severely handicapped by the Korean war and the decision to buy weapons at any price. These were enough to make anyone neurotic, and the slim Parliamentary majority was scarcely helpful. But, quite apart from these extenuating circumstances, there was a succession of minor decisions, like the imposition of Health Service charges, the abandonment of a large part of the Exchequer share of social insurance and the faint-hearted singling out of the cement and sugar industries for nationalization, which showed how quickly the Labour Party had reached a dead end. It was not simply that the two most formidable leaders, Cripps and Bevin, had been lost, nor that the Bevanite split had occurred without offering adequate alternative leadership, nor even that the Party needed to recover its breath before resuming the assault. No one knew what to assault. Instead of realizing that their work was only beginning the Labour Party leaders thought it was at an end. They seemed to be drained of initiative by the effort of legislating. They no longer believed in any tangible social aim and had increasingly lost touch with ordinary people. These were the two frightening facts at the start of the 1950's.

From 1948 to 1951 I was at Cambridge. In 1949 Orwell's *1984* was published. In the next year or two few undergraduates failed to read it. The impact of this book, coinciding as it did with the tragic death of Orwell himself, was very great. It is a masterpiece of cynicism. Orwell had shown how the highest political ideals could be, and had been, perverted. He had revealed the mechanisms by which the unsophisticated could be, and had been, misled. More than anyone else, and despite the many occasions on which he laid himself open to mockery, he had taught that Socialism was a code of conduct to live by and not an uneasy compromise with vice. His last book gave the final twist in the wounds of 1950 and 1951. Those who had discussed the plans for a new society so ardently during and immediately after the war found their hopes sadly deflated. They were completely disillusioned.

During the last seven or eight years this disillusion with Socialism has persisted. I think it can largely be explained by the meaning given to the simple, but crushingly cold and complacent phrase, 'the Welfare State'. I want to attack this phrase, and all it is supposed to represent, first because it suggests, or rather, is taken to mean, that a country which is a Welfare State is soft and makes people soft, and second, that in a country which is called a Welfare State there can be, in some strange way, no just causes left.

The strict values of the unbending spinster have always had a cherished place in British society—the peculiar and varying disciplines of the public school, the Church of England and the outside lavatory have seen to that—and it is not surprising to find them being expressed with peculiar vehemence as soon as the new health and social security services began to operate in July 1948. The general satisfaction created by the legislative achievements was quickly undermined. Britain, so the argument went, was going soft and everyone was being supervised from the cradle to the grave. Wage-earners had been granted improved insurance and assistance benefits in sickness and unemployment: no doubt they would be feckless and stay off work. Mothers were actually being paid a

small allowance when they had two or more dependent children:
no doubt they would spend it on perms or the pictures. The middle-
aged and old were making extraordinary demands for wigs, spectacles and dentures: no doubt they would acquire them irrespon-
sibly to entertain their grandchildren. Services were wasted on
people who could not be trusted, who toddled off to the nearest
doctor or National Assistance officer to get what they could when
they needed nothing.

All this may read like exaggerated parody. I only wish it were.
The line of criticism could be documented at tedious and uniformly
depressing length. When, in February 1958, the Director of the
Conservative Political Centre wrote in *The Future of the Welfare
State* that we were 'squandering public money on providing indis-
criminate benefits for citizens, many of whom do not need them
and some of whom do not want them', he was simply repeating,
in a characteristically vague way (which benefits? which people?),
the complaint that has been made down the years in the correspon-
dence and editorial columns of the *Telegraph*, *The Times*, *Economist*
and, perhaps most revealing of all, *British Medical Journal*.

It is quite remarkable what happens when we submit the various
charges to the cool test of evidence. What about 'malingering' and
'abuse', for example? Everyone knows, or thinks he knows, of the
individual instance, but is it significant nationally? Early in 1958
The Lancet published data showing that in one area a small minority
of people made claims for sickness benefit said to be unjustified by
the doctor, but the money they received was only three per cent of
the total paid. A year or two previously the National Assistance
Board took a special look at those who had drawn assistance for
long periods during unemployment. Its officers found that about
2,000 of the total of 32,000 were 'work-shy' (less than one per cent
of the unemployed, or 0.001 per cent of the total working population at that time). What is more, nearly *two-thirds* of this tiny
group were physically or mentally handicapped. As for the run on
spectacles, dentures and the rest that took place after July 1948,
no proof has ever been offered of the widespread belief that many
people were queueing up for these for no other reason than that
they were free.

It is important to ask for the evidence. It is also important to remember historical precedent. The same severe views have been pressed with considerable force for generations by one section of society. The Poor Law reforms of the nineteenth century and the Old Age Pensions Act of 1908 were attacked as bitterly as any recent measure by those who saw them as 'undermining the sense of family responsibility' and who fought to preserve the distinction between the 'deserving' and the 'undeserving' poor. They believed firmly in charity and in the division of the population into first and second class citizens. In his film masterpiece *Intolerance*, made in 1916, D. W. Griffith mercilessly satirized the 'uplifters' of his day, who perpetrated so much cruelty under the guise of charity. I shall never forget those women, acting like agents of the Lord's Day Observance Society—sternly moral, if not openly pious, inflexible and frequently outraged.

The journals of the Establishment, such as *The Economist*, *The Times* and the bank reviews, have taken the criticism a stage farther. They have given a good deal of support to the idea that the social services are an indulgence or an extravagance which should be withdrawn as soon as possible. With increasing national prosperity, it is said, more and more people should look after their own health, education and social security; the dwindling numbers of the destitute should be covered by selective services which assuage guilt by employing more palatable means tests. This is the 'self-liquidating' theory of the social services. So far as I am aware it has never been expressed in practicable details suggesting how the chronic sick, the disabled and the poor can pay for their own services and how State schools and hospitals can be handed over to private individuals. It is little more than a semi-articulate protest drawing on self-interest and class mistrust.

This has not stopped the theory from being used freely in recent years to support the sustained attack on the social services and on taxation. Nowhere from the political Right or Left has much resistance been shown. Ironically enough it has been left to Enoch Powell, in one of the few intelligent statements about social policy ever to have been made by a member of a Tory Government (perhaps that is one reason why he is no longer in office), to stress that the social services are as necessary to modern society as sewage systems to Victorian society.

I have discussed one assumption about the Welfare State. The other, that there are no just causes left, is more pernicious. It implies that everything has been achieved. But were the achievements of 1945–48 as remarkable as so many people suppose? Future historians will, I think, pick out the uncritical acceptance of the Beveridge recommendations as one of the most significant phenomena of domestic politics from 1942 to 1946. Here was a set of proposals for social security which caught the imagination of the public. Central to them was the idea that benefits should be enough without other resources for subsistence, yet this idea was never scrutinized. Beveridge took over the kind of measure used by those who had carried out surveys of poverty before the war. It looked bogus, was bogus and has been shown to be bogus, yet right up to 1954 successive Governments stuck to it bravely and pretended that they were trying to live up to it. The subsistence standard, even as Beveridge worked it out, has never, by a good many calories and proteins, been attained. How many people know that the unemployment and sickness benefits for a man in 1958 form a much smaller percentage of the average wage than they did in 1938, or indeed in 1912? Full employment and not social insurance has been responsible for the reduction in poverty since the war. The Beveridge scheme tidied up numerous anomalies and extended social insurance to the whole population (largely, it must be said, to the benefit of the self-employed and the middle classes, some of whom now qualify for the full retirement pension of £2 10s. for a single person or £4 for a married couple after only ten years of tax-free contributions), but it belonged to the past, to the 1930's and not the 1950's. It is difficult now to understand the enthusiasm of only ten or twelve years ago.

All Governments pretend to the public that their achievements are greater than they are. In a democracy one hopes the pretences will be probed ruthlessly by an alert Opposition. But where are the informed critics of today? Labour politicians have been happy to exaggerate the achievements of the Welfare State because they feel they can gain most of the credit. Tory politicians have been loath to disavow them because they can follow less guiltily a policy of cutting 'marginal' social service expenditure and reducing 'redistributive' taxation. 'Nothing,' as they say, "is sacrosanct." This policy has indeed been followed since 1951 : up to that year the proportion of the nation's resources devoted to the social services had been growing steadily, and then stood at about eleven or twelve per cent (compared with about nine and a half per cent in 1938). Even now, in its Health Service, Britain is strikingly ahead of most other countries, but in many other services it has fallen strikingly behind. Germany, for example, is now spending half as much again as Britain on social security from a smaller national income.

The achievements in what is unreflectively called 'income redistribution' have also been exaggerated. Were the post-war trends so much in favour of the working class as both Socialists and Tories supposed? During the war differences in living standards had narrowed sharply and only grudgingly did the Labour Government begin to let them widen again. That seems to be as near to the truth as we are likely to get. A 'redistribution' of income occurred in the war rather than afterwards. Not for some time did the middle-class counter-revolution come into full swing. Not until 1947 was the first important step taken to increase regressive, and lighten progressive, taxes. Bank chairmen have now talked unceasingly about the plight of the impoverished middle classes and the *Manchester Guardian* and *Observer* have joined the other journals in printing lengthy discussions. Gradually an elaborate protective system has been built into the tax system and industry. Successive Chancellors of the Exchequer have loosened the rules by which tax is collected. Allowances have been granted for more kinds of dependants, for some dependants for longer, for superannuation and life insurance. Income tax consultants have become prosperous and more individuals have become aware of the expenses which, quite legitimately, count for tax relief. Just before I began to write, the 1958 Budget has introduced allowances for subscriptions to professional societies. Many of these changes may be reasonable in themselves, but the cumulative effect should not be forgotten.

The changes outside the tax system have been even more important. Indirect income benefits today have reached such a pitch that mere comparisons between two persons' incomes tell us little about the real differences in their standards of living. There are luxurious cars bought and maintained at the expense of the firm, meal vouchers, season tickets, subsidized and free housing, salaries paid in full during sickness, large superannuation contributions, holiday expenses and free travel abroad. The recent Royal Commission on Taxation recognized all this, but failed to appreciate its significance. Examples are not hard to come by. Claims for as much as £28 for one lunch for four people are not infrequently made by the executives of one big company. I know of one extreme instance where the expenses for forty people for a lavish four-days conference in a seaside resort amounted to over £8,000. At a time when the number of people with incomes over £5,000 a year is supposed to be small the increase in the number of very expensive cars on the roads is impressive. The production of Rolls-Royces has more than trebled within the last ten years. In April 1958 *The Times* was advertising a new Rolls-Royce for £9,015 and a Bentley for £8,388. Admittedly these appeared to be the prices for rather exceptional models. Those who were prepared to rough it a bit could get by with the standard Rolls-Royce for £5,500 or the Bentley at £3,700.

Subsidies to income explain part of the middle-class counter-attack. Capital gains explain another. Throughout the last ten years inflation has meant a large series of non-taxable capital gains. The seven- and eightfold increase in undistributed profits since 1938 has given a powerful boost to the value of shares (partly concealed by free and cheap issues of new shares to shareholders) and so a much bigger proportion than previously of the shareholder's income has come from capital gains than from dividends. Moreover, heavy death duties have caused the rich to look for ways of avoiding them. They can pass on their wealth late on in life, more than five years before they expect to die; or they can buy agricultural land and expand the family business, on which they pay less tax. The recent history of the reaction to the high tax rates of the war and early post-war years teaches that no economic measures intended to narrow income inequalities can last unless the Chancellor of the Exchequer remains both Socialist and vigilant.

All this could be documented in great detail and far better than I could pretend to. But would it go far enough? Would it answer those like A. J. P. Taylor, who recently wrote an article for the *Manchester Guardian* entitled 'Nothing left to Reform—Political Consequences of 1945-50'? The arguments I have used are destructive rather than constructive. What *is* there to reform? To answer this question we have to know more about people's needs and how they live.

I work as a sociologist. I should like this to mean that I explore, and write about, present-day society so that others may understand it better. I should like it to mean that I spend a good deal of time observing and interviewing small cross-sections of the population before writing detailed reports which aim to keep human beings to the forefront. Above all, I should like it to mean studying very carefully the life of the poorest and most handicapped members of society.

Why do I emphasize this last point? In the British population of 50,000,000 there are nearly 5,000,000 retirement pensioners, 500,000 widows receiving special benefits, nearly 2,000,000 war pensioners, not far short of 250,000 people receiving industrial injuries and disablement allowances; 450,000 unemployed (at present) and there-fore around 1,250,000 men, women and children dependent on unemployment benefit; and, on any average day, nearly 1,000,000 wage-earners and their families dependent on sickness benefit. Altogether about 2,250,000 people are dependent at any one time on National Assistance allowances, most of them for extremely long periods. There are many more people, particularly the old (as a number of studies make clear), who would qualify for National Assistance, but do not apply. There are 300,000 mental defectives and persons of unsound mind, most of whom are in mental hospitals and other institutions; over 750,000 disabled persons, including spastics and the blind; there are hundreds of thousands of persons in chronic sick hospitals, institutions for the aged, chil-dren's homes, and even more chronic sick living at home. There may be nearly 1,000,000 old people who cannot leave their homes unassisted. Finally there are many adults and children in large families, among whom recent surveys have confirmed nutritional deficiencies; many young and middle-aged widows with children to support and many working men still earning less than £7 or £8 a week. The figures I have given may overlap in some instances but if we are trying to estimate the proportion of the population with special difficulties over a long period, who cannot and could not be expected to overcome their problems on their own resources, we should think in terms of the submerged fifth and not the submerged tenth. The total numbers are nearer 10,000,000 than 5,000,000. Did Mr A. J. P. Taylor have them in mind when he said there was nothing left to reform?

Mine is a utopian view of the definition and scope of sociology. In fact the name covers an enormous range of different subjects. A fully fledged university lecturer in sociology addressed one of the few meetings of the British Sociological Association during the present year on the subject of 'Protestantism and Capitalism in Sixteenth-Century Germany'. Articles in the sociological journals with titles like 'The Dimensions of Syntality in Small Groups. I: The Neonate Group,' 'Suffragium: From Vote to Patronage' and 'Palaeolithic Religion and the Principles of Social Evolution', are by no means rare. Many sociologists are in fact interested only in social philosophy, in history or social evolution or in rather mechanical experiments in closed laboratories. These interests have their place somewhere, but one wonders whether the balance is right and why so few research workers study the submerged fifth. Among the last hundred main articles in the *British Journal of Sociology* only twenty report research into present-day society, six of these twenty dealing with overseas affairs (three with the social background of African students), six with social status and ranking of occupations, and two with the employment of sociology graduates. Clearly the graduates are not much employed on surveys of everyday life.

The few who are doing social research often seem to concentrate unduly on the specialized techniques of questionnaire design, coding and computing, and administrative tasks like the supervision of junior interviewers. This is one way of acquiring professional status, as market research agencies have been quick to appreciate, and of building up recognition for an academic discipline which has taken rather a lot of beatings and which does not even exist in Cambridge (and only in the barest outline in Oxford). However, the preoccupation with method and with status is symptomatic of a disease which goes much wider than sociology. This is the general problem of professionalism in Britain, whereby groups of specialists with a technical training, their own language and their own ethics multiply and form their own protective associations. It is one of the long-term problems we have hardly begun to identify. A professional association seeks privileges at the expense of the common good. It attaches more importance to respect for seniority, conformity to professional rules of conduct and the growth of tradition than it does to individual freedom and inventiveness. Its members are conditioned to interpret their duties more in terms of professional skills than in terms of the needs of clients. Professional people must not get involved in their clients' affairs; they must be wholly detached, formal and objective; they must be neutral and never, never get mixed up in politics. Perhaps this is why the strongest associations tend to be so reactionary.

The same pressures are now exerting themselves on the sociologist, yet the more he tries to study and interpret contemporary society the more difficult it is for him to isolate his work from daily politics. If he visits a cross-section of people in their homes and tries to understand their lives and problems he is made aware of their needs and of how government affects them. It should be terribly hard for him to write his report without revealing, or at least implying, what their needs are, even if he shirks the separate duty of going on to suggest how these needs may be met. This difficulty is much more acute for him than for an anthropologist concerned only with a remote non-industrialized society or for an economist, still less for a biologist, a historian or a physician. It may cost him his bread and butter. Is it surprising to find wealthy foundations shy of giving money for social research, or university specialists tending to concentrate on subjects which they hope are politically neutral?

It may be best for the sociologist to admit this dilemma rather than pretend it does not exist. He may then be less inhibited about studying social needs; readier to concede that Government officials and politicians always will, and perhaps should, look to sociology for evidence on which to base reform; and readier too to face up to his own worst failings and prejudices, rather than conceal them by depending too much on the reports of others.

I have never realized the importance of these things more clearly than during the first more-or-less formal interview of my life. I was supposed to be trying to find out what had been the effects of prolonged unemployment in 1952 on many thousands of people living in the Lancashire cotton towns. Already I had talked to officials of the National Assistance Board and of the Ministries of Labour and National Insurance and done my best to penetrate the fog of their statistics; I had done the rounds of borough councillors, trade union secretaries, personnel officers and welfare workers without finding much enlightenment. I could avoid the hardest job no longer. The first address I had chosen at random proved to be a dark, terraced house and I remember the whitened doorstep and the tall chimneys rising above the roofs in the distance. Twice my courage failed me and I walked past without knocking. My hands were thrust in my raincoat pockets and I can still remember fumbling with some scraps of paper and tearing them into minute pieces while I stood at the corner of the street and pretended to be looking for a bus.

I knocked hesitantly and when the door opened explained myself rather abjectly to a woman in her early twenties. She was friendly and showed me into a rather bare sitting-room where her two-year-old son was romping around. She had another boy of five who was at school. My questions were bad, my manner worse, and I felt a complete charlatan—a bungling amateur with no right to scientific pretensions. Yet somehow she patiently coached me through my interview, tactfully answering the really important questions which it had not occurred to me to ask. She and her husband had both been weavers earning a combined income of £12 a week (the grandmother used to look after the children). Both had been unemployed for twenty weeks and while their social security benefits totalled £3 14s. their unavoidable outlay on rent, rates, life insurance and fuel totalled £2 12s. (including 10s. to keep alive a hire purchase agreement on a suite of furniture). No more than £1 2s. was left for food, clothing and the rest. Early on in unemployment they had spent their few pounds of savings on tinned foods and for four months the family lived largely on these and on bread and jam. No meat was bought, no butter, eggs or fresh milk (the children relied mainly on tinned dried milk, though one had started getting fresh milk at school and the other had lived for several weeks with a better-off relative), only part of the bacon and margarine ration, no sweets, little fruit, few vegetables and practically no clothing (indeed, some clothing was sold). Although the 2s. a week on the football pools was abandoned, husband and wife bought a few cigarettes and still went occasionally to the cinema. 'Life wouldn't be worth living without *something*.' The family had developed its own idiosyncrasies during this time of crisis. They went to bed early to save fuel and electricity and they had entered vainly for newspaper crossword competitions. When he had no chance of trying for another job the husband stayed in bed until lunchtime so that he would need no breakfast. Relatives had given them food from time to time but were mostly in no position to help. The family had not sought National Assistance although they qualified. 'That's for the people who are really poor.'

As I called at other homes I began to understand something of the problems of the submerged fifth, even though I had not learned to be at ease during an interview. (I tried to identify myself with the people I met, yet half realized I never could.) One person I met was a widow with three young children and no close relatives. Another was a mother with two illegitimate children. A third was a widower living in a hostel who suffered from double incontinence. Then there was a couple with two boys at grammar school—'when our children were born we made up our minds that they would never go into cotton'; a bachelor living with his parents—'the dole is nowt at all for a single man'; two middle-aged spinsters, one with chronic bronchitis; a family with a long history of tuberculosis, and many others. Again and again I found I was wrong in assuming that doctors, social workers, local government officers, trade union secretaries and others who spent most of their lives working in the area would have firsthand knowledge of the peculiar circumstances and problems of the people living there. For one thing they were often acquainted with no more than one odd corner of local society. On matters of detail falling within their specialized field of work they were helpful; on general matters involving the life of whole sections of the population, whether children, young families, the unemployed or the chronic sick they were unbelievably wide of the mark. Many seemed to have little comprehension of the needs and circumstances of people living right under their noses. A trade union secretary said he knew of no one in his union who would qualify for National Assistance, yet he was wrong in at least five of the ten instances where members of his union were interviewed. It is extremely hard not to be misled by people thought to be so much more eminent and knowledgeable, especially if they are charming and share some of the same sentiments. I found this very hard to understand. Go easy. Ask for the evidence. If you want to believe it, don't. What people like to happen, what people say happens, and what in fact does happen, are very different things.

The journey through Lancashire had left me in a confused but excited frame of mind. It had come in the middle of a two-years period of research among White Papers and Blue Books and I determined to seek the earliest opportunity to do more continuous research among people living in their own homes. I had set off with some questions I had been unable to answer. I returned with different questions, with a deeper respect for people like Charles Booth and Mayhew and also for D. H. Lawrence and George Orwell, and with a greater mistrust of the Welfare Establishment subscribed to by Socialists and Tories alike. At that time criticism was, however, so rare that it was easy to doubt one's judgment and Richard Titmuss was the only university person of repute to give confidence and inspiration to a number of people like myself who were beginning to feel their way towards some evaluation of progress since the war. In fact he was the only person who seemed to understand what had been happening. The public debate about social policy had a strange air of unreality alongside the facts of people's lives. Some of the strengths of working-class life and many of the needs of the submerged fifth had been overlooked.

In 1954 Michael Young started the Institute of Community Studies to do a job the universities were not doing, and I had the opportunity to interview old people in Bethnal Green. What struck me hardest was the extraordinary diversity between people of similar age living in the same locality. It was deeply puzzling. All the stereotypes in one's mind had to be taken to bits. By the time I had finished counting exceptions to the politician's traditional picture of Darby and Joan living on the old age pension there was nobody left. It was hard to fill in a truthful picture. At one extreme I met a man who was one of twenty-two children, married to a woman who was one of eighteen, and between them they had seventeen children, of whom twelve were alive. They had about

sixty relatives living within a mile and on every occasion I called
the house was alive with grandchildren. The family kept a stall in
the local market and had many friends. At the other extreme was
an elderly spinster who was the only child of an only child. Her
father died when she was a baby and her mother some fifteen or
twenty years ago. Since then she had had literally no relatives
whatsoever. She lived in a single room at the top of a tenement
block and consistently refused to apply for National Assistance.
She had virtually no friend in the world and no close contacts with
any of the neighbours. Her holiday consisted of visiting Southend
once or twice a year just for the day; she sat on the front by herself and watched the crowds. I found it almost impossible to believe
she was so isolated and I was not convinced until I visited her on
Christmas Eve and found no sign of Christmas but a sheet of wrap-
ping paper from Woolworths pinned up above the mantelpiece.

Between these two were the widest variations imaginable. Dimly
I tried to make sense of them and to group people so that generalization might be possible. All the time I wrestled with and never
properly resolved the apparent contradiction between the comforting conclusion that the majority of old people lived reasonably
secure lives within an affectionate family and the disturbing conclusion that a frightening number of physical, financial, occupational and social needs went unmet and, what is more, undetected,
particularly among the minority of isolated or semi-isolated people
with few or no relatives. I wondered vaguely whether the surprising range of people was not due to my catching people towards
the end of life, yet when I did another spell of interviewing with
people of all ages in a single tenement block in Stepney the diversi-
ties seemed even wider.

One day's experience may show what I mean. First of all I
climbed a stone stairway and knocked on a brown-painted door at
the end of a gloomy passage. It opened almost before I had lowered
my hand. Standing there, with her head cocked on one side, was
a small stocky woman with a mop of yellow-grey hair splaying out
from her head. A bedraggled blouse was held together with at least
four safety pins and below it a misshapen velvet skirt had dropped
three or four inches to reveal a vest partly concealed by a red sash.
Her face was fleshy and pallid and she kept placing stubby fingers

against a cheek in thought. She rambled disconnectedly in reply to my explanation of my call, talking in one breath about washing her hair and the problem of an H-bomb world, but she motioned me inside.

The room was small and an inside door led to an even smaller room, not much bigger than a large cupboard. There was very little furniture and, except for one strip of old lino, the floor boards were bare. There was a terrible armchair, dilapidated and broken with a rope mat thrown over it, a small table in the centre, a wooden chair, a small iron bedstead, and little else. The bedstead possessed no mattress. A carpet lay on the springs and there was a grey pillow and coverlet rolled up at the foot. Slung under the mantelpiece and above an old open firegrate was a large cardboard box in which there were all kinds of knick-knacks—pins, cotton-reels, bits of wool and cloth, and scraps of paper. By the fireplace stood a single gas ring on top of a cylindrical tin which in turn rested on another tin. On one wall was a magazine-illustration of an eighteenth-century lover wooing his lady by a lake; it was clipped to a board with three clothes-pegs. In the middle of the small table I noticed a child's toy lorry in which had been placed a few tiny flowers, dahlias with the stalks nipped off.

The woman put a bowl of cold water on the table to wash her hair, went behind me to fetch a bar of soap and later transferred some hot soapy water from a zinc tub—in which she had been washing some clothes—into the bowl on the table. These actions were spread over the half-hour I was there. At first we were in semi-darkness and she shuffled around the room, eventually finding a small step-ladder, which she placed against the door in order to reach the gas meter and put a shilling in the slot. She left the step-ladder against the door and, with momentary alarm, I saw her place a heavy gas fire and a flat-iron against the door. 'You're in a strange world. It isn't England at all. They say they want to put a stop to wars . . . but with all the bombing everyone got unsettled and we had to leave the shelters. It all started with that. . . . It's very hard to live and perhaps you'll call tomorrow. But it's always nice to welcome friends.' Her brother and her only daughter lived in the next street and saw her every day. One provided her with a small cleaning job and the other often gave her meals. But for their support and perhaps the considerateness of her neighbours it is reasonably certain she would have been in a mental hospital. She answered some questions lucidly, but then trailed off into confused meanderings. She kept speaking of her separation from her husband. 'You keep wondering, wondering where he is, right now. Wondering if he's with someone. You're used to married life and you want a partner. You can't go down the road and have a drink unless you've got a husband. They say absence makes the heart grow fonder. It's true. Your heart aches. But you've got to dismiss it.' And she began busying herself with soap and water.

I then called on a middle-aged married man who had several relatives in the same block and many more in the neighbouring streets, and he and his wife seemed to be meeting dozens of them every day. There was another couple with nine brothers and sisters and twenty-six uncles and aunts, many of them in the immediate neighbourhood, who also led a tight family life. Then there was a young couple waiting to move out to Crawley New Town and away from their family; a young single woman who had taken a room in the next street from her parents to be sure of a home after her marriage a few months hence, and an enormously fat widow who had that utter casualness of many working-class Mums and who cross-examined me shrewdly, if not mercilessly, about my own life. Finally there was a neurotic man living alone who was separated from his wife. He was one of the real desolates of society who seem to turn up in poor housing in fairly large numbers. He had left his wife and family in Liverpool years before and had had no contact with them since. His room smelt stale. He complained of 'breakdowns' at work and kept rubbing his head. Nevertheless he was intelligent and talked knowledgeably of the people in the locality who had many relatives. 'You have to be careful what you say. You'll go to a pub and you'll be talking about someone and he'll suddenly say, "He's my cousin". There's so many people related to each other in some way—it's like a little village.'

Besides those who were very poor perhaps as many as a fifth or more of the inhabitants were isolated and handicapped. They were elderly bachelors and spinsters whose parents and contemporaries had died, or merchant seamen who had drifted in from the docks, or divorced, separated or deserted people whose family life had

been disturbed. Then there were the few who seemed to have led
a hermit-like existence because of some deformity or disability or
whose past was something of a closed book. Many of them were
pathetic individuals who had found cheap shelter in a place where
their anonymity could be preserved, where there was a general air
of sociableness but of respect for privacy, where they could be
accepted with indulgence but not interfered with. 'He's a poor old
soul.' 'He means well. He can't help it.' 'She acts a bit queer, but
she's very quiet. I think it was the war.'

Around them was preserved the main texture of working-class
society, the people whose parents lived there, whose brothers and
sisters worked around the corner and whose children either lived
there or near by. Some two-thirds of the inhabitants were closely
related to several people in the same block, parents, brothers, and
sisters, children, and grandchildren. Relationships ramify, and many
people were aware of distant connections to other extended families in the same block and nearby. Thus part of the sense of community, of solidarity and of neighbourly restraint arose and was in
fact created by the ties of kinship.

What lessons are there here for social policy? I believe that it is
possible to get a better understanding of what are the needs of the
submerged fifth and how they can be met by learning what are the
strong features of working-class life. That is why the analysis of
social diversity seems to me to be so important. The happiest and
most secure relationships between adults in a family, for example,
seem to be those in which all kinds of services are exchanged, as
when the old grandmother cooks meals and cares for the grandchildren, and her daughter does the shopping and cleaning and
works part-time outside the home. One-sided dependence is disliked and the ability to give, to be of use to others, to do one's share
and to be independent, is venerated. This simple fact explains a lot
of things. It explains why working people (supported, incidentally,
by the trade unions) have always preferred to pay for social security
by specific 'contributions', because they earn thereby their right to
benefit in a way that they feel would not be possible through
ordinary taxation. It explains why social services administered by
systems of charity, patronage or means tests have never succeeded

and always will be disliked if not hated. A man does not want to get anything according to his degree of misery or destitution for that is humiliating. It affronts his dignity.

Yet it is difficult to reject the hand of the unbending spinster and her world of the privileged and the unprivileged, the strong and the weak, the deserving and the undeserving. She turns up in unexpected places and in unexpected guises. She never admits failure. More important, she never wants to succeed. Hers is an ambivalent attitude, wanting to do good works providing the reason for doing them is never removed. So long as she does not expect to gain, so long will there be inequality. It has taken us more than a decade to realize that beneath the New Look of social security the same old lady lurks. For, shrewdly adapting herself to the slogans of progressives, she has adopted wholeheartedly the policy of the national minimum.

The central choice in social policy lies in fact between a national minimum and equality. Support for the establishment of a national minimum in some or all social services has a long history, and especially from the work of the Webbs at the turn of the century to the present day. All one has to worry about, so the belief runs, is the need to raise health and living standard to a bare minimum, a subsistence level from which individuals can themselves build by their own efforts. It is in the State's interest to ensure that this minimum is attained: to go farther would be to interfere with individual freedom and to waste national resources. In theory the idea seems wonderful. In practice it evaporates. It is extraordinarily difficult to define what can be meant by a 'minimum' (bread? tea? cake? newspapers? books? cortisone? 'invisible' hearing aids? plastic surgery?). It is all the more difficult to readjust one's ideas continuously during a period of inflation. Even when a pound is worth ten shillings the fact takes time getting used to. Has anyone tried running up a downcoming escalator? Supporters of the national minimum are all too likely to find themselves defending a policy which widens rather than narrows the gap between living standards and depresses the opportunities for recovery of the poor, the sick and the dispossessed.

The source of confusion is that the national minimum has been held to be the badge of equality. How noble for all citizens to be treated alike. What could be more equal than flat-rate benefits for all, financed by flat-rate contributions? Unfortunately this is a perfect example of doublethink. When the rate of benefit is kept below a 'national minimum', when the national insurance stamp takes a far larger share of the wage of the lowest paid than the salaried earner, and when part of the population is allowed to exploit the tax system through a plethora of private insurance and 'top hat' pension schemes to gain very generous extras, the result is the opposite of equality. According to a recent *Manchester Guardian* supplement half the pension contributions of those earning a few thousand pounds a year would otherwise go in tax. 'The greatest gainers are those with the highest rate of surtax. Thus the man with an income of £15,000 a year would lose only £7 10s. of net income per £100 premium, the remainder of the premium being offset by tax saving.'

Two separate standards of social value exist at one and the same time. In old age the living standards of the poor now fall more sharply than do those of the rich. I have interviewed middle-class people whose incomes were about the same or higher after retirement than before. They had paid off the mortgages on their houses, some had received large tax-free gratuities; and some were getting the advantage of the generous tax concessions now allowed on any further earnings. Their difficulties are as nothing compared with those of people now living on £3 or £4 a week who were recently earning a wage of £10, say, or more. There are millions of people living on £3 or £4 a week—and some on even less.

The problem for the future is to refuse to tolerate two standards of social value and apply one: to see that the privileges of the few can be transferred to the many. One obvious course is a complete recasting of social security, to reduce poverty and gross inequalities in living standards. The Labour Party has tentatively approved the principles of a national superannuation scheme with graduated contributions and benefits which favours the lowest paid. The plan could be the biggest contribution to social equality since the end of the war. I say 'could be' because the interpretation of a few of the crucial principles of the scheme remains in doubt. It will be interesting to see how far the traditional opponents of social equality can undermine the scheme. But the changes in social security cannot stop there. The same principles will have to be applied to sickness, unemployment, widows' and industrial injuries benefits. They may be applied partly by obliging the employer to pay full wages (as well as full salaries) for the first months of sickness and also by obliging him to make adequate redundancy payments (one day's notice and one week's pay are still all too frequent). Children's allowances (both direct family allowances and tax allowances) need to be revised and increased. This general reform would logically entail the drastic revision of the tax concession laws and the eventual withering away of the National Assistance Board, with people whose needs cannot be met by social insurance being transferred to the care of casework agencies.

Too many social services, and not only those concerned with payments of money, are still governed by the belief in a 'minimum'. These clothes will do for the boys and girls in this children's home; they are cheap but hard wearing. The meals in this institution only cost 15s. a week per person but they give adequate nutrition; the inmates are used to simple meals. The children in this school are far from reaching eleven-plus standards (what do you expect in such a district?); that is why they are housed in an ancient building in classes of fifty. The people queueing up outside this surgery (housing office, labour exchange, welfare office) have been waiting a long time; but they are used to waiting.

We have hardly begun to understand how to abandon the double standard of values in the social services and treat people as we ourselves would like to be treated. What can be done? To a large extent the deficiencies can be remedied by good legislation and government. Take housing, for example. As many as 2,500,000 households in this country (seventeen per cent of the total) have no piped water, well over 3,000,000 no water closet (twenty-three per cent) and 6,500,000 no fixed bath (forty-five per cent). When we know that millions of people must live for decades in old housing why is there no adequate plan, supervised by the Ministry of Housing, for its modernization and maintenance? Why do we allow slum clearance schemes to remove many solidly built terraced houses (sometimes, as in Bethnal Green, to make it easier to view the hideous old tenement blocks of Victorian England which are the worst slums and about which nothing much is being done) and to be carried out with gross insensitivity to community and family life? Housing management seems to be almost as much of a national scandal as the procedure by which patients lodge complaints against doctors and others in the Health Service. Local authorities should perhaps be answerable to regional housing associations (with consumer representation) set up by the Ministry of Housing.

Or take the services provided in the home. Part of the business of treating people as we ourselves would like to be treated is respecting the desire to be independent and to live a normal home life. Throughout recent years there has been growing professional emphasis, in the medical and psychiatric as well as the social-work world, on the value of care at home rather than in an institution. Most children taken into care by local authorities and by voluntary societies, old people in need of care and attention, and young and old in mental and general hospitals may be better cared for in ordinary private homes within the environment of a normal or substitute family rather than in institutions. For one thing the self-less devotion of institution staff makes more acute the separation of patients or residents from society. The idea that others are giving up their lives for your benefit and you can do nothing much about it makes you give up trying, or it makes you aggressive because you want your independence. The trend towards smaller hospital wards and smaller old people's homes (including many single and double rooms); the establishment of more contacts between institution and community (shown in the more generous visiting hours and more frequent 'holidays' outside institutions); the development of boarding-out schemes for both children and the aged taken into care—all these are indications of a complete change in outlook. Experiments in Worthing, Nottingham, Oxford and elsewhere give a hint of the enormous role which the domiciliary services will play in the future. The growing number and proportion of old people in the population strengthen the argument for a new policy.

In the first place, therefore, priority should be given to the home and community health services, including district nursing. By comparison with hospital services (except for mental hospitals) far too little money is being spent on domiciliary health and preventive services. The development of health centres and group practice has been much too slow; and the education of general practitioners barely touches on psychological and social medicine and thus offers no training for over two-thirds of their future work.

In the second place, a Family Help Service should be created. The purpose of this would be to enable the old, the sick and the handicapped to lead a normal life at home within an ordinary community, by supplying those who have no relatives or who are separated from them with the services normally provided by the family—like shopping, cleaning, cooking meals, washing laundry and so on, and by giving support to those relatives bearing a heavy burden of care—through personal attendance allowances, for example, or relief at night and during holidays. In the population there are many with few or no relatives. About a quarter of the old are unmarried or childless. There is the nucleus of a home help service and no doubt this would form the basis of the new service. It would have many additional functions, like the systematic visiting of the isolated aged by skilled workers to assess need, the supervision of special housing schemes and welfare homes and the provision of occupations for the homebound. The emergence of a major new service to take its place alongside Social Security, Health, Education and Housing may be justified.

If there is any lesson in the experience of the last ten years it is that no social aim can be achieved merely by planning, and passing, the necessary legislation. The various services do not exist as self-perpetuating systems untouched by worldly sin. They need money and they need good staff. They therefore depend on political decisions about priorities and on all the subtle twists and turns of social, and human, change. Almost imperceptibly since 1945 the needs of the submerged fifth have grown and the differences between the rich and the poor in their living standards have widened. Powerful arguments can be advanced, as I have tried to show, for a new and ambitious policy, geared to the principle that the best possible standards of service should be available to all on the basis of equal sacrifice. This could be followed with imagination, hope and enthusiasm. There is just one condition. It is useless paying lip-service to equality. Better nothing than that.

You cannot live like a lord and preach as a Socialist. Equality of sacrifice is not an ideal which applies to others but not yourself.

It is essentially personal and is not just a matter of avoiding osten-
tatious displays of wealth. To be scornful about cigars, extravagant
receptions, hunt balls, or a Rolls or Bentley with its superior number plate (like the elegant Bentley—UUU100—which I recently saw
parked outside the House of Commons) would be easy. The real test
comes in all the trivial details of life—in choosing whether to dodge
some taxes, use the firm's stamps for personal letters, add a pound
or two to the bill for expenses, or jump the queue at the hospital;
in asking repeatedly whether certain of our privileges look as
reasonable to others as they so often do to ourselves. How many
business lunches cost more than the National Assistance Board is
paying a man to keep himself for a whole week? How many professional people, and how many workers, have four, six, or eight
weeks holiday, a working week of less than thirty hours, and a
centrally heated and carpeted workroom? The more privileges you
have the fewer there are for others.

Everything turns on the way people behave to each other. The
handicapped, for example, still are treated too often as second-class
citizens who have no rights and no feelings. I once went round an
old people's home with a matron who swept into rooms and lavatories without making any apology to the people who were sometimes there. I saw one of her staff changing an old man's trousers
in full view of thirty other people in the room. In another home
the warden, an ex-army officer, took me into a room where there
were a dozen aged women. He stood and pointed at each one in
turn, saying in a loud voice, 'That's eighty-five, that's eighty-eight,
that's ninety-two . . .'

It is more than a personal ethic of self-respect, of fighting hard
to avoid conforming to a double standard, and failing often. It is
also a faith in people, in the fundamental goodness of man. People
live very differently and it is sometimes hard to understand what
drives them to act as they do. To give them the benefit of the
doubt, to assume they have good rather than bad motives when we
know little or nothing about them, and to concern ourselves with
their needs rather than their failings—these are generally regarded
as being Christian virtues, and yet they are the essence of Socialism.
They come naturally to some people. I have never known my
grandmother bear a grudge against anyone. As the eldest in a large

family in Middlesbrough she worked hard to help her own parents. She lost her husband when she had three small children, took in washing and tried to live on £1 a week. Yet whenever I meet anyone who knew her then, I hear stories of her helping neighbours in illness, injury and death. Throughout her life everyone has imposed on her, yet I never remember her making a single complaint. Even now, at the age of eighty-three, she is looking after her widowed son of sixty who lost his legs in the 1914 war. Perhaps, because of my love of her, I exaggerate her qualities. Yet there are many as unselfish.

It is more difficult for those who have to make a conscious effort of will to achieve as much. The sort of Socialism advocated by William Morris, or any simple expression of faith in the goodness of man, frightens and embarrasses the intellectual. He does not want to be taken for a sucker in public and you rarely find him saying anything so straightforward and naïve. He is much too cynical and self-conscious. Yet if he is not prepared to live his Socialism it stands little chance of attainment. He wants to stand apart from the crowd, to be original, to wear an outrageous shirt, condemn the mass media and talk of commitment, positivism and free cinema. He wants to reject many of the values of society. He may be right but continually he runs the risk, in his thoughts and actions, of alienating himself from ordinary people. There are few harder conflicts to resolve. Somehow he must preserve his independence and his right to criticize and yet keep in touch with people of every age and class, and laugh and cry with them, in his private life as well as in his public utterances. This is his one hope of becoming a constructive and not simply a destructive critic of Society. For to believe in people is to subscribe to their strengths, their pride, their capacity to recognize humbug or to shrug off propaganda, their fair dealing, their unselfishness and their willingness to bear pain without fuss, but above all the strengths given them by their lives within their families.

Traditionally Socialists have ignored the family or they have openly tried to weaken it—alleging nepotism and the restrictions placed upon individual fulfilment by family ties. Extreme attempts to create societies on a basis other than the family have failed dismally. It is significant that a Socialist usually addresses a colleague as 'brother' and a Communist uses the term 'comrade'. The chief means of fulfilment in life is to be a member of, and reproduce, a family. There is nothing to be gained by concealing this truth. The really great moments of life come not only in falling in love but in marrying, in having children and in maintaining one's love for one's parents. Herbert Spencer bounced one grandchild on his knee and said it was worth far more than all the books he had ever written. A good deal of a man's public activities, especially as a politician, can be explained by his possession or lack of a family.

Terms such as 'equality,' 'privilege,' 'the establishment,' and 'class' are imprecise and call up different images for different people. One is conscious of the risks in using them. But if that overdone phrase 'a classless society' means anything it is a society where differences in reward are much narrower than in Britain today and where people of different background and accomplishment can mix easily and without guilt; but also a society where a respect for people is valued most of all, for that brings a real equality.

At a Bank Holiday Fair on Hampstead Heath I was once watching a stolid, heavily-built man in his late forties heave at a rather ancient collection of horses, motor-bikes and cars which comprised a child's roundabout. After he had got it going he continued his labours on an iron wheel at the centre of the roundabout. It was then about 4 p.m. and he had been at it for hours. His forehead shone with sweat, yet despite this and the waiting throngs he was giving the children a fairly long ride for their sixpences. The small daughter of a young woman in slacks and a cashmere cardigan—probably the wife of a writer or a university lecturer—started wailing. The man stumbled between the circulating toys of iron, caught the child gently and handed her to her mother, placing his body in the way of the missiles so that he could do so. Humbly matter-of-fact, he took a terrible blow in the middle of his back. His expression did not change and he moved clumsily back to the wheel to continue his job. The woman and her husband had not thanked him, had not even looked at him. 'We shouldn't have brought her,' the mother said to her husband, 'she's so sensitive.'

RICHARD HOGGART

Speaking to each other

As I was preparing to write, one scene
came more than any other into my mind. It shows the classroom of
a bright new secondary modern school on a public housing estate
outside a busy provincial city. Almost all of the large class of
thirteen-year-olds look healthy and are decently clothed; their
young teacher wears what is by now almost a uniform—sports
jacket and charcoal-grey flannels. A sense of vocation still gives
something of the glow of idealism to his face, though it is confused
with signs of strain. He is taking a poetry lesson and finding it at
times surprisingly rewarding, at times extremely disillusioning. He
knows most of his pupils go to the pictures at least once a week
and watch television for two or three hours a night. They tell him
about the programmes in a friendly way; they know he hasn't a
TV set. He is an ex-scholarship boy, by choice committed to educat-
ing people whom he knows as deeply as one only knows those one
was born among—and whom he yet feels he does not know.

Most of the cultural aspects of our complex social revolution
can be seen there: the emerging Britain of a modest and fairly
widely diffused prosperity, of a new kind of 'working class' and
of the mass-media; a Britain which has superimposed on its many
other changes a significant stream of inter-class movements through
educational opportunity; a Britain which has not yet learned
to speak seriously to its new self. If we have no war and no
considerable economic breakdown it is likely that some of our
social assumptions, and much in our forms and manners, will be
very different by the end of the century from those we knew as
children. My general assertion is that we are moving towards a
cultural classlessness; that if we understand these changes better
the new society could be a great improvement on the old; if we
do not, it may be worse.

The present boundaries of the move towards cultural classlessness can easily be illustrated. Our national morning newspapers are by tradition politically divided. As, during the last few decades, the popular press has become more and more a form of entertainment this political quality has weakened. But a typical British resistance prevents the classless morning daily from emerging at present. The point we have so far reached can be seen in the *Daily Mirror* and the *Daily Express*, which between them account for more than half the total sales of our daily national morning newspapers. There is some overlapping in readership, but substantially they appeal to two bodies of people who still like to think of themselves as distinct —say, to working-class and lower-middle to middle-class people respectively. The two papers use different properties and forms of speech because these differences are still significant to their audiences. But the quality of the life each embodies and promotes is roughly the same; a cultural classlessness can be seen emerging there, held at the moment from greater assimilation by a residual sense of difference.

In some respects television would be the best instance of the emerging classless culture. But we can continue to draw illustrations from popular publications since in one part of that field the culturally classless world is already here. The colonel's lady and Judy O'Grady are sisters under the skin and their reading—though previously class-divided (all the way from *Peg's Paper* to *The Lady*) —has never been much concerned with either politics or the arts. *Woman* is the first truly classless journal of the new Britain.

All classes are on the move but one class is most strikingly moving, emotionally and often physically. The great body of urban working-class people are beginning at last to leave the dark, dirty, squalid back streets and the often confined imaginative horizons which the economics of life there encouraged. There is no need at this stage in the argument to look back in nostalgia. If we remember the conditions of life for these families—many of them our own families—fifty years ago, then we have much to thank our radical forefathers for effecting. Our children are going to be healthier and fresher, and have more opportunities according to their gifts, than our parents ever had. In this sense we are indeed heading for a better Britain, and I hope we have the sense and honesty to welcome it.

But what kinds of outlook will a technological, commercial, mass-communications society encourage? What qualities will the new class of consumers, embracing the large majority of the 37,000,000 adults in this compact and literate country, exemplify? Will they express a modern version of what we are used to thinking of as aspirant lower-middle-class attitudes? In some ways the pressures of a consumers' world do turn people away from traditional working-class attitudes towards those of the aspirant lower-middle-class; 'sticking together' tends to be replaced by 'keeping up with the Joneses'. But I think the prospects both better and worse than this. Better, because the new society is likely to be more widely tolerant, pleasant, open and unaggressive. Worse, because it may become what the Americans call, speaking of trends in their own environment, 'bland'. And 'blandness', which is a sort of imaginative boiled milk, will be lying in wait for all classes, not only for those we are used to calling working people: the new society could become homogeneous in a new way, except for a small group of dissidents.

This peculiarly challenging situation is further enriched by two native abilities: first, our slowness to accept change (in working-class areas today there is little evident difference in the styles of emotional life from those of fifty years ago; and a conversation with a provincial lady Conservative usually illustrates how hard our sense of the importance of distinctions dies); second, because of the Establishment's power to maintain or to remake itself by sheer receptivity, flexibility and flair—its ability to absorb almost anyone into the British socio-cultural Happy Family. But though these qualities do make change slow, they do not finally prevent it; under the surface change is taking place all the time . . . in the life of that provincial town and housing estate, in that class of boys and their teacher.

If we look back to the activities of those who were concerned with social problems at the turn of the century, at the sureness with which prospects were assessed and expressed—often in statements which are now classics of their kind, or in new social agencies—we are likely to decide that there must have been giants in those days, or to wonder whether their problems were simpler. Perhaps social and economic needs were in some ways easier to decide; it is easier to see a hole in a shoe than to assess the outlook encouraged by the television set which the emancipated worker has bought and turned his eyes to. No doubt those earlier documents were given vigour by the more plain relation, to both authors and audience, between evident needs and assured or assumed values. But I think they remain vivid and memorable chiefly because of their great intellectual and spiritual energy and breadth.

We could have at least the same sense of occasion; our challenge is in some respects a finer one. There is more dignity for the human spirit in questioning inward problems of *choice* than in opposing obvious economic injustices. The present offers a rare challenge—to affect the future of a society which is now, by its very success in material improvements, in danger of weakening its hold on its own moral strengths. The size and nature of the problem, its risks and its opportunities, should make us all feel historic. It is important to say this firmly because a society can be bemused by its own slogans. A society which repeatedly tells itself that it is tired and second-rate (neither of which seems to me true of Britain, though there is a superficial level at which they may seem to be), will begin to act that way.

Changes of attitudes are needed generally. But first a word about changes needed in some common attitudes on the Left. The British Left too often exhibits a bull-headed parochialism towards cultural matters. At one extreme this is the brass-tacks insensitivity of many local and national party and trade union officials, ready to associate anything artistic—or even intellectual—with upper-class gentility; 'Don't teach my boy about poetry; he's going to be a union boss', might be their form of an old statement. At the further extreme we find the assured narrowness of some intellectuals, a doctrinaire, anti-imaginative, Fabian-sterile single vision. Such people tend to dismiss the evidence for an emerging classlessness by pointing out that, economically, the Insiders are still very much in control, or that only one working-class family in ten has so far left the dirty districts—and then round matters off by calling the argument only another form of neo-Conservatism. They prefer situations imaginatively simplified. They would still like to find visible villains—in the Establishment, in the Press, in the other media. Teasing out the interactions of greed, self-delusion and weakness all the way through workers, intellectuals and men of power is a less satisfying process. A tycoon is a more satisfactory enemy than an able, pleasant, amusingly disillusioned—and probably mildly Left-wing—advertising copywriter.

But we need to concentrate on more widespread inadequacies in our attitudes. First, towards mass communications today. The basic facts of the situation are now well known : that during the last few decades the instruments for mass persuasion have undergone three main changes—a great absolute increase (e.g. in daily newspapers, which might have been expected to decline under the pressure from radio); a considerable centralization (chiefly because Britain is so small geographically); and an increasing concentration (e.g. we are reading fewer *different* publications). The pressures are mainly commercial. But the mass-media primarily reflect larger forces, and the event which did more than any other to encourage the whole process was, in fact, the last war, when mass means of communication had to advance very quickly if the common effort was to be improved. Still, that pressure is now largely relaxed; we are back at an open society with all the media available to it. That type of society will show certain specific tendencies in its use of the media.

These tendencies will not all be unfortunate ones, and we should count first the possible gains. It is right and important to remind ourselves, without sentimentality, of the strengths in our traditional and homogeneous class-groups : whether the fidelity and gentleness of face-to-face working-class communities; or the devotion and un-self-seeking responsibility which the best upper-class training could produce. But there is room for a lot of light in the narrow and cramped places of the English imagination. We tend to be spiritually insulated, insufficiently flexible and mobile (both physically and emotionally). We would do well to get rid of some of our emotional *gaucherie*, the prevailing half-light in the English soul at all levels of society. I believe we have that adaptability, if we try to find our own way and do not allow ourselves to be pushed in *their* way by the men from our version of Madison Avenue. We are capable of throwing up strengths relevant to our new situation as, say, working-class people threw up new strengths

125

in the difficult days of settling in to the harsh Victorian cities. We can do this on the housing estates, even though economic pressures do not put a premium on mutual trust, and though the gossip over the dustbin yields to the face on the screen in the living-room.

I do not think the mass-media of communication can do much to make any one of us think or feel the better; they are, after all, mediators, parasites. But they can widen our sense of other people's lives, irrigate our ingrown sense of humour, reduce our curtain-twitching narrowness, stimulate us in a number of useful ways—and occasionally bring us to the point where we begin the slow and personal business of discriminating.

What of the other side of the coin? We know enough by now not to attack the mass-media on the grounds that they are crude, violent and sensational. Their temptations are not these. They are on the side of the angels as popular art has traditionally been; they are often decent and large-hearted. Their new society will be a very moral one.

I have suggested that the mass-media must, whether consciously or not, work towards the emergence of a culturally classless society. Stratification keeps the potential customers in separate groups. Mass sales are helped by suitable mass attitudes, and these the mass-media must encourage. They cannot move quickly, for they are bound to reflect what most people will accept at any one time; and this means that they have to express what most people thought yesterday or this morning, not what some of them might move towards thinking tomorrow. They must roughly show us as we at present are or, more important, as we like to think we are. But their mirror-image progressively distorts. Clever alterations of angle and deceptions of lighting can slowly bring about a change; we begin really to believe what the mirror says and do not notice its subtly progressive changes.

At present the attempts to win consumers may be seen as an interacting process of appeals to old attitudes (many of which are common to all groups, though their forms may still differ), and appeals to the 'popular philosophy' of democracy in a debased form. Traditional working-class values such as group loyalty, tolerance and idiosyncratic nonconformity can change into the gang sense, 'anything goes' and a spirit of 'no flies on Charlie'. Basic democratic ideas such as freedom, equality and progress can change into the notion of freedom from rather than freedom for anything, a little man's lowbrow levelling and a bandwagoning progressivism.

The writer who wishes to appeal across class divisions still has a difficult problem since physical properties and manners are heavy with the overtones of class (from the posh to the low in almost every aspect of life). He has to find a level and forms which will not arouse the irritations of unconscious class prejudice. Separated, therefore, from the often fruitful ability to draw upon genuinely local and particular situations, whether in Camberley or Hunslet, he has to invent a world acceptable to the greatest number in which his characters can move and have their being. So there emerges the copywriters', illustraters' and storytellers' bright unreal world, a smart-young-wife-dominated world of smart young couples moving among contemporary splay-legged furniture to prepare a modish new meal out of a modernistic can. Oddly enough, one sees, the old class-defined way of life had advantages. We knew where we were and this allowed us—unless we belonged to the aspirant minority—not to waste much time in being anxious about questions of status and identity. Life had an assured formal or dramatic pattern. We usually knew in our bones how to behave : that this was an occasion for bringing out a special bottle of wine, or for getting the three-shilling tin of Grade 1 salmon off the kitchen top-shelf. There will be no gain if we are to be constantly running to the latest issue of *Good Housekeeping* to find out what 'place-setting' goes with what guests at this 'stage' in our career.

There is not sufficient space to elaborate fully on the way this process proliferates and feeds on itself. One may quickly point to such interesting aspects as the glossy narrow fragmentation of *Reveille* compared with the bitty but comparatively wide curiosity one used to find in *Titbits*; or to the hypocritical double-eye of the newer kind of Sunday sex papers; or to the way in which the old sense of the personal is graduating from the backyard fence to become the larger-than-life personalization of the soap-operas or of the 'national personalities' thrown up as a classless substitute—Lady Docker, Royalty as it is at present treated, the ubiquitous TV pals and all the other friendly persuaders. When the locally concrete is no longer usable—as it always is in serious art—you are thrown on to the artificially projected.

But the central dangers to the quality of emotional and intellectual life are stereotyping, the pseudo and narcissism. If we are affected by head-counting we will play for safety and be pushed towards the simpler and bolder generalities of expression. We will not dare to introduce the complexities and qualifications of life, even though most of us can sense these complexities without necessarily being able to articulate them. The *Daily Express*'s stage-stereotypes include the nice little semi, the small car, those dreadful teenagers earning £15 a week and the workers with TV in practically every room: the *Daily Mirror* has the pools, the push-bike, the honest pint. I hope the middle classes are not one and all such acidulous relatives of Mrs Dale as the *Express* suggests: I *know* the *Mirror*'s working man is not true to life. The deficiency here is particularly illuminating. As the *Mirror* insists, working-class people do often show gusto, tolerance, big-heartedness and a scorn of pomposity. But they are also—and this the *Mirror* does not illustrate—sometimes very discriminating, often cautious and canny, and altogether much more phlegmatic than the *Mirror*'s intermittent hysteria of manner would lead the outsider to suspect. We are being presented with a simplified and abstracted inflation of some undeniable working-class virtues—which are only meaningful in relation to a great number of other virtues and vices in the reality of dense and concrete life. The *Mirror*'s stereotype is no more like the body of English working people than a stage cockney.

The movement towards block or prefabricated responses is general. Recently I saw both a Conservative and a Labour Party political television broadcast. Both exhibited the same imaginatively stereotyped assumptions as the commercial mass-providers about the very people they were so strongly claiming to speak for—standardized bright new British interiors with bright new families; an unctuousness in the interviewer asking the father what he wanted from life (and turning the answer to his party's profit), a phoney toughness in the journalist put up to challenge the Minister in the name of the common man.

Behind all mass communication is an inhibiting condition: nervous awareness of the audience. One need only reflect on the

different sense of imaginative freedom one would have in writing a
novel (not a would-be best seller but a novel one really wanted to
write) or in writing a script for television. The pressures begin with
questions of sex and go on to almost anything which might
shock anyone who happens to be in the audience. They all tend
towards holding the limits of response at what is already acceptable; whatever is, is right. An artist's world has to be one of continuous intellectual and imaginative reassessment before the experience, not of deployment before the audience. The mass-media
cannot but insensibly encourage a conservatism and conformity of
the spirit in both their providers and their consumers.

But since there is, because of the competitive need to attract more
consumers, a pressure to find excitements, we see also a constant
tendency towards pseudo-sensationalism: towards the sex-in-the-
head thrill of contemporary pin-ups; towards the shadow-boxing
'radicalism' of the popular press when it goes on a 'crusade';
towards the idiosyncrasy of characters who, going through the
motions of nonconformity, produce an unrooted bloodymindedness
—the truly *in*-significant nonconformity of the professional grum-
blers. None of this would matter much were it not probably helping to deflect the urge towards the real qualities it imitates, and we
could do with more of these just now.

All this leads to what we can only call a narcissism of the
emotions. I spoke earlier of the way the older and class-based
popular art was able to root itself in local, particular and concrete
detail. So may highbrow art, because highbrows are classless whilst
reading; they are then truly disinterested. A sensitive working-class
youth can read *Anna Karenina* with the same sort of attention as
he reads *Sons and Lovers*, whereas the *Daily Sketch* or some popular
middlebrow and middle-class novel would arouse intense irritation.

Moral values become meaningful to us in concrete situations; we
come to know what tolerance means by living through to it in a
succession of demanding situations. Good art, whether highbrow
or popular, embodies its moral sense in specific details. The modern
mass-media, inspired by the desire to reach across all classes and by
their undervaluing of what people are capable of appreciating, are
led towards a sort of cracker-motto hymning of certain values
in themselves. They become self-consciously narcissistic. *This is*

Your Life and *Have a Go* are particularly regrettable programmes because they exhibit this narcissistic indulgence in emotions in and for themselves ('aren't we nice people—we are so tolerant—or kind to the aged'; not 'life is such and such . . . so tolerance well becomes us'). Such programmes are a world away from the moment when Gracie Fields sang about tolerance, very sentimentally, to a Northern audience, for whom a sense of the virtue of tolerance had been forged in the complexities of day-to-day life. Virtues repeatedly named as flattering incantations are likely to lose fibre.

This whole process is more developed here than most of us wish to realize. Americans are shocked by our popular press whilst we still tell ourselves that the worst features in modern mass-media are all in America, that it can't happen here. We point to our checks and balances; the Trust quality-press; the Third Programme; the public libraries—forgetting that the advertisements on television are really more symptomatic of middle-twentieth-century trends. We tell ourselves that the 'intelligent minority' has increased from about two per cent to about four per cent of the population in the last fifty years, and fail to assess the centralization and concentration in the provision for almost everyone else. We might inquire how many local councils have increased the library rate to meet this increase in the proportions of the 'intelligent minority'. We might say to ourselves at intervals: in the fifties commercial television was introduced, several decent journals died and the British Museum library continued to close at five o'clock because the country 'couldn't afford' to keep it open. Though we are scarcely even maintaining our checks and balances we use them as illustrations of our continuing cultural health—like a man who refers to his maintained membership in a good club to suppress the thought that all but one floor in his house is let off to non-U tenants.

Worse, we often show an open-mindedness which looks superficially like a mature tolerance but can be a weakness, fed by an unease towards the mass audience and a guilt about being 'highbrows' at bottom. This is a knowing, permissive treason of the clerks which supports itself by not getting very close to the reality of recent developments. I think here of numerous instances: of M.P.s, dons and writers for intellectual journals who confess that they enjoy *Reveille*; it is not as stuffy, they say, as the clever publications they write for: they talk about *Reveille*'s roots in the full-blooded tradition of British popular art.

Or there is that reaction to the advertisements on ITV which takes the form of saying that, far from objecting to them, one quite enjoys them. But of course they are amusing; this is only one form of gimmick in the second-stage of self-conscious mass-persuasion. Amused intellectual patronage of this sort is a long way from the laughter which can express a nonconformist refusal to buy an obvious line.

Or one thinks of the people who admit that they have a soft spot for the *Daily Mirror*; 'it's got gusto', they say, and when it speaks out is in the direct line of the old Radical tradition. One does not need to deny that the *Mirror* is much pleasanter than the *Express*, or, of course, the *Sketch*; or that it expresses a kind of generosity: but one has to realize also that it expresses a travesty of the fullness and complexity of working-class life and of Radicalism. Intellectuals who make this mistake are here as crude in their judgements as the stockbrokers who took a vicarious thrill in the Suez adventure because the old lion was at last showing its teeth again.

It all helps to consolidate a situation in which one group of graduates produces the mass goods and another excuses itself for dealing in a more highbrow brand—and compensatingly hastens to defend the first group. Or occasionally someone attacks mass-entertainments with an irrelevance to the real cultural issues which suggests that he is inspired partly by pique because he has not found either the wealth or the fame which mass success can bring. I suggested earlier that it could be a mistake to look for initiating 'villains'. Yet, the refusal to face issues can cover many peculiar activities, and one cannot ignore the fact that today old Etonians and Wykehamists often direct mass-entertainments.

It is plain that we shall not assess the probable effects of this process unless we seek a firmer knowledge of the imaginative reality of 'ordinary' people's lives, of the complex interaction of family, neighbourhood and workplace relationships, of older and newer attitudes, in those local areas now being flooded with centralized goods and ideas. Life in those areas did not provide emotional equipment for meeting all situations; but it provided for a great many and provided surprisingly well, by a kind of unconscious absorption. On balance it evolved an unexpectedly mature pattern of sanctions, responsibilities and freedoms, from the exigencies of a life predominantly hard and unendowed. Behind its appallingly dull appearances it had a quality of melodrama, of the histrionic and heroic which—so middle and upper class is our predominant literary culture—one rarely finds accurately reflected in, for example, the English novel during the last half-century.

To realize this can easily lead to sentimental over-valuing; but that danger has to be met if we are to get away from the self-flattering attitude which thinks of working-class people as almost blank slates, with none of the rich and elaborate manners of the middle and upper classes. The stereotypes and clichés of intellectuals can be as powerful as those of the copywriters: the dulled automata of the mass-media or the upright workers waiting only to be turned into tidy lower-middle-class figures are as unreal as the hearty boozers of the advertisements.

If we do not gain this closer knowledge we shall fail to allow for what must surely be the most hopeful group of elements in older attitudes—the power of resistance and resilience, of scepticism, nonconformity and irony; and the immense fund of decency which these support when they interact with traditional charity and tolerance. We have heard a great deal during the last few decades about 'the decline of family life.' If we look more clearly we shall see that in fact the family holds together extremely well. Similarly we shall gain a better sense of resilience, of the power to remake or to assimilate new elements in their own way, if we look without patronage at working-class amusements today. It is easier, because the activity has an antique music-hall flavour, to admit some of the strengths in working-men's club singing than to see the signs of life in skiffle and teddy-boy clothes. These elements may not amount to a great deal but they can show a kind of independence, vitality and choice. And even as one says this one realizes that such a widening of view only increases the responsibility for discrimination. We have to remember that such instances of vitality are usually taken over very quickly by the mass-media, wrapped in cellophane, and then presented as the real thing. And we have to be careful not to confuse the more flexible view with cultural slumming or with a highbrow's anti-highbrow attitude, a disguised *nostalgie de la boue.*

Irony, scepticism and nonconformity; they have not yet become a cynicism though they could be turned that way. At present these and a great many other elements add up to a life of such texture and body that most of our assessments and missionary efforts seem thin and drab by comparison. British people still exhibit a strong capacity to ignore the emotional changes expected of them, to laugh in the wrong places, to go on with their complicated human routines whilst the electronic computers and the electronically transmitted persuaders buzz all round them. Or they prop their mugs of tea on the computers and use them to work out their horoscopes. We shall meet better the change which is nevertheless going on all the time if our understanding is based on an unsentimental respect and reverence, on a depth of humane feeling which plays over as much as we can each encompass of the realities of people's lives, so that we do not mistake the material now given to them in their name for their true inwardness.

The whole problem is further complicated by our very great and understandable difficulty in assessing what—if not a consumers' glossy culture—is to succeed a culture which was, in places of power, predominantly high bourgeois in tone. To assume that it is possible to spread widely the traditional kind of European high culture leads only to an impasse; which is why Ortega's superb *Revolt of the Masses,* once well pondered, should be seen as the last fine statement of a position now largely irrelevant.

More of a nuisance, because more widespread, is the assumption that one is really seeking to develop a sort of middle-class culture-vulturedom. Group excursions of selected scholarship boys to Arts Council exhibitions may be enjoyable and valuable; but they are not the only nor even necessarily the best successors to working-men's club concerts or Frankie Vaughan. And *Jude the Obscure* will not really have done more than get out of one trap and into another if he becomes a middlebrow semi-intellectual, specializing in opinionation rather than fragmentation, graduating from *Titbits* or the *Weekend Mail* to the *Readers' Digest* and *Any Questions.*

When this uncertainty co-operates with the lack of knowledge and slight guilt towards 'the people' which I have already described it tends to produce a peculiar deference in many intellectuals when they speak or write before a mass audience. So on the one hand we find the Intrusive You ('you too can . . .') or Wot Abart It Chums of the popular mass-media; on the other hand, the 'I'm sure viewers will agree . . . a good argument even though no questions were settled . . . ventilation . . . friendly exchange . . . etc.' of intellectuals who also are hesitant at the thought of the Great Public outside, who smile and smile in a way that we never smile at our under-graduate students in seminars. It is a strained desire to be accepted which reminds one of a colonel who has been advised by his adjutant that he really must have a drink in the men's mess at Christmas. And every day is becoming Christmas now, what with the quizzes and the forums and the brains trusts. Too often we mitigate such force as our convictions have as much—well, as much as the fighting men of the popular Press. If only we would dare to risk being dull or intransigent. We might then be interesting in a new way.

After all, there does exist the waiting group I indicated at the beginning of this chapter, in the figure of the young uprooted teacher. Here we may be dealing with small numbers, and my own illustration may well lead to the suspicion that I am now going to talk about some small and dissident cult. This is not so, and two considerations should make clear why. First, that the dissident or concerned (no word is entirely satisfactory here) exist in all classes and have a variety of backgrounds and of intellectual equipment. One of the best fruits of the considerable educational and cultural changes of the last few decades has been the increase in the informed minority in all parts of society. I suggested earlier that the proportion of this group in the total population has been roughly doubled since the First World War.

Second, and much more important, we need to realize that most of us at some time, with some part of our experience, belong to this group. There is no firm or final division into the eggheads and the rest. We are all in some ways more discriminating than the image of us which the mass-media put out; we are all at intervals among the dissident, the concerned, the serious. No other thought can possibly be more encouraging—or should do more to discourage us from timidly flattering that abstraction 'the people'—than this: that it *is* possible, even among all the noise, now and again to make contact with people other than through the simplified generalities of the mass-media.

For all that, I should like to refer to the peculiar problems of those who can be described as an uprooted minority, since they throw into relief some of the special complexities of our emerging classlessness and some possibilities for growth of a good kind. One of the most difficult feats for an Englishman from below the upper-middle classes is simply to become educated or an intellectual. In seeking this condition he is pushed towards a whole new set of social forms, a whole new range of ways to speak, write, laugh and cry. In the degree to which he is sensitive he is likely to be carrying on throughout a running love-hate duel with social manners. And this is not altogether a bad thing. One of the advantages of the culture-and-class mixture is that we are not strongly tempted to think of ourselves—simply because we have cultural or intellectual leanings—as the bearers of a sort of Cain's brand, creatures whom the power-groups or money-groups in our society are quite unused to accommodating. We are not greatly pushed towards the heroics of alienation and despair, towards becoming self-consciously esoteric or towards a sense of separation from practically all our society's everyday life.

Still, the disadvantages are considerable, especially in a society changing as comprehensively as is ours. There is little difficulty in illustrating that so far this challenge has not been greatly appreciated. Why are the sixth forms in our grammar schools not bursting with a very special energy and sense of commitment at this time? Why are our provincial universities, which have greatly developed in stature during the last thirty years, still generally regarded—for all the public assertions to the contrary—as inferior imitations of Oxford and Cambridge? Or we might recall the recent U and non-U controversy. It had its amusing side, and one might seem over-solemn in regretting it. Yet how sadly parochial it was. The fact that it roused so much interest indicates that this kind of frozen irrelevance matters far more in English life than it should. No doubt we all know local authority schools where the junior mistresses, scholarship girls from local training colleges, spend a lot of time teaching the children to say that they want to go to the 'toilet'. On the other hand, I used to think that American and Irish voices were popular on the radio because they sounded tough or folksy; I think now that they are liked because they are free of class overtones. Eamonn Andrews can speak to English children in a voice with an aura quite different from that of the Sussex prosperous uncles we often hear on the B.B.C. We could begin to tackle the general problem bit by bit, by sorting out such specific confusions : by deciding that we at least will no longer type-cast regional accents by class or comedy (every Lancashire man his own George Formby); and that lazy speech is bad, whether it shows as the urban working-class glottal stop or the pale-pink 'Oxford' drawl of assistants in genteel shops.

These are only instances of numerous factors which lead many people who might become informed and active to stay in a cultural no-man's land, suspecting the 'fancy' forms which so often seem to be concomitant with the condition of being 'cultured', suspecting also the imaginative inadequacy of the active Left wing which claims to speak to their condition. This represents a considerable loss of power in analysis and action. We are not short of sources of information and intellectual stimulation : we are desperately short of people who try to choose and discriminate *consistently*, and here might be a very good point to start. If we learn to speak relevantly to such listeners, we might also express ourselves more satisfactorily when we try to communicate more widely, to people not specifically in this group. We have nothing to lose but our fear of 'the masses' and the mass-media. We can afford to be more highbrow; we can hardly afford not to be, on peril of losing what small virtue we have. All communication is a moral activity, and when a society reaches the point where some of its most successful citizens can speak of 'the faith of a salesman' then its language has become blurred and so has the hold on its own moral life. In this part of the problem we are committed to increasing the area of consciousness. We have to think harder of ways to keep open that decent middle range in communication which is truer to the talents of most of us than the 'wotcher-cock' populars. The distribution of readers for the more serious publications suggests that, for the first time in our history, cultural and intellectual matters need no longer be associated almost entirely with selected social groups. Here is a particular and fairly precise point at which one good kind of classlessness might begin to emerge, a classnessness neither that of outsiders nor that of massed consumers.

Here, as elsewhere, there is no need to be depressed. During the last few years in particular there have been many signs of life to refute our own clichés about Welfare-State softness. What has become known as the angry young man movement, has, in fact, some very positive aspects at bottom. But we can point to some less-publicized recent activities. It is worth while pondering on the success of the group of enterprises associated with the *Universities and Left Review*, a journal which began with the hope of attracting about two thousand readers, chiefly in Oxford and Cambridge, quickly found six thousand readers from all parts of the country, and regularly fills a large hall in London with young people anxious to discuss aspects of contemporary British life. Or one can recall the 'free' films made by such men as Lindsay Anderson and Karel Reisz, films which take a fresh look at Britain and which have evoked a considerable response. I do not mean a modish response: my experience is almost entirely provincial and I can say that such things—for these are only examples—have aroused an interest which, though comparatively quiet, is as powerful as I have known since the more striking excitements of my own youth in the thirties.

The ideals of the young teacher we saw at the beginning of this chapter, though now somewhat inhibited, are strong and well-rooted in the tradition of British nonconformist idealism. At the moment he has been led into a sandy delta; but he could emerge. Luckily, he has usually a pleasant saving irony towards himself—his own type of scepticism—which should prevent him from becoming, in the meantime, an amateur Cassandra and, when he does begin to act, could save him from the callower progressivisms in much of our progressive social thought.

My argument has been that we need to think more imaginatively and firmly in three main areas: about the use and misuse of the mass-media; about our remarkably persistent old strengths; and about the whole business of change in class formulations, its strains and its promise. We are almost spoilt for choice and can each take what most draws his energy. It is all a matter of reassessing our own view of ourselves, our own depressingly false formulations or irrelevant romanticisms. Between the grey Britain often conjured up by depressed intellectuals and the export-Britain of Elstree, the British Travel and Holidays Association, the British Council (too much Galsworthy and clubmen), or the artificial heroics of such a film as *The Bridge on the River Kwai*, there already exists in part, and there could grow stronger, another and more genuine Britain, not at all so grey and limited, and a great deal tougher and more resilient.

This period is full of the most exacting and potentially fruitful tensions. If we still have some belief in the democratic ideals which were partly responsible for bringing us to this point of change then we have no cause to be unduly alarmed. We are likely to become in a certain sense classless. It need not be left to the free operation of blind forces to encourage a classless conformity of consumers. By a close and constant discipline of thought and feeling, working from the grounds outwards, we shall be better able to take stock of our lines for growth. We often accuse the Americans of false democratic *bonhomie*. To me the most chastening aspect of life over there is the realization that people at all levels of wealth and power really can, at times, look at each other face-to-face, that in a deep sense they can believe that each is as good as his fellow. When two Englishmen meet for the first time, by contrast, one can almost hear the built-in complicated fruit-machines of class-assessment whirring. Yet we *can* arrive at a decent classlessness, one fed not by the admirable American dream but by a merging of the considerable lived-into virtues still to be found in all classes.

NIGEL CALDER

The revolutionary in the white coat

SCIENCE AND SOCIALISM. I began to write this in an infants' schoolroom in Reading where some of the Aldermaston marchers were camped for the night. The next morning we had to cover the remaining ten miles to the Atomic Weapons Research Establishment, using our feet to protest against an outgrowth of advanced physics which promises to destroy the species *Homo sapiens* and leave *Rattus norvegicus* to come out of the sewers and inherit the earth.

In a hydrogen bomb neutrons breed neutrons by way of a chain reaction; the cause of the explosion is the rapid rate at which the neutrons multiply. In our society, discoveries and inventions are similarly breeding discoveries and inventions in an explosive manner. Whether you call it exponential growth, compound interest or simply a rat-race, our technical civilization is blowing up in our faces. The H-bomb itself is lumped, in this bigger chain reaction, with ballpoint pens, the discovery of the structure of myoglobin, and all the rest of our *know-how*. I look to Socialism first and foremost for the *know-what*, for seeing that science is properly applied, and for taming technology before it devastates us or drives us mad.

As human communities grow and mutate the advantage seems to lie with those in which the individuals specialize in their work, as do the differentiated cells of the higher animals. Knowledge and skills are atomized among the people, and they will only be properly used if the individuals co-operate like the cells of their healthy bodies. Competition, in a highly sophisticated society, is like a cancer—and nations believing in free enterprise have frequently to indulge in self-medication. On the same analogy, dictatorship supposes that the brain, by taking thought, can direct the growth of a limb. Perhaps it can, but not without mutilation.

Anyone who is literate knows that our useful knowledge springs

139

mainly from scientific research and development. Yet the references politicians make to the discoveries and inventions of past and future are mere crusts thrown to feed the duck-billed platitudes. How many British Socialists have awoken to the fact that the real revolutionary in our midst is the man in the white coat? In pubs, coffee-bars or common-rooms they talk of Marx but never of Watt; of the Webbs but not of the Braggs; of Bevan but not of Brundrett.

Forty years ago a generation of young men were as pygmies beside the perfectors of Maxim's gun; today you and I are dwarfed by the anonymous troglodytes of Aldermaston—we needn't be, but we are. On the brighter side of human affairs, the great reforms for which radicals have claimed the credit have largely depended on technical change. Votes for women owed more to the cotton looms, the typewriters and the shell-filling factories than to the shouts of the suffragettes. The study of nutrition by Le Gros Clark, Boyd Orr and others formed the cornerstone of the Welfare State. And advances in tropical medicine are today changing the face of the world. The worker's standard of living, too, depends as much on technical capacity as on the way it is shared. Throughout history a haircut has cost roughly an hour's wage. Against this, Jean Fourastié cites the case of a mirror, six feet square, which cost forty thousand hours' wages in 1720 and only three hundred hours' wages in 1952.

There is nothing new in what I am saying: the dreadful thing is that it should still need saying in 1958, on the road to Aldermaston. As a Socialist I regret the present ignorance about science because it prevents intelligent, democratic control of the uses of science. As a scientist I fear the day will come when the anti-science of Shaw and Forster will take hold of the people and they will burn the laboratories to the ground. I was astonished to be told by a graduate's wife that she found Zeta, of all things, 'rather frightening'. Yet Margaret Mead's study of American high-school pupils shows that many of them think 'the scientist is a brain' who, among other things, neglects his family and behaves in a generally anti-social and sinister way. This may be a grossly unfair picture of the individual scientist, but is it such a false image of science as a whole? However noble its intentions, science is, after all, a pursuit undertaken by individuals for the gratification of their own egos, and we have to take the consequences, for better or worse.

Those of us who are most anxious that discovery and invention should continue are forced to admit that modern science has been poisoned. Like a plant treated with a hormone the precious seedling of Newton and Faraday is shooting upwards; but the bottle is clearly marked 'Nationalism'. These are the evils that result from the poison : unbalance, corruption and secrecy. Much more support and effort is devoted to the physical sciences (physics, chemistry and related subjects, which are important in war and in the wealthier industries) than to the biological sciences. The branches of applied science are outgrowing the roots of pure science : scientists are paid to assault Nature rather than woo her.

The hack scientist has little conscience and less social imagination. This man will sell his skill to anyone in exchange for good working conditions, a house and a motor car. Very useful he is, too, to the Communist and capitalist states, where he tries to be a good citizen and a good husband. As Einstein said : 'The man of science has slipped so much that he regards the slavery inflicted upon him by national states as his inevitable fate.'

All too often the concomitant is the professional degradation of the scientist, by the barbed wire and the Official Secrets Act. Secrecy has no rightful place in science or in a democracy. It is the enemy of both. At its lowest it is wasteful : scientists working for different companies or different countries have to duplicate their work, while fruitless projects are kept going under cover of security. But what is far more important, secrecy prevents us from knowing what is being done in our own country, in our name. We have no way, for example, of telling what biological weapons are being developed, or how soon colour television receivers are likely to appear on the British market.

Yet, in spite of these diseases, science is a wonderful thing. What glories had the dead civilizations to compare with the discoveries of the atomic nucleus or of the colliding galaxies in Cygnus? What skills to compare with the aircraft designer's or the medical research worker's? What instrument of the mind to stand beside experiment and inductive reasoning?

The chief interest of the socialist should be the point at which discoveries are taken out of the laboratory and put to work. It is not as easy as one might think to draw the line between 'pure' and 'applied' science. Cosmology clearly falls on one side and brewing technology on the other. Yet the helical nature of the protein molecule, so suggestive for modern biology, was discovered during studies in wool technology, while the immediately useful X-rays emerged during academic research on the discharge in gases. Even a fundamental thing like the accurate measurement of time using the 'atomic clock' is important for getting a guided missile from the U.S.A. to Moscow, or from Siberia to Seattle. But one can write down a list of the major industrial and medical advances of a given period and call them 'applied' science. The long list for the first half of the century would include such things as the catalytic cracking of oils and what is nowadays called automation. During the second half the under-financed but skilful efforts in pure biological research are beginning to pay enormous dividends. The medical and agricultural scientists are saving lives and preparing for the birthrate bulge to end all bulges, while their more academic colleagues are hatching such discoveries in the realms of the nucleus of the living cell, which, in application, will make the antics with atomic-nucleus seem a mere diversion.

The gross results of applied science are plain enough. We can now choose between having more grandchildren or trading them for a higher standard of living—neglecting for the present the third possibility, universal death. In biological terms the fitness of the human species has improved. This is a genuine achievement, even though there are some neo-Malthusians like Sir Charles Darwin who are frightened of the idea of too many people with too much leisure and independence. Darwin predicts famine on the one hand and compulsory P.T. for the masses on the other: but unless we bungle things there is not the slightest reason why we should be reduced to either.

To my mind, the chief characteristic of the scientific way of thought is the enormous number of practical ideas which it produces. There is a great deal of nonsense spoken about scientific objectivity and the scientific method. In fact, from Columbus, who fudged his figures in an attempt to prove that China was not so very far away, to Maxwell and Bohr, the master-manipulators of illogic, the scientist thinks there are no holds barred. He has the *habit* of producing original ideas and of testing them. The most dreary and dangerous thing about our present condition is the dearth of fresh thinking. That is why the politician should take a leaf out of the scientist's book: no self-respecting scientist would go for a year without making at least one original contribution of lasting value, yet politicians on the whole seem to have fewer ideas than housewives.

Who is the man who controls the purse-strings of science? The witch-doctor in striped pants, the pillar of the Establishment, the universal super-ego of our time. It is he who, in his ignorance, has made 'science' a dirty word. He may be a Civil Servant, or an industrial executive, or a renegade natural scientist on his way to a knighthood. But his outlook is always the same: he believes in political truth rather than political honesty, and this truth, on analysis, turns out to be that what's good for his sort of people is good for you and me. Hence bags of money, chaps, for defence research, for nuclear sciences and for television—and let the cancer and TB researchers go sell flags in the street. At for the Ministers who endorse these allocations . . . well, to be charitable, have they the faintest idea what they're doing?

In many respects we are still back in the Dark Ages. Our newspapers continue to tell fortunes: a great blow was struck for unreason when the *Daily Express* astrologer correctly predicted that Mr What would win the Grand National. The expression 'scientifically proved' is today a fairly reliable signal that one is about to be hoodwinked. Our Nobel laureates find themselves in a community where feelings run high against speed traps using Doppler radar, because they remove the benefits of imprecision, and where Colin Wilson can make his most fatuous remark: 'I too was trained as a physicist, until I was seventeen.'

In this atmosphere of magical thinking, Science, like Democracy, Freedom and even I'm afraid Socialism is a word that has become part of the incantation. At the same time as they mistrust science, people at large expect the scientist to come down in his helicopter and remove that inconvenience here, prove that point there. They *believe* too much in science.

Small wonder then that the nationalist, basically Tory rules by which science is planned are making a mess of things. Not so long ago, the Queen, several leading scientists and the Press at large were involved in the biggest confidence trick for some time. Calder Hall, a nuclear munitions factory for making the core material for hydrogen bombs, was hailed as the first great peaceful use of atomic energy. The fact is that when you make plutonium you release heat and you cool it with a gas: you can either throw the heat away, as at Windscale, or you can use it to generate electricity for driving the gas over fuel rods. With ingenuity you can declare a sizeable bonus of electricity, which you pass to the grid.

Poor scientist! Once he has sold out he will rarely get the credit when things go right, yet he will take all the knocks that are going—while the man in striped pants rubs his hands and says: 'Ah, well, Science you know, it's got to go on.' Perhaps this was what Blake anticipated when he wrote:

> Now the sneaking serpent walks
> In mild humility,
> And the just man rages in the wilds
> Where lions roam.

So far I have expressed what one Socialist at least sees when he watches modern science. Now, I look at the social tasks and opportunities that spring from science.

But first I ask: what is the aim of social co-operation? The Labour Party ran out of ideas in 1950, at one of the most exciting moments in history. One reason, I think, was that it had too long been obsessed with the sensible purpose of righting obvious social ills. Doctors and psychiatrists can now define minimum standards of welfare on a rough-and-ready technical basis. But surely keeping fit is not the be-all and end-all of human life? The terrible greyness of contemporary liberalism and art results from such a morbid fascination with wrongs, with backward-looking reform, not forward-looking change. Yet the bright flash of Harwell's Zeta, with its promise of power and fresh water from the sea *which is nobody's property*, is as fine a torch for world Socialism as any yet lit.

Man is distinguished from the animals by his remarkable ability to control his environment, and by his skill in manipulating symbols. These are the weft and warp of his greatness, from which he weaves his fabric of discovery, technology, art and religion. Once man's animal needs have been taken care of, these are the things that matter. If this brings the charge of 'narrow intellectualism' on my head I will retort that if every man had not an intellect I would not be a Socialist. The only fragment of a Utopia which I possess is that every man and woman should be B.A. or B.Sc.

If we correctly determine Britain's role in the world of science, and set our sights high enough, it is my belief that domestic reforms will follow naturally. In contrast to the early Fabians, whose Socialism was essentially domestic and unconsciously dependent on the Royal Navy, we must formulate our policies in world terms and then translate them into English. It should not need the knowledge that London is within I.C.B.M. range of Peking to drive us to this attitude.

Not only must we look farther afield but we must look deeper. The botanist today rushes off to the south-east Pacific to study the natural flora of the islands, with their clues to evolution and continental movements, before they are irretrievably disturbed by the clumsiness of man. Not long ago, it was the anthropologist who hurriedly snatched his impressions of unsophisticated communities before the trade and the missionary had undone them. The environment to which we as living creatures have to adapt is largely man-made, yet we must never lose touch with the natural world from which we spring. In our anthropocentric way it is very easy for us to do so. Roads and steel-frame buildings, processed food and petrol pumps, umbrellas and D.D.T.—all these save us from the inconveniences of nature, as surely as powdered cow's milk can save the baby from the natural consequences of a dry breast. The rubber technologist protects us even from the consequences of sex.

Tomorrow, perhaps, we shall control the weather, breed dumb chicks so that we need not listen to them cackle, and invade even the fastness of the deep sea for our practical ends. There is no reason why we should not do all these things and very much more, provided the human world remains adapted to the natural world on which it depends, and so long as human individuals remain adapted to their human world without going off their heads.

Like Buffalo Bill and the men who built the railways across London River, we shall destroy more than we create if we look always to the superficial needs of man. We must know what it means when hybrid corn gives high yields at the expense of soil fertility, when malaria mosquitoes develop resistance to chlorinated insecticides, when the big-game hunter shoots the leopard and leaves behind a plague of baboons. We should at least take note of the fact that the use of cosmetics, plastic surgery and slimming techniques may alter the balance between the nubile, less fecund woman and the plain, fecund one and so lead to a change in the birthrate.

There is nothing magical about the balance of nature—it can come into equilibrium at any number of levels. But as medical science takes the brake off human multiplication we must strike a satisfactory balance or die. So we must learn from the expert— in this case the ecologist. Yet beware, for every ecologist there are dozens of physicists, chemists and engineers who will instruct you in terms of kilowatts and bulldozers but who would probably be hard put to it to explain what natural selection means.

The economist, on occasion, may be an even greater menace. It is not with the ineptness of his predictions that I want to quarrel at the moment, nor even with the Economism, with its essentially capitalist-materialist values, that seems to have become a substitute for Socialism. It is the absurdities which stem from his habits of thought. It may be sound economics to ship automobiles from Coventry to Detroit, but it is ecological nonsense. So is the philosophy of waste whereby men and women are urged to buy more than they need and even things they did not know they wanted in order to keep the wheels of industry turning. The economist worth his salt is the one who shows, for example, how a pound spent in medical services can save more than a pound's loss of production, and who can cut through the magical quasi-scientific words and theories of his fellows and see men at work, minerals being taken out of the ground and actual human beings using or misusing their skills.

Enough of attitudes. To come to real business, let me make a fairly obvious list of world priorities.

Staying alive.
Conserving and enlarging our resources.
Sharing knowledge and resources throughout the world.
Making the most of scientific discovery.
Injecting reason into human affairs.
Exploring outer space.

Staying alive is not going to be easy; it will demand energetic action on the part of those who wish to do so. The characteristic willingness of men to die for an idea is notorious, and it persists even now that the age-old fear of vengeance on the third and fourth generations can be translated into radio-genetic terms. Perhaps it is a pity that the outpouring of adrenalin which comes to a man when he faces death, and drives him to activity, is denied to us when we merely watch an H-bomb test on television.

As weapons become more and more devastating, they themselves become the major cause of war. The I.C.B.M. with an H-bomb warhead is by no means the limit of devilish ingenuity. The full refinements of the automatic war are not yet with us: when they come, there won't even be a button to push. And even if successful disarmament-with-inspection schemes could be worked out for nuclear and conventional weapons, the subtler techniques of biological warfare could be developed in secret almost anywhere.

Short of removing all possible reason for war, the only security will lie in making oneself not worth attacking—in particular, by voluntarily doing away with aggressive or retaliatory weapons. If all measures fail, the only biological answer is to entomb, at the first sign of real trouble, a number of volunteers equipped and provisioned for a generation, who will repopulate the earth when the poisons have been leached away. This is not science-fiction stuff; it is the reality of the situation at the time of the Aldermaston March.

Conserving and enlarging our resources is also part of the policy for survival. Our new medical knowledge imposes on us the clear duty of making people well, even if as a result the world's population doubles in fifty years. Couple this, however, with the way the advanced nations are squandering their resources in the quest for a good life, and it is at once clear that conservation of soil, water and

147

metals is a matter of the utmost importance for rich and poor alike.

With conservation, of course, goes the attack on pollution. The pollution of rivers and seas with chemical wastes, sewage and oil is bad enough. The World Health Organization has named air pollution as the biggest single public health problem in Europe, yet the pitiful clean-air measures in this country are based on quite inadequate instrumentation. Even more serious is pollution with radioactive material, at any rate in prospect: if power from nuclear fission ever becomes a major industry, we must face the problem of having to dispose of several H-bombs'-worth of fission products every day.

There are several ways of enlarging our resources; we can open up the last virgin territories, we can drive the crops farther north into the Arctic, farther into the desert, and clear space for them in the jungle. By geological and geophysical prospecting we can transform the geography of mineral resources. The oceans have been barely tapped, either for food or for minerals. We can find ways of extracting minerals from poor deposits, of getting food from poor soil, and we can find substitutes for the traditional resources—plastics, synthetic fibres and so on. And, of course, we can economize in their use.

The geography and technology of copper and wheat, of oil and desert should be part of every Socialist's equipment. We should not be content to argue about how the High Aswan Dam should be financed, nor even to marvel at its proposed thickness (1,300 metres). We should also ask: is it in the right place? Or have political considerations carried more weight than arguments about evaporation loss from the proposed broad reservoir?

Sharing knowledge and resources throughout the world is what one most wants to do, now that it is in our power to release a thousand million of our fellow-creatures from the bonds of poverty. But the economists sound the warning: vast capital sums are needed. The neo-Malthusians wring their hands, and eat every steak as if it may be their last. But make no mistake about it, the underdeveloped regions of the world are going to get developed—but fast. The economists, and more particularly Professor Blackett, point to the fact that the annual rise in the living standards in the West is comparable with the total living standard in India and elsewhere. They see this making nonsense of all attempts towards world equality: on the contrary, I see it as proof of what can be spared. Not that it is being spared at the moment. Those who are ill-fed are worse than before the war; the better-fed even better. This is not surprising, since industrial countries can easily increase their food production by snatching nitrogen from the air, by breeding better strains, and by developing chemicals for controlling weeds, diseases and pests. But just as the British Labour movement demanded and won a fairer share of wealth, so the black and brown and yellow men, knowing what modern science can achieve, will not stand silent while their children die. We cannot afford to disappoint them; they can say, in the long run, pay up—or else.

The enormity of the task is itself a challenge to the 'cleverness' of the white man. In the next forty years, world food production must be multiplied four times, with a notable increase in the proportion of the more expensive protein. And though tropical disease is now going out by the back door, it will re-appear at the front again unless living standards rise sharply. At mid-century forty-four per cent of the world's adults could not read and write.

Now count the assets. Firstly, human beings as intelligent as ourselves, released by medicine from the dead weight of centuries—raring to go. Men and women, too, whose productivity at the moment is zero or even negative (too many people on the land) and who can therefore be employed on new work without loss to the old work. Secondly, power. If most of the world's fossil-fuels lie north of the Tropic of Cancer, most of the hydro-electric potential lies to the south of it. Thirdly, there is human ingenuity. A British nutritionist told me of a technique he has used in African villages. He looks around until he finds the inevitable odd man out, who remains well-fed while the rest of the village go hungry; he then examines his diet and finds out where he got it from. Whatever it is, it is from local resources and available to everyone else.

The fundamental technical obstacles in the present mammoth exercise in world Socialism are few, except in so far as human selfishness determines that one dollar must be made to do the work of fifty. It is true that the West has advanced from the days when we burnt wheat on the prairies: nowadays we are more sophisticated and we turn it into hardboard. But such practices must cease, as the populations of nations press ever more closely on the biological limits . . . until the hoped-for day when increasing living standards reduce the natural selection for high fecundity, and world population levels off at perhaps five times its present numbers.

Somehow or other, with the impetus of science and the momentum of human indignation, the underdeveloped territories are going to crash through the Money Barrier. Then they will need machines and chemicals: not nylon, but fertilizers, not television but telephones, not supersonic airliners but helicopters, not fast tankers but long-range trawlers (ninety-eight per cent of the world's fish-catch is at present in the Northern Hemisphere). More exactly, they will need the plant with which to make these things for themselves. The market for capital goods will be enormous, and I think we would do well to gamble on it, because if this prediction is wrong, in the terrible disaster that will overtake mankind, industrial dislocation in a country like our own would be a minor accident. This sharing of knowledge and resources always seems at first sight very one-sided. Yet, as geological surveys are intensified, new mineral resources will appear, to the benefit of all, and worldwide education will vastly increase the number of working scientists and engineers.

Making the most of scientific discovery is, in the long run, the key item in my list of six, because with so many human and material problems to be overcome in every country in the world, it is only with the utmost ingenuity that we shall avoid heartbreak, and before that we need more knowledge. I have already mentioned the disease of modern science: nationalism, with its symptoms of unbalance, corruption and secrecy. It is most urgent that we should restore to science or, at any rate, pure research, the international, honest and almost carefree character which it had before 1914. There are various ways in which this could be done, given co-operation from a reasonable number of governments. But, to my mind, the best solution, in legislative terms, is to internationalize the universities under the auspices of UNESCO. Roughly speaking, this would mean that the subsidies at present paid by governments to university buildings and research would now be paid by them indirectly through the United Nations. Not only would the opportunities to study abroad be increased and UNESCO achieve much-needed stature, but the universities would here find a neat way of dodging the otherwise inevitable tightening of State control—more particularly, this somewhat superficial alteration in administration could have a profound effect on the outlook of research-workers and teachers alike.

Another thing which needs watching is the problem of scientific communication. Even without the curse of secrecy research is often duplicated or overlooked because of the rudimentary difficulties of reading all the scientific papers which are published; language differences only make the problem worse. Indeed, there are signs that the rate of scientific progress will be checked for these reasons alone. Of course, it is not only the research worker who is being submerged in piles of paper with which he cannot cope. The engineer, the lawyer, the politician and the businessman are getting into the same predicament. However, just when it seems that civilization is in danger of succumbing to a log-jam of information in all its forms, along comes the digital computer, and the techniques of data-processing, automatic indexing and mechanical translation. Information services for the scientist and engineer now can and must be greatly improved. But do not forget one of the scientist's greatest assets—the natural internationalism of his subjects. At the big conferences he will exchange information with his opposite number from the other side of the Iron Curtain, if need be, in the lavatory. The experimental philosophy is the same the world over, and the facts are the same in any language.

Injecting reason into human affairs, especially into government, will call for many needles. The sharpest of these is the study of human nature by scientific methods: 'We do this,' in the words of Lord Adrian, 'in the hope of preventing its failures.' The study of the nervous system and of the mind puts us on our guard against fundamental irrationalities. Somewhat blunter, but equally important, is the examination of human societies. I hope it is not just the arrogance of a natural scientist when I say that I think sociology will acquire neither respect nor effectiveness until physicists, chemists and biologists experienced in their own fields are put on to the job. Operational research, that branch of sociology concerned with optimizing performance in military and industrial operations, has already established this point. The social sciences have had a hard time trying to prove they are sciences, and trying to get financial support. Here is the way out for them. Thus, perhaps, we shall begin to deal with world affairs in scientific terms. But I must stress that observation is the basis of science, and that the collection and analysis of data are much more important than grand theories of human behaviour. As the doctors say : 'More mistakes come from not looking than from not knowing'.

Conversely, we must also translate science into human terms. Its basic ideas must be taught to every citizen, and its advanced ideas to every statesman. It must be seen for what it is, the keystone of our culture. By study and by imagination, the human consequences of invention must be anticipated, and the sociologists and politicians put on their mettle to match them with social inventions. Children should grow up self-reliant and ready to re-orientate themselves to an ever-changing world. For that matter, they should also be prepared to resist the blandishments of novelty, so that no longer need the words ring true : 'Invention is the mother of necessity.'

Exploring outer space strikes many people as a futile occupation when there is so much work to be done on this poor old planet. If the choice were ever strictly between an expedition to the moon and the life of a single child, the answer would be simple. But we can't all nurse him or build him a hospital. I hope that rocketry of the peaceful sort will figure high in Socialist policy in future. We in Britain should participate in the planning, building and launching of escaping manned rockets, as a United Nations venture. Perhaps Britain would make the special contribution of the thermo-nuclear motor needed to reach the planets.

My first reason for advocating this is that it is high adventure. That in itself would be sufficient, but there is also a political reason —it is psychologically most important that the flag planted on the Moon should be a United Nations one, and not the Stars and Stripes or the Hammer and Sickle. I would regard it as vital to peace in the future, however schoolboyish it may seem. Man is bound for space, and he must go as the representative of the human race. The time to start planning for it is now.

So, out of all this, what is the policy for Britain? We are living in an underdeveloped country, which will have to reconstruct and modernize its industries, or starve. The world does not owe us a living. We can if we like redouble our efforts in the rat-race—more and more invention, development and production to less and less real effect, always struggling to sell enough to pay for our food. If catastrophic or seeping disaster is averted, and there is something left to argue about, there will be large-scale disarmament and the advanced countries will find themselves before long with more manufacturing capacity than resources and demand can possibly sustain. At the same time, political and economic pressures on world food supplies will grow—with Britain in as vulnerable a position as she already occupies in respect of oil.

Should we not adopt a very different policy, based on the biological realities rather than on the economic superficialities?

Our first aim might well be to become potentially as self-sufficient as possible, to provide ourselves with a firm base during the world-wide technological revolution. Agriculture moves high up the priority list: our contribution to world food supplies could be a 50–150 per cent increase in our potential if not in actual produce. This capacity could then be used, as need be, to offset the dislocations to normal trade that are bound to arise in the future. This is not a Little England policy, nor is it 'yokelization'—scientific and technical measures needed to achieve it at a reasonable cost would stretch us to the limit of our ingenuity, and there would be a bonus of knowledge for a hungry world. At the same time we should exploit nuclear and water power to their utmost. Electricity should become our prime mover, and we should look forward to extremely fast mono-rail transport rather than congested roads and airways.

I reject the well-meant idea that Britain should become the 'Laboratory of the World'. Caltech and M.I.T. could swallow our universities whole, and when the great Soviet scientific machine loses its inhibitions it will move extraordinarily fast. It is already on the move. Individually, our best scientists are second to none and our contribution will always be great, but even to hold our own, if such language ought to be applied to what is essentially an international affair, we shall have to expand our laboratories and scientific staffs several times over. If we have any special role to play it is doctoring to a sick world.

Capital goods industries, with the maximum scientific content, should be our chief concern: better ways of making things rather than new ways of consuming them. What we make should be built to last. The aspect of automation to which we should look is the self-regulating, pre-programmed machine tool (extremely flexible, just the thing for custom-built jobs) rather than to the transfer machine and mass production. The markets in the underdeveloped territories, on which we could be gambling in this scheme, would in any case take time to develop: meanwhile we could be encouraging the semi-developed countries from which we buy our food also to aim at being more self-sufficient by building up their industries.

Whatever path we take, our industries, our administration and our social climate must become better adapted to the scientific age. We must not be misled by our successes in aircraft and atomic energy: many of these have been expensive gambles underwritten for the sake of military aircraft and nuclear bombs. On the whole our industries are backward. A far more determined policy is needed in science education: the brightest, not the dullest, scientists are needed for this work, and they should be induced to spend up to a third of their time out of their laboratories, in the classrooms. Every part of the school science syllabus should be available on film, while television should be used for stimulating curiosity outside the syllabus.

The organization of scientific research would depend on whether or not the universities were internationalized, as I proposed above. But a principle I should like to see applied, if only as an experiment, is this: every graduate who is of research-student standard and above should be given a certain *per capita* grant for his research expenses at an approved laboratory. It would then be up to the scientists to make their own arrangements for co-operative research with one another and with their professors. This would give them more independence of thought and action and would, *inter alia*, help to correct the bias against the biological scientist, though a limited number of 'earmarked' grants for certain expensive and important projects would still be needed.

The most central thing is to cultivate our ability to predict technological trends and their social consequences. I hope that this can be done by international studies but, if not, we in Britain must make our own arrangements. Probably what is needed on the technical side is the ruthless logic of the computer applied to existing knowledge, combined with the perspicacity of the better science-fiction writers. Invention is becoming more and more formalized, and there is no reason why individual inventions should not be anticipated with a high percentage correct. But the study of the social consequences and ways of softening them will depend on something we have not yet got: a larger programme designed to give the social sciences stature, competence and a reservoir of trained manpower. In particular, we must invent new operational methods for the study of man in society.

Yet the ultimate choices about what we are to do with our knowledge must rest with democratic government. The only sure way of seeing that industries do what is right for the community and for the world is the Socialist way. Indeed, the very idea behind my present thesis, that one should look not for quick profits but for an anchor in a heaving world, is not calculated to attract support from the capitalists. I hope I am too much of an optimist to believe that if progress towards world Socialism is not made very rapidly we shall perish—but there is something pretty inexorable in the nuclear chain-reaction, the exponential growth of technology and the population bomb.

So this march to Aldermaston has been only a part of a very much broader picture. I want to see Socialists trying to understand what the white-coated revolutionary is up to, and what he could be doing. We must adopt something of the scientist's way of thinking, and slap down unreason and magical opinions whenever we encounter them. 'Doubt everything' is the best maxim for a democratic Socialist, so long as it is applied equally to old ideas and new.

It should not be our purpose to order the experts to step back and make room for humanity. We must enlist their help and stir their consciences in the name of humanity. We must woo them with Einstein's words: 'Concern for the man himself and his fate must always form the chief interest of all technological endeavours. Never forget this in the midst of your diagrams and equations.'

We must begin now. Otherwise we shall find ourselves in the position of that other philosopher, Immanuel Kant, who called on a lady to ask her to marry him only to discover she had left the district twenty years before.

HUGH THOMAS

Outside the office door

I WAS A SPY in the Establishment for two
and a half years: from 1954 to 1956 I worked in the Foreign Office.
The Establishment's counter-espionage service had presumably
noted that I had called myself a Conservative at Cambridge, without realizing that my conservatism had been romantic, Gothic
almost, pre- rather than anti-, capitalist. Perhaps it was also impressed by the obvious good character of my uncles, among whom
there are a general, a colonial governor, an anglican monk and an
American. But it overlooked another uncle, an editor of the *Daily
Mirror*. While one of my grandfathers was a Cambridgeshire rector
(very sound), the other was an unsuccessful portrait painter with
a violent temper and a respect, at least, for wine. The Establishment might also have realized that the seven-month period I spent
in Paris between Cambridge and London is quite adequate for
revolutionary, as for genetic, gestation; and certainly by the time
I left Paris I had become, thanks to the fresh Left-wing winds then
blowing along the Left Bank where I lived, if not exactly a Socialist,
at least a passionate opponent of the European Defence Community
and of German rearmament, of Mr Foster Dulles, of colonialism,
of the policy of the 'deterrent'—those things which I found myself
called upon immediately to support, when, in August 1954, the
Assistant Secretary-General of the Establishment called me in,
thrust the Official Secrets Act into my hand, gave me his provisional
imprimatur ('H'm, I'd take a game of squash when you can'), and
sent me into the Foreign Office's United Nations department.

At first I was rather impressed. The whole fandango of diplomacy
had always interested me—at Cambridge I had specialized in the
history of the approach to the First World War—and I was able to
distinguish a *démarche* from a *détente* almost on my mother's knee.
The great governmental machine of the Foreign Office was an

absorbing study—the idiosyncrasies, its occupational habits, the jargon—the phrase I liked best was 'under flying seal', which merely means a letter sent to the head of another government with the envelope unstuck so that the ambassador in the country concerned —who would be delivering it—can read it first. Being of a historical frame of mind, I could not help being amused at the surviving formal character of the diplomatic minuet, the letters for the 'bag' the busts of past Foreign Secretaries in the Foreign Office corridors, and the language which dates from the Council of Vienna : 'I am, Sir, with great truth and respect, your Excellency's most obedient and humble servant . . .'. To any social anthropologist, also, the hierarchical character of the profession is a subject for much brooding : for in the Foreign Service there are not only four *branches*, but a varying number of *grades* within each branch, and two systems of ranks, one for home, one for abroad, covering the grades— rather like those houses which are not only No. 99 Crescent Drive but boast a name, such as 'Ti Wa Wa', as well. Then the telegrams, copies of which are circulated three times daily to the different departments in the Office, give one immediately an agreeable sense of proximity to the centres of power, as did minutes by Ministers on the papers which one was handling. Further, it was satisfying to look down into Downing Street from my office window to watch the Ministers go by, to walk soberly across St James's Park with measured Establishment tread, to play about with big words like 'security', and 'the policy of strength', and 'H.M.G.'s vital interests are at stake', and dictate all this to a pearly secretary —an *Establishmentère*, of course. But really, from the start, it was an affair of false moustaches, black patches, borrowed clothes. Publicly, for quite some time, I gave the Establishment a chance, as a child will pretend that it believes in Father Christmas, long after it has discovered the cardboard box under the bed, so that its father can enjoy himself a bit longer. And it was clearly and specifically on questions of policy, not habits, that I quarrelled with the institution in which I was working.

There were naturally other aspects of the Foreign Office which seemed ridiculous, unnecessary and undesirable : but one learns to tolerate, certainly to expect, in England, the idiosyncrasies of overgrown public schoolboys—such as the private lavatory for the under-secretary—an intellectual approach comparable to that of a football changing-room, and the self-importance and unthinking assertiveness of those who have suddenly achieved a measure of power. Anyone who knows anything of England will have seen such behaviour and customs on a thousand occasions, and will also know and perhaps even have some understanding for, the timidity and vacillation of those 'safe' men whose unexceptionable conduct has brought them advancement with which they are unable to cope. No, all this would have been tolerable, if the policy had not been wrong. Which policy, you ask? The Middle East policy, the Cyprus policy, the German policy? Or the disarmament policy, the Chinese policy, the policy on European Security? I mean the lot. It was *all* wrong. *Nothing* was right.

In the autumn of 1954 Her Majesty's Government's policy, and America's policy, and the policy of the rest of the alliance, was to build up the West to such an overwhelming strength that, it was argued, the Soviet Union would be forced to bow down or take the consequences. *They* needed co-existence more than *we*. This meant, of course, German rearmament. No 'lowering of the guard' was possible until that had been secured, no talks with Russia, that is, although the idea of a 'summit' conference had been broached by Churchill sixteen months before. I thought this was wrong and said so as often as I could. The reaction of my colleagues was usually one of private agreement, with a despairing shrug of the shoulder: 'but the Americans insist . . .'. After I had been in the Office three weeks, E.D.C. was defeated in the French National Assembly. The Office was aghast and astonished. Since there had never at any time been a majority for E.D.C. in the National Assembly (as any moderately well-informed journalist in Paris would have told them, if the British Embassy was unable to do the necessary addition sums of the different parties), it is incomprehensible that anyone should ever have supposed that it could have passed, much less professional diplomats, who, even though they may have been actually working on something else, might have been expected to know more than the man in the street. But the surprise was apparent even among those actually at work on European affairs.

In the meantime I had begun my proper work. I was first of all engaged in trying to reach a definition of aggression. This matter was to be debated at the forthcoming meeting of the General Assembly. British policy was to get the question shelved for another year: it was premature to reach agreement at so early a stage. After all, a series of special commissions and committees had been sitting on the matter only since 1951. I did a series of drafts of the brief for the U.K. delegation, and the final draft was sent off to New York. This first diplomatic move in which I played a part was supremely successful: the question was shelved for three years, not one. At this I was shifted on to become, as I was told, 'a cog in the disarmament machine'.

On disarmament there now seemed to be a clear chance of a 'break in the log-jam': for on 30th September, 1954, Vyshinsky accepted an Anglo-French plan on the timing of a disarmament agreement as the basis of a disarmament treaty. Early the next spring, the U.N. Disarmament Sub-Committee was to meet again in Lancaster House, and we passed the winter preparing for this. During this time, I was above all struck how every proposal which we contemplated putting forward was finally approved not by the Foreign Office but by the Ministry of Defence. This reveals an important and generally ignored fact about the contemporary diplomacy of the West: the frightfulness of modern weapons has enormously increased the power of the Service departments. The foreign policy of the fifties reflects, and does not—as it should— direct military thinking. To politicians, no doubt, there is something comfortingly simple about the advice given to them by their Service advisers. It is free from the qualifications, the subtleties, the fastidiousness of the arguments of Civil Servants and diplomats. Military thinking—if one does not dignify the profession overmuch by using such a phrase—is neither arrogant nor self-assertive: it merely states as calmly and rationally as possible the facts of essentially irrational conduct—the settling of disputes by the use of force. And the dream-world of a future nuclear war permits of very clear statements indeed, which cannot be contradicted, because, as Professor Ayer would say, they are neither true nor false. I do not deny that diplomacy and strategy are interrelated. But they should be interrelated on the diplomats', and not the strategists', terms. The contrary juxtaposition is, if anything, more alarming than military dominance over civilian politicians by more obvious abuses. It is a juxtaposition particularly inappropriate at present when, to most sane people, nearly all accepted military assumptions, such as the whole concept of nuclear war, are unthinkable.

I labour this point because this seems the first and most dangerous of the fetishes by which the Foreign Office is at present blinkered. Wherever you go in trying to understand contemporary foreign policy you will find the military fetish: the assumption that the soldiers know best, and not merely in respect of disarmament plans. The error is seen at its most glaring in the claim, docilely accepted by all but a few Western diplomats, that, as the 1958 Defence White Paper put it, 'the balance of military power and deterrents . . . constitute almost the sole safeguard of peace'. But diplomats, who are quick to sneer at the opinions of those they dub as amateurs—and they include retired diplomats such as George Kennan under this designation—should not be so humble about themselves. It was skilful diplomacy and no deterrent that prevented world war in 1950 over Korea, in 1954 over Indo-China, and in 1955 over Quemoy and Matsu. Nuclear weapons played no part in the Berlin crisis of 1948 nor in the Suez-Hungary crisis of 1956. I doubt if the deterrent has deterred Russia at any time since 1945 from embarking upon any action which would have risked a conventional war in the deterrent's absence. The very existence of diplomatic corps on the Western model, each aping each other's habits and using each other's jargon, interlocking with each other in a thousand ways, is a far stronger safeguard of peace than any 'balance of mutual fear', and it is high time that Western diplomatic services got up and said so, and ceased leaving the speaking to military dreamers. After all, there is peace in the world not only between some other countries, where the deterrent does not apply, but *all*. The only wars at present going on are civil wars and not wars between properly constituted states. This is an extraordinary change from the whole of past history and one for which diplomacy must take the chief credit. But it does not.

So much for the military fetish. No sooner had I first encountered it in the Foreign Office in the spring of 1955, than we heard that Britain was about to make a hydrogen bomb. This decision was announced only a week or so before the Disarmament Sub-Committee was due to start. It would have been difficult to have timed an announcement less appropriately. Naturally the Ministry of Defence did not care, because disarmament was hardly something for that department to take seriously. One might have supposed that some others in the Foreign Office besides the small disarmament group itself would have cared. Not at all. We were throughout regarded as being involved in an 'exercise'—the very word indicates the military influence in the Office—harmless, and eccentric, and of no great importance, and not only by our colleagues in other departments of the Office, but others in our own department also. The chief reason for this indifference was the prevalence of another fetish—that of *laissez-faire*.

Old-fashioned diplomats always used to call their memoirs something like *Leaves From A Diplomatist's Scrapbook*, and *More Leaves*, by the author of *Leaves*—with some judicious words about the wisdom of 'dealing with situations as they arise'. This is sheer micawberism in the twentieth century, even if it was possibly justified in the nineteenth, when Britain was the world's greatest power and could stay out of international imbroglio if necessary. The classic statement in this vein was made not by Palmerston or Salisbury, but by Lord Halifax who in 1938 told France, on 12th September, 1938 (he had been asked what Britain would do if Germany attacked Czechoslovakia, as then seemed inevitable), that the British Government was 'unable to make precise statements of the character of their future action . . . in circumstances that they cannot at present foresee.' The great advantage of having worked in a government department is that one knows for certain that this kind of Establishment pomposity is nonsense and that one is entirely justified in saying, whenever one hears it, 'come off it'. People who have never seen the inside of Whitehall are inclined, because of their good nature, to give the Government the benefit of the doubt in these instances: they must never do so—for these cover-up phrases simply and straightforwardly reflect sheer intellectual laziness, however easily they may go into silver Latin. But, as a result of this fetish, there is deeply imbedded in the Foreign Office an occupational dislike of planning, of looking ahead, of doing anything except waiting for the papers to come in and living on the receiving end of events. Hence disarmament, involving the attempt to secure, to however limited an extent, a new world, is naturally not regarded as a high priority by the top men. The *laissez-faire* fetish has, incidentally, two forms. The first, which closely resembles a rather depressing brand of English Toryism, is melancholy: it despairs of any 'change in human nature', it finds a certain glum comfort in thinking about 'natural law', and finally, in denial of all positive thinking, concludes that 'whate'er is best administered is best'. The other form is optimistic, and is closely connected with American liberalism: whatever happens, all is going to be all right: despotism is on the way out and the democratic way of life will inevitably triumph, regardless of any temporary setbacks. The grand oscillator between these two attitudes, the one sad, the other hopeful, is, of course, Mr Foster Dulles, whose views on natural law are frequently intermingled with recollections of Jefferson.

When the Disarmament Sub-Committee met in February 1955, I was to come up against a third fetish. However, its nature only became clear over the course of a year. During this time, the Sub-Committee met sixty-four times, mostly in London, for a while in New York. I was present at nearly all these meetings On two occasions—in particular on 10th May, 1955, and 27th March, 1956 —the Russians made clear attempts to reach a compromise with the Western Powers by accepting proposals that we had been arguing for up to that very moment. The first occasion when this happened, in May 1955, was the most heartbreaking event at which I have ever been present and it made a very great impression upon me. There we had been, talking for months, and then suddenly our proposals were accepted almost entirely. What happened? The golden moment passed. We spent the rest of the summer wondering what to make of this astonishing Russian change of front. The Americans, on the prompting of the Pentagon, put all their proposals in 'the deep freeze', and we, for fear of quarrelling with them, followed their lead. The 'summit' conference came and went, and, in New York, America refused to talk any disarmament except President Eisenhower's Open Skies plan, which provided for no disarmament at all. Thus we killed the 'spirit of Geneva'.

The scene shifts. Another spring, another meeting of the Sub-Committee. Now, at the Geneva meeting of Foreign Ministers in

October 1955, Macmillan, then Foreign Secretary, had hinted broadly that, because of the difficulty of securing a one-hundred-per-cent guarantee of the elimination of all nuclear weapon material, Britain would put forward not a 'comprehensive' disarmament plan but a 'partial' one, providing only conventional disarmament. This hint was repeated in the General Assembly in December and again as late as February 1956 in the Defence White Paper of that year. Accordingly, when the Sub-Committee met, the Russians produced, on 27th March, just such a partial conventional plan as Macmillan might have been envisaging. But the British Government had changed its mind again, and actually embarked upon the absurd course of attacking the Russians in the Sub-Committee for not including any proposals for dealing with nuclear weapons—an argument that sounded hollow indeed when one recalled the arguments and counter-arguments of the previous ten years. It was not as if this Russian plan omitted the need for control, for it included the most far-reaching inspection provisions ever included in any Russian document. And both this plan and that of the preceding 10th May had disengagement plans attached, which, if carried out, would have altered the entire history of Eastern Europe. The blood of the Hungarians is therefore partially lying on the hands of those responsible for the rejection of those documents.

Of course, I know that the Soviet Union may have been 'insincere' just as it may have been 'insincere' in the thirties when Litvinov made eloquent speech upon eloquent speech in favour of collective security—or in the winter of 1957–58 when so many proposals for disengagement came from the pen of Marshal Bulganin. But we don't know because we never tried to find out. We cannot impugn Russian motives since we refused to take the opportunity offered us. Why?

Partly, the military fetish was at work. Once a military position has been established, innumerable reasons can be concocted for preserving it in no way related to the original cause for that position being taken up. Thus, if a disarmament treaty or a disengagement treaty were to entail the radical alteration of NATO, then such a treaty would have to be avoided, though, ludicrously, the facts and assumptions upon which NATO was created would have been removed. The *laissez-faire* fetish was also at work. Disarmament would mean a planned world, even a Socialist world, one where the United Nations would inevitably be a body of great prestige and power. And a co-operative, international world is bound, at least subconsciously, to seem distasteful to the *laissez-faire* diplomat. But there was another fetish—the morality fetish. This argues that no agreement of any kind can ever be reached with the Soviet Union since between Russia and the West there is an impenetrable, himalayan chain of moral, intellectual and religious barriers of the kind that, say, divided Christianity from Islam in the Middle Ages. Any agreement with the Communist countries would, under this reckoning, inevitably be an agreement with the devil, the surrender of some private offshore island, a departure from the policy of strength; in a word, appeasement. This is an attitude taken over, in fact, from the Communists themselves, largely, one suspects, through a rather superficial study of Communist texts. Communist propaganda has consistently emphasized the exclusiveness, the difference in kind of Communist societies from those of the West, mainly, one imagines, to justify to their own people the continued existence of Soviet dictatorship. Western diplomats, perhaps to give the impression that they have brought themselves intellectually up to date, possibly to satisfy an unsatisfied craving for religious belief, have, over the past ten years, taken over this absolutist interpretation of the world's condition, and may now often be heard muttering to themselves about a 'war of ideas', or 'the ideological struggle', or a religious war 'comparable in many respects with the battles between the Protestants and the Catholics in the sixteenth century'. The oddest aspect of this fetish is the ease with which those who subscribe to it identify support of two-party government not only with Christianity but also with the capitalist system. Of course, this moral, black-and-white, heathen-and-Christian, evaluation of the world is quite false. We fear Russia not because we dislike State control of industry, or a censored Press, forced labour, or atheism—all these can be found in countries to which we are allied—but because Russia is powerful. We are afraid of the great size, the population, the industrial potential of Russia, and the fact that, under a totalitarian regime, these resources can be swiftly mobilized. If only the essentially power-basis of our relations with Russia could be admitted, and our diplomacy could be stripped of its self-delusory, religio-moral approach, real negotiations could be undertaken with a hope of success : for it is not as if the barriers are like those dividing the Christian and the Islamic world in the Middle Ages, or those dividing Western peoples and those whom they conquered and enslaved in the early days of colonialism. The whole world is now organized almost entirely according to ideas originally put forward in the West. Developed and under-developed countries, Communists and capitalists, neutralists and absolutists, are living in the same continuum of communities, are subject to the same compulsions towards Western aspirations such as high productivity, leisure, security of home and employment, and, though they are at different stages of historical and economic development and are meeting new challenges in different ways due to historical and geographical accidents, are all now inextricably linked together. How Britain will ensure that once man does not have to fight for survival he does not die of boredom, will be relevant, eventually, to Asia and Africa also. Marx has had nearly as much influence over the development of Western societies as he has over Communist, and Russian scientists have not ignored an old *bourgeois* like Einstein. This infinitely complicated world situation gives rise to all sorts of questions of social control, of military power, of centralization, of how far human beings with low standards of living prefer (and what do you mean by prefer?) security to the liberal freedoms; of fear of novelty and hatred of the past, but not at all to any ideological struggle. Naturally, however, if you divide the world into black and white, you will find it difficult to bring yourself ever to reach any agreement with black.

This moral fetish is partly the reflection of a deeper uncertainty about aims of foreign policy on the part of those most involved in it. Dig your way to the back of any Establishment diplomat's mind—and you'll need a trenching tool to get past the heavy fudge of platitude, stalling communiqués, stock phrases—and you'll find what? Anything? Only very rarely indeed a passionate conviction that the sum of the world's content, or freedom, or achievement, should be pursued at all costs, and at all times, and that the positive use of diplomatic skills is one of the means by which this can be secured. Who is there in the Foreign Office who will refer an inquirer to George Kennan's advice: 'to my own countrymen who have asked me where best to apply the hand to counter the Soviet threat, I have had to reply—to our American failings—the things we are ashamed of in our own eyes: to the racial problems, to the conditions in our big cities, to the education and environment of our young people, to the growing gap between specialized knowledge and popular understanding . . .'? How many English diplomats, if asked for the *raison d'être* of their activity, for the excuse for their big motor-cars and tax-free whisky, for the ultimate motives behind the forms of words, the truth behind the emergency telegrams and the whispers in confidence, would suggest, in any way at all, that they were involved with the only worthwhile objects of any form of public activity—the extension of the areas of freedom from social, intellectual and economic tyrannies? I can only think of half a dozen men at the most at all concerned with such matters in the Foreign Office, and, of these, one is already dead.

After the meetings of the Disarmament Sub-Committee in 1956, I was transferred from the United Nations department to the Southern department, where I looked after the affairs of Austria, and, later, of Italy and the Holy See, and Albania, and, then, for a time, of Turkey. This kaleidoscopic series of changes of work derived from the preoccupation of the Foreign Office with a fourth fetish—amateurism. What I was expected to be was not an expert of any great quality on any of these countries, but merely to be a practitioner in the craft of diplomacy. This argues that, whenever any problem arises in this or that country, it will always be possible to apply a certain formula which has been previously applied elsewhere. Hence, the argument goes on, there is no need for anyone to stay very long in any one post—indeed, that might possibly be dangerous because the person concerned would become really involved with his subject, would get to know too much about it, develop ideas about it, or gain too much power over it. Hence the personnel department of the Foreign Office plays an elaborate game of musical chairs, whereby everyone is supposed to get as much experience of as many different subjects and posts as possible, staying, however, only in one post for just long enough for him to become almost an expert, then to be removed again to become a novice again somewhere else. No doubt this policy makes it very difficult to decide who should go where—and when. My qualifications for looking after Austria, Italy, or Turkey were absolutely nil, and I wasn't even encouraged, much less subsidized, to brush up my German to deal with the Austrians. An indication of the frivolity of some of the postings can be seen by the fact that, on occasions too numerous to mention, persons with similar names have been planted down next to each other—Dodds and Dodgson, for example, as private secretaries to the Minister of State, Pink and Scarlet sent to Berlin together, and Comfort and Joy were plumped in the same room in the same department. It is easy to see that the effects of this dilettantism could have disastrous consequences, if a really serious crisis should break out anywhere where the key person is either new or not particularly well qualified for the job.

Most of the time I was in the Southern department the great crisis in the world was that of the Middle East. It culminated, of course, in the Suez débâcle. During the course of this crisis all the fetishes already noticed showed themselves fairly clearly and early on. The military fetish made the Foreign Office see the Middle East as part of the world jigsaw of 'positions of strength', into which as many countries as possible were to be fitted: hence the Bagdad Pact, to defend a non-existent free Middle East from a non-existent Soviet military threat. The morality fetish made the Foreign Office think that those Middle East countries whose rulers refused to join us were inevitably the tools of Moscow. The *laissez-faire* fetish led the Foreign Office to do nothing to prevent the chronic Arab-Israeli dispute breaking out into war. The amateur fetish made the Foreign Office suppose that nothing had changed in the Middle East for thirty years, that Arab nationalism could be ignored, and that Englishmen had only to keep their snowy steeds following the Southern Cross to be loved for ever in the Gardens of Allah. The paradox of the Middle Eastern crisis was that I, like, I think, most of the Left, spent the first part of 1956 wondering how Israel could be saved from the consequences of the absurd Western policy of attempting to outbid the Russians in offering arms to Egypt, and the second half of 1956 protesting against the Anglo-French threats, and then action, against Egypt. By this time I had lost all illusions about the Office, the jokes had worn thin, and, though this sounds pretentious, for me it was simply a question whether I would not do better to stay inside and attempt to moderate policy from within, eventually perhaps, by luck and sycophancy, fighting my way to a position where, after many years, I could actually hope to make policy, or whether I would not be better outside the walls. The Middle Eastern crisis decided me in favour of the latter course.

The nationalization of the Suez Canal on 26th July, 1956, put the Establishment at bay. All its tricks seemed to have failed. There remained the two weapons of violence and guilt—guilt, that is, for the old Establishment crime of Munich, the spectre of which was to be invoked throughout the ensuing crisis. Many members of the Establishment in the Foreign Office did not follow their natural leader, Sir Anthony Eden, all the way. Violence is no fetish and the Foreign Office as a whole is naturally not in favour of settling international disputes by force—a resort to force being an obvious admission of diplomatic failure. Consequently, the Office, whose mistakes in the Middle East had led to the outbreak of the crisis in its most acute form, was largely ignored by the small group of militarists in charge of policy. The Office later was able to rational-ize its pique at not being consulted as opposition to the whole enterprise, though on grounds of expediency rather than ethics. When I say 'the Office', I mean the expressed opinion within the Office by the majority of people. A few were passionately opposed to the whole Suez action from the start, but most seemed merely to watch and wait to see how successful it would be before making their judgment. At the moment of the intervention, at the end of October, it was not, I think, the use of force which caused dismay in the Office; but the series of lying excuses given for it. 'Knock Nasser on the head' was all right; what was absurd was 'separating the combatants' or 'preventing a Soviet plot' or 'a forest fire'.

It was typical that I heard about the impending disaster from outside and not from within. At about 3.30 p.m. on October 31, I was telephoned by Paul Johnson. He told me that Claude Bourdet had just called him from Paris to say that the British and French proposed to drop parachutists by the Suez Canal that night. This news was the most extraordinary of an extraordinary week—a week which had begun with Gomulka's victory in Poland, had continued with the, at first, seemingly similarly successful rising in Hungary and then, that very morning, with the Israeli attack on Egypt. Disaster, of course, always brings a feeling of excitement to start with, and I confess that my immediate reaction on hearing the Bourdet story was that, if true, it showed that our leaders were just as mad and bad as I had been saying that they were at least since July. But was it true? I made a brief tour of the Office, finding an air of great activity in various key spots. At the lift on the ground floor, I met a close friend. He said, 'They have my unbounded admiration'. He spoke of the Israelis, whom he pictured streaming towards the Canal. I told him my news. He was incredulous. I walked across Horseguards Parade with him in the biting wind. By the time I was back in the Office, Eden's speech in the House of Commons was coming over the tapes, announcing the terms of the ultimatum to Egypt. The ultimatum was so loosely phrased that one felt that its author didn't care if anyone read it or not: he simply knew that it wouldn't be accepted.

I resigned from the Foreign Office and the Establishment shortly afterwards. I think this decision was finally forced by one incident in particular: I had to talk to a European diplomat about a problem which was (and no doubt still is) a bone of contention between our two countries. I had to argue that, while privately we would have liked to help his government to reach a horse-deal on the subject, international law dictated a different course. Naturally, I had to add, Her Majesty's Government could not contemplate any thing which would conflict with its obligations under international law. His eye quivered—with amusement, I think. I smiled also. But it was too much. It was quite clear that the longer I stayed in the Foreign Office the more compromises I would be forced to make. I wanted very much to be outside in the political arena—I had joined the Labour Party—and, above all, I wanted to be free, and have my pen and tongue free to say what I thought, to be able to throw stones at the windows, not be all the time closing the shutters against the splintering glass. I do not, I hasten to add, claim this as in any way a moral act: it was a question of temperament.

Outside, what can be done? It is frequently said that the only means of reaching decisions about foreign policy is to be in the

Office and influence it from within. Historically this is far from true. Even in the Suez crisis, public opinion, once roused, exerted, through its informed spokesmen, great influence. The Labour Party might adopt certain detailed measures of foreign policy as part of its election programme with great advantage, for the size of the public meetings at the time of Suez and over the H-bomb has shown the extent to which the public can be interested in matters of diplomacy. But better still would be a clear statement from the Labour Party that it intended to make a clean break with the whole paraphernalia of traditional diplomacy, and throw away all the old catchwords such as the 'balance of power' and 'the preservation of national self-interest'. What is required is a radical new departure in foreign affairs, seriously and simply aimed to create a better world. The immediate goals and assumptions would be simple—the realization that Socialism must be internationalist or die, the pursuit under all circumstances of international co-operation in all ways, art, sport and health in particular; the concentration on the economic growth of all countries and not just one; disarmament; the setting-up, so far as is possible in as many countries as possible, of mixed, non-absolute, social-democratic regimes comparable to our own : the great change would be to have a goal, to set aside consciously these things as being of first rather than second priority, and to pursue them with tenacity and courage. Give the Foreign Service a series of goals and make one or two alterations in the system of posting, while all the time altering the character of the society of which the Service is the product and the reflection, and the fetishes named here will soon drop away. A fixation has only to be realized and fully documented to be cured. But if nothing is done, the fetishes will stay to poison international relations, and probably cause us eventually to blunder into war.

PETER MARRIS

Accessory after the fact

Kenya on new year's day, 1954: sitting
on a log in the early morning, learning the names of trees. A tuft
of cloud caught on the summit of Mount Kenya and, in the fore-
ground, the stately forest trees ranged along a ridge among planta-
tions of wattle and banana palms. I asked one of my Kikuyu police
what trees they were—names which half an hour later I forgot.
But the botany lesson accorded with the serenity of the morning,
and took my mind off the business in hand.

A boy and girl had been killed the day before. Lovers, they had
been dragged out of a hut in the middle of the night, and slashed
to death as informers, the bones of their arms and legs showing
yellow through the gashes in their skin. Under the girl's breast we
had found a sheet torn from a schoolboy's exercise book, held in
place by a bullet.The paper was crudely stamped in violet ink:
'United Swords Liberation Army, Camp Barafu 56', and under-
neath someone had written in pencil: 'Mount Kenya C.I.D.' Glumly
indifferent, the neighbours would give us no clue to the murders.
So we hired some ramshackle lorries from an Indian trader,
gathered the Kikuyu guard from nearby posts, and organized a
manhunt.

From the log where I sat, the Kikuyu guard were deployed at
an interval of ten paces along the ridge—old men in frayed khaki
shorts and cast-off overcoats imported from a London dealer, a
spear in their hands and a broadsword in their belts. A whistle blew
and, as we advanced down the hillside, the sunlight on the spear-
points and blue headbands gave our iron-age army a certain air of
menace.

Two hours later, the cumbersome exercise was nearly over, and,
as usual we had found nothing. I was eating an orange in an
orchard, my mind on beer and fried eggs in the police mess, when
someone began firing a Patchett gun from the slope above. A young

Kikuyu ran into the road, his hands above his head. A police officer seized him by the hair and swung him round, the snout of his gun poking at his belly, crying, 'Where men? Where men?'—the only words of any African language that he could recall in his excitement. But his captive could only scream in a falsetto frenzy of terror. Another lad darted from a thicket beside me, dodged behind a hut, and tumbled in a plot of beans. He was about eighteen years old, unarmed, and dressed as a schoolboy, with a Boy Scout belt and a macintosh coat. The policeman who had been giving me the nature lesson—who was an engaging fellow—was pushing him about with an officious show of sternness. While my back was turned, he shot the lad dead: he pumped bullets into him at a yard's range. One shot passed through his mouth, and I remember the torn flap of his cheek pulsed slowly, as if he were still breathing.

I thought first of the waste in ammunition. Then I rummaged the dead boy's pockets, in search of some evidence on which a court would have sentenced him to hang. His sudden death would then have seemed more merciful. Someone produced a round of .303, but whether it was really found on the corpse, no one seemed to know. I could think of nothing more to do. I might have arrested my policeman for murder, but all the experiences we had shared together rose in my mind to prevent it. I remembered the afternoon when I was manœuvring a car out of a ditch on the edge of a ravine, and he had been the only passenger to keep his seat; and another, when we had both disgraced ourselves as soldiers—he had left his ammunition hanging on a tree, I had dropped mine in a river. Besides he was by nature gentle and affectionate, with a jolly wife and three inquisitive children, and I did not want him hanged for a moment of hysteria. I was too astonished to be angry, and too unprepared to simulate anger in a foreign language. So we climbed up the slope to the road, where the operation ended. It had been, unexpectedly, a modest success.

The incident is of no special importance. But it remains more vivid in my mind than any other experience of the two years I spent as a District Officer in Kenya. I had not realized one could commit a crime so simply—between breakfast and lunch, as it were, with his mind on the names of trees, beer and fried eggs, and the files waiting in an office tray. For the rest of my life I shall be, legally, an accomplice after the fact of murder. And this, too, is of no special importance, except to understand how good intentions can end so.

How did we come to kill the lad in the Boy Scout belt? I had arrived in Kenya with that confidence in the effectiveness of my moral integrity which the best education provides. I had intended, where I held any authority, to prevent just such a senseless destruction of life. And why should my policeman, whose ambitions were to plant coffee, drive a car, and be a friend of all the world, have been possessed by the lust to kill? And the lad we killed—one of those earnest young men whose prayers for freedom, neatly copied in an exercise book, we used to capture from time to time, together with rules against smoking, drinking and sleeping with women, each with a savage penalty attached—why should he have confused the dedication of his life with the cruel antics of a bandit army?

We were caught in a conflict beyond our control, and, taken unawares, we forgot ourselves in the parts assigned to us—terrorists and security forces, fox and hounds. But if we were not ultimately to blame, who is? The settler who stood by his privileges, the demagogue who roused the rabble, the missionary who forbade tribal dancing, the well-meaning official who papered over unpleasantness with a soothing report? They too have excellent excuses. The settler made a farm in an arid plain, brought wealth and work to a poor country, and claims the safeguards without which his achievement will be taken from his children. The missionary must preach his gospel. The official can point to the fruits of patience and compromise—his schools and hospitals, local councils and model farms. And the African politician cannot lead his people by a sweet reasonableness they are in no mood to follow. Faced with the tragedy of our good intentions, we look for a scapegoat. But the blame is diffused, the original sin lost in the power politics of nineteenth-century Europe, and our bitter accusations only obscure the essence of a colonial crisis.

I wish to emphasize this, because I think much Left-wing criticism of colonial policy is so preoccupied with accusations that it distorts the nature of the problem. It seems to imply that if only the settlers were less arrogant, the police less brutal, if the judiciary

were more independent and the administrators spoke the verna-
cular, the crisis need never have arisen. But the origins of rebellion
lie not in the people who govern, but in the nature of the government itself.

When Captain Lugard carried our colours across the map of
Africa, he was less concerned to spread our civilization or our
religion than to forestall the Germans and the French. We wanted
to control the hinterland of the Niger, the source of the Nile. To
reach the Nile we needed a railway from the coast. To build the
railway, we imported labourers from India; to make it pay, we
encouraged settlers from England. So the people of Africa became
drawn into a complex pattern of international relations. Where
there was a paramount chief, a king, the imperial power took him
under its protection: where there was no central authority, we
provided it. In either case, effective government passed into our
hands.

The colonial crisis now begins to develop. Traditional codes of
behaviour could not be adjusted to include relationships outside
the scope of those which they had evolved to control. The ending
of tribal warfare, the introduction of a money economy and a
European conception of political authority destroyed the basis of
traditional values. Inferior in knowledge and skill, and powerless to
challenge the foreign civilization, tribal culture began to collapse.
With its collapse, people lost their sense of identity with a social
group. Hence the feeling of rejection which torments colonial
relationships.

Those who grow up under colonial rule have no culture of their
own in which they can take pride, to compensate them for their
ignorance of the foreign culture. They can only judge themselves
by European standards, having no other—and by these standards
they seem inferior. Hence they can only recover their self-respect
by acquiring our knowledge as quickly as they can, and then asserting their equality on our terms. They are less concerned with
knowledge for its own sake than with its concomitants of power
and status. They may even belittle the pre-eminence of European
skill—as the Mau Mau, for instance, claimed that a Kikuyu had
invented matches, and had his hands cut off for his pains—since
the less it is, the sooner they can acquire it. From this eagerness for

knowledge grows a class of more or less educated men who can find no place in their own society. Their education gives them prestige amongst their own people, yet alienates leaders from followers. They can find few professional opportunities outside government and European concerns, and the more wholeheartedly they devote themselves to their work, the more they are distrusted by Africans and dependent on European patronage. They are impatient of the remnants of traditional authority, yet they cannot identify themselves with the alien bureaucracy. They belong to a nation not yet born and, in their frustration, only the task of creating such a nation can command their allegiance.

The crisis now approaches its climax. The colonial power is reluctant to compromise its cautious devolution of authority, to appease men whom it regards as an impatient and irresponsible minority. It claims that there are far too few educated men to staff a government, however precarious. The leaders of the colonial people see this as a deliberate attempt to humiliate them personally, and a proof of the hypocrisy of the imperial power, whose real aim is to exploit them.

Can the crisis be resolved without tragedy? If the imperial power does everything it can, by promise and example, to prove its good faith; if every unnecessary humiliation is avoided; if political concessions are made before agitation becomes embittered, then there is hope that the colonial relationship may be replaced without bloodshed by a relationship between sovereign peoples. But if this is not done, there will be revolt. And in the end, the revolutionaries must always win, because we lack both the resources and the moral sanction within our own culture to hold the country permanently by force.

Political concessions cannot be timed to suit ideal standards of preparedness. They are determined by a balance of two forces— the urge of colonial peoples to recover their self-respect, by asserting their equality with the people whose culture they are committed to mastering; and the desire of the foreign administrator not to abandon his task of creating a modern society before it is done. In this conflict, an appeal to the analogy of education only confuses the issue. You cannot teach people self-government, since they will not realize the nature of their responsibility until they hold it.

You cannot teach even the most practical skills once you have lost the goodwill of your pupils: even the inoculation of cattle becomes a political issue. The question is not, when will the people be ready? But, how long will they wait? The administrator may believe that in giving way he is betraying his work: but if he resists the demand, he will find that in any case his efforts are frustrated, because he loses the co-operation that would enable any further progress to be made.

I believe, then, that the colonial crisis is inspired above all by humiliation. In robbing people of their self-respect, we take from them something that they value even more than liberty, something that they can only recover by creating a society of their own, under their own leaders, with which they can identify themselves. The movement for independence gathers its strength from the snubbed graduate, the semi-literate clerk whose cosmic letter of application moulders in some Government file, the lad who hangs about the city streets without work or land, the peasant woman trudging to the road gang with her baby on her back, the prostitutes and jail-birds, chiefs without authority and farmers without farms, everyone who feels himself dispossessed and relegated to a marginal status in a society where the only confident citizens are white. Humiliation finds relief in the vainglory of the swashbuckling terrorist general, the controlled bitterness of the African leader, the lads who swear in a forest ritual to murder their fathers and their mothers for the sake of freedom. The lad in the macintosh and Boy Scout belt knew we would kill him if we caught him, but he risked it for the sake of a few weeks in which his life acquired some meaning.

Once frustration has broken out in revolt, the restoration of order can only increase bitterness. I was in Kenya again recently, and a phrase which I heard from both Africans and Europeans sticks in my mind: 'Of course, Kenya is virtually a police state.' Of course, since nothing has changed but the determination with which the government asserts its authority, and the sense of purpose with which a new challenge gathers strength. Only a policy bold enough to concede the abrogation of colonial power, within far fewer years than Governments have hitherto considered, can save Kenya from more violence. Not that it is easily done: minorities, even privileged minorities, have rights. And there is no way in which we can guarantee the rights of European settlers within the framework of independence. Partnership provides no answer: I cannot conceive any form of society in Africa with which both races could equally identify themselves. Neither will concede enough: they share little but the mutual determination to dominate their homeland. In the face of deep conflicts of aspiration, the ideal of racial partnership dwindles into a plea for better manners and a rigged vote. Europeans can only remain in Africa on sufferance or by force, and we can therefore only appeal over our broken promises to the doctrine that ultimately African interests are paramount.

But the presence of European settlers does not create a colonial crisis; it only exacerbates it and complicates its solution. I have tried to show that the crisis must be latent under all colonial rule, since wherever people cannot identify themselves with the Government which controls their lives, they feel intolerably dispossessed. I have discussed Kenya only because there I experienced the reality of such frustration, and discovered how futile in the face of it was my well-meant liberalism.

The first object of colonial policy must be, then, to restore to the colonial peoples their social identity. However valuable the skills and public services—from wheels to international airlines—acquired through colonial rule, no wealth of technical resources can reconcile a people to the loss of their self-respect. To have destroyed that respect is perhaps the gravest harm that any people could inflict upon another; and it cannot be recovered without autonomy in the only form the world will recognize—that of a sovereign State. National independence is an ideal in its own right, not merely the means to democracy. Indeed, liberty may for a while be less well protected in the emerging nations than it was under the detached eye of a District Officer from Wellington or Rugby. Colonial rule acts as a catalyst, crystallizing into a nation heterogeneous tribes circumscribed by unnatural boundaries: they lack even a common language. And once independence is achieved, all the rivalries and discontents assimilated to an overriding purpose revive to flourish their unredeemed promises. The task of creating a society with which its members can identify themselves has only begun. As the concept of government, independent of party, has to be established anew, the right of opposition easily becomes confused with an attack on the central authority itself. The threat of anarchy and secession may drive the Government towards a one-party dictatorship. But the more we protest, from the comfortable security of our own inviolable constitution, the more we damage the prestige of that Government and drive it towards the very measures we protest against.

This is why I do not argue my defence of colonial nationalism in terms of freedom and equality. The less secure a society is, the less can it withstand the disruptive claims of freedom, and the more it must reward those who commit themselves to the new state. If for this reason we turn our backs on the newly independent nations, we shall destroy our influence for the sake of a self-righteous inflexi-bility. The more wholeheartedly we encourage them, the greater their chance of remaining faithful to the ideals which, almost in spite of ourselves, we have managed to pass on to them.

Our own recent history has been so dominated by the demand for liberty within the social order that we tend to interpret all political issues in terms of individual rights. In asserting the claims of nonconformity, we have continually challenged the established order. But we have only been able to achieve this without destroy-ing ourselves because our cohesion as a nation was fundamentally so secure. We can tolerate conflict because we contain it within our institutions. However bitterly Government and Opposition, or trade union and employer may attack each other, they remain faithful to the conventions which determine how their quarrel shall be decided. We rest secure in our loyalty to each other as members of the same society, scarcely able to conceive of any conflict, how-ever strident, strong enough to shake our stolid patriotism.

But the newly created nations have no such assurance. They are societies within which the values that can command a common allegiance have not yet become articulate. What justifies the claim to leadership—a majority of votes, the inheritance of traditional authority, the prestige of wealth or education, or pre-eminence in the struggle against imperialism? May one region claim autonomy, if it enfeebles the State? Is a present to the judge who tries your case a traditional courtesy, or a crime? The rights of every relation-ship remain to be established. The constitution itself is a legacy of colonial rule, as much an expression of the ideals of the imperial power as of the people themselves. The function of trade unions has to be disentangled from the confusion of racial politics. Even marriage, over much of Africa, has yet to be defined, since for the most part it is neither Christian nor traditional, an unstable association of men and women almost devoid of institutional sanction. A society struggling to realize itself is under great pressure to suppress conflicts which it cannot immediately resolve. Few men can find a meaning in their lives, unless they identify themselves with others whose purpose they can share. And while they are urgently seeking to establish this sense of a common purpose, the man who demands to go his own way seems a traitor.

I do not mean to suggest that the nationalism of former colonies must always end in dictatorship but only that the more disrupted a society has been by colonial rule, the more the explicit conflicts of a democratic constitution will strain that society's confidence in its identity as a nation. The appeal of Communism to newly independent nations lies, I think, not in its doctrines but in its promise of unity. It justifies its ruthlessness in the name of an overriding national interest: dissidence becomes treachery, and all the nagging uncertainties of democratic choice are swept aside in a mood of massive dedication. But people cannot for long commit themselves to a purpose which they have not chosen of their own will. Appeals to patriotism degenerate into menaces, and the attempt to create a society sustained by a compulsory allegiance collapses in persecution.

The form in which authority and liberty are reconciled can only be established by experiment. The nature of the dilemma will be clear to anyone who has attended one of those tiresome Christmas parties where a new game is invented. The guests are all anxious to play, but each has his own ideas of what the rules should be. The argument seems endless, and at last they submit with relief to the man who will be the first to lose his temper if his rules are not accepted. But after a while the losers may recall their original reservations and withdraw in protest; the game has lost its point. For a contest is meaningless if the players do not accept the rules, and equally meaningless without rules to accept. So is a marriage meaningless, unless the bride and groom accept their obligations, and there are obligations to accept. And so is a society meaningless, unless its members commit themselves to some purpose which unites them.

In their struggle for self-realization, the new nations will be the more intolerant of internal conflict the more incoherent they feel their society to be. If, as in our Suez campaign, we appeal to the people over the heads of their acknowledged leaders, we shall only threaten their sense of their national integrity, and convince them that their leader's claim to absolute power is justified. But if we accept these nations wholeheartedly as sovereign independent powers, we shall contribute something towards their sense of security, and so to the tolerance with which they work out the basis of their national life. I mean more than the dispatch of available royalty to unfurl a flag, read conventional messages of congratulation, and bestow gracious approval on a few public buildings, more than the annual good-fellowship of a Common-wealth conference. I mean a genuine eagerness to be of service wherever our good offices can help them, and especially to back them with the capital they need to develop their economy. The excuse that we lack the resources sounds hollow from one of the world's prosperous nations: the injustice of great inequalities of wealth is not absolved by frontiers. Nor can we justify our reluct-ance by insisting that all investment be conceived in strictly economic terms. Industry is more than a means to prosperity. Since it is bound by no traditional loyalties to tribe or region, it draws together men of all kinds into a complex organization which reinforces the coherence of society: and it can become, especially under State sponsorship, a powerful symbol of a national purpose. We, who have spent millions to acquire the unprofitable prestige of nuclear armaments, cannot convincingly dismiss some giant hydro-electric scheme as a grandiose daydream, because a more cautious deployment of resources might offer a more businesslike return. Is a project therefore suspect because it makes a powerful appeal to national pride? The more a society achieves, the more will its members commit themselves to it, proud to associate themselves with those achievements.

Nationalism is not, then, an aberration of political immaturity. The need to belong, to find yourself within a society whose ideals you can share, to contribute to its achievements and appropriate its aspirations, is as profound a human impulse as its opposite, the desire to protect your personal integrity from the distortions of enforced conformity. The right of association is as fundamental as the right to justice and a livelihood. And in a world which recognizes only nations as sovereign social groups, nationalism is as necessary to human dignity as liberty itself. Jingoism and the strident brandishing of authority do not express the strength of nationalism, but rather its weakness. The more confident a nation, the less it need fear the limitation of its sovereignty by international agreement, and the less arrogantly the Government need assert itself in the eyes of its own people. Nationalism is not the enemy of freedom and international understanding, but their prerequisite. A weak Government cannot protect liberty within its frontiers nor guarantee its undertakings outside them; and the man who puts his trust in his rights as a citizen gets short shrift in the office of the local boss.

I believe, then, that we should encourage and support nationalism, and that by this we could do more to create a world open to our conceptions of liberty and social justice than we have ever done as a colonial power. Not that we should therefore condone every act done in the name of national unity. We cannot muffle our distaste for arbitrary arrests, censorship, intimidation and jobbery merely to save political leaders from embarrassment. But our protests will be impertinently glib unless we understand the nature of the dangers against which they have to guard. Only in the struggle against colonial rule, when government and imperial power are one, will the aims of independence and democracy necessarily agree. Once independence is achieved, it takes an adroit statesman to reconcile the needs of an emerging nation with the practice of parliamentary democracy—and even so, he will need the sleight of hand of his personal prestige to keep his contract. I have tried to show that national freedom can itself be a cause worth supporting, even if at first it does not also secure personal freedom; and to us, as a colonial power, it is the only relevant issue. No one can defend a people against themselves.

When I began my service in Kenya, I discovered in myself a vein of uninhibited rhetoric. I launched upon a campaign of speeches in which I passionately denounced the cruelty of the terrorists, appealing for loyalty in the name of their murdered and mutilated Kikuyu victims. It used to anger me that my audiences remained so indifferent to my humanitarian arguments. The women would fret over their babies, bored and restless; the young men would ask pert questions with a mocking smile. Sometimes the terrorists themselves would take advantage of the opportune crowd to make a stump collection. I discovered in time how ambivalently even loyal chiefs and Kikuyu guards felt toward the Mau Mau movements. In spite of the gross obscenities and outrageous cruelty of the rebellion, it compelled the sympathy of the Kikuyu people: it was at last something of their own, through which they could recover, however paradoxically, their respect for themselves. And so great was this need that it overcame their repugnance for the arbitrary terrorism of which they were themselves the victims. If people will sacrifice so much for their national aspirations, I thought, no wonder they are bored by my trite appeals to decency and the peaceable rewards of co-operative pig farming. Good government is no substitute for self-government, especially since good government, in the face of revolt, ends by using the methods which are used against it. Speechmaking gives place to the punitive razing of crops, the tyranny of secret informers and mass arrests, the masked accuser pointing his finger at whim along a line of suspects, children starving while their mothers dig fortifications, and undiscriminating manhunts in which no prisoners are taken. Good intentions end in the tragic futility of estimating your achievements by the tally of the dead. And to this end must come all those who claim the right to decide the welfare of others against their wish. It is a warning, both to ourselves, and to those who come after us. But our successors can draw on a fund of goodwill which we have exhausted.

The time is short

I WAS SEVENTEEN YEARS OLD in 1939; and if you can think of a worse year in which to be seventeen you will surprise me. Successors to the self-styled lost generation, we could with more accuracy have been called the conscript generation—and not in a merely legal or official sense: the generation that never knew what it was to be without duties. The war directed and shaped our lives just when we ought to have been learning to think. Since being demobilized, and with the exception of those of us who found it simpler to sign on as regulars (with or without uniform, in one army or another), we have applied ourselves to this accomplishment. We have found it doubly difficult, just as it takes more effort to learn to type with correct fingering if you have been banging away to your own satisfaction for years with two fingers.

It will be evident that, when I speak of the war, I mean more than what the proclamations called 'the duration of the emergency'. For those of my generation concerned in politics, and concerned on the side of the Left, life has been one long emergency as far back as we can remember. The trumpet-call to which we listened was not, as in happier ages, one of opportunity; no, the characteristic and irresistible note of the late 1930's was of urgent and sinister menace. There are two expressions of this appeal that will never lose their power for me. One is the phrase, 'It is later than you think'. The other is the final stanza of Auden's *Spain*:

> "We are left alone with our day, and the time is short, and
> >   History to the defeated
> May say Alas but cannot help nor pardon."

Reading again this long and beautiful poem, which perfectly conveys what thousands felt, the *necessity* of fighting in Spain, I am struck by the absence in it of any expression of what the Spanish war was about. I know that a poem is not an editorial. Nevertheless, I find this significant. When I wrote just now that my generation did not learn to think, I may have offended some readers and puzzled others, who picture the thirties as a time of furious intellectual activity. So it was; but thought never achieved its proper mastery over action. It was not found possible to work out ideas and follow them to the actions which they suggested. Actions and events generated ideas, as resistance or as justification. The time was short, and the events were usually those in which Hitler and Mussolini took the initiative.

It will be noticed that I have not got far without mentioning the Spanish war. The Reichstag fire trial, the persecution of the Jews, the resumption of the arms race—these were the first political events of which I was aware. But Spain (in how many autobiographies have you read this sentence?) was the chief emotional experience of my youth. I might have worked it out of my system if I had fought there, but I was too young, and had to make do with the Second World War. This may sound odd, until it is remembered how much more generously the Spanish war filled the need of 'a faith to fight for'. In fact, like other young men in my position and with my convictions, I spent the war years fighting Fascism, to the bewilderment of those in adjacent slit-trenches who were fighting Germany, or simply fighting.

For what are called the politically minded—a weak phrase indeed to describe an obsession of the whole spirit and personality—certain events achieve the impact of personal experience. Those of which we read in the newspapers are as real as though we had been directly involved, and both move us as keenly as the triumphs and disasters of private life. Any such person, if he was about seventeen in 1939, will compile nearly the same list of such events: the defence of Madrid, the fall of Vienna and Prague to the Nazis, the defeat of Spain, the outbreak of war, Dunkirk, the invasion of Normandy, the liberation of Paris, victory, and in recent years Suez and Hungary.

All, of course, to do with war and violence. But why 'of course'? Even in this bloodstained epoch, other things happen, and we know, once we think of it, that social and economic changes, scientific advances, and the emergence of new nations will bulk larger in the histories than the clashes I have evoked.

It is partly a matter of being that precise age. The turn toward political awareness in the early thirties was impelled by the slump and mass unemployment; only those for whom politics began with Hitler allowed their field of vision to be filled by the issues he raised and the struggles he made inevitable. Partly it is a matter of class; contempt for bread-and-butter politics is the luxury of those with enough bread and butter, and I was among those more likely to meet an exiled Jewish savant than a miner on the dole. And partly it's something we still do not like to admit. Issues like Spain and Suez are, in every way, easier than issues like equality in education and democratic control of nationalized industries. The former lend themselves far more convincingly to solutions expressed in slogans, to the type of action that precedes thought, and to the marking out of lines drawn to divide all the good people from all the bad people, with consequent licence for uncritical admiration and unrestrained denunciation.

This temper of mind was invited, and so excused, by the plain and incontestable facts. There really is nothing very complicated about Fascism—it is wrong and must be opposed. Action has the genuine spur of urgency; if nothing is done, it will be too late. And even if every actor in a given conflict isn't admirable or detestable, quite enough of the principals usually are.

All this is true; and yet, because we have seen no other truth, we stand now in a greater danger than ever before, and are ill equipped to meet it. If we are to escape and survive, I believe that our first need is to think afresh.

To suggest this appears to many worthy folk a kind of treason, and understandably enough, for no threat was ever more manifest than that of the hydrogen bomb. The warnings have achieved a literal truth of which their authors did not dream. In the contest of survival with extermination, there will be no history to say anything to us if we are defeated.

As I write, the headlines are tall with crisis. I shan't, of course, discuss this particular heat-rash on the world's face. If you are reading in printed form the words I am now typing, we shall have turned this corner. But that is no guarantee that we shall take the next corner, or any of the others into which we speed with screaming tyres.

So if I urge that our need is for thought, and only for action as thought dictates, I am not by any means saying that either thought or action can wait. There must, indeed, be a difference in mood and argument between this essay and the others published with it. When they call for a new approach to economic policy or to education, they may well insist that it should be adopted quickly, both from intrinsic need and to overcome the stagnation of what Norman MacKenzie has called the stalemate state. Yet if the new ideas do not triumph in 1959, they must be pressed in 1960. If even then they are resisted, there is still 1961. One cannot make such assumptions in writing or thinking about the hydrogen bomb. The time is too short.

The international policy of Great Britain is built upon the determination, in certain circumstances, to start what even the cool-headed Dr Kissinger calls a thermo-nuclear holocaust. I write 'start' because this is not made to depend on the enemy's using nuclear weapons first; and I write 'determination' because I flatter our policy-makers with the assumption that they are neither so cynical nor so foolish as to try to bluff Krushchev. That this can bring us no conceivable advantage, that it will in fact bring catastrophe on a scale not yet imagined in our history (even if it does not kill us all, which is probable)—so much is admitted. We have a Minister of Defence who tells us flatly that the country is indefensible, and a Prime Minister who utters the profound thought that if the deterrent is used, that will prove that it has failed.

But the reasoning which underlies this astounding resolution is accepted by all the political parties; by all but a dozen Members of Parliament; by every large-circulation newspaper, except the *Daily Herald* in a moment of honourable aberration. What are we to conclude?

I am by nature a romantic and an optimist, which is one of three possible ways to continue active in Left-wing politics. (One can alternatively be a cheerful cynic, or outstandingly imperturbable and persevering, but I cannot mould myself effectively into either of these personalities.) However, I have seen Spain and Hungary flattened under the tanks; and I do not believe that right must triumph over might, or that thrice is he armed that hath his quarrel just, useful though these phrases are on the platform. Nor do I think that the will of the people is invincible, even under our system of government, which is not precisely democracy (since, by the meaning of the word, the will of the people *would* then be supreme) but government by conflicting pressures (election results and the use of free expression being the most obvious, and certainly precious, but not always the most potent). Finally, there is still less warrant for imagining that the course dictated by reason is sure to be followed.

So, although my whole temperament rebels against the conclusion—as I suppose his does also—I think Bertrand Russell is right when he says that the human race has no more than an even chance of surviving to the end of this century.

Why do the rulers of great nations, with the support or the inert acquiescence of at all events a large section of their peoples, behave in a way that is likely to lose us this melancholy wager? We had better try to understand, if we want to bring about a change.

Lord Russell, as his critics unkindly point out from time to time, suggested in 1946 that it might be wise for the West to threaten Russia with an atom bomb in order to enforce a change of Soviet policy. However objectionable in several respects, such action was feasible. The atom bomb did not have the incalculable destructiveness of the hydrogen bomb, and America, of course, had a monopoly of atomic might. Today such threats are meaningless. Despite his advanced age, Lord Russell's views have altered with the changing situation. The trouble is that those of most politicians do not. In the language of psychology, they repeat their obsessional actions despite a growing estrangement from reality. Thus, Mr Dulles and Mr Selwyn Lloyd maintain, in utterly changed conditions, the *cordon sanitaire* instituted by M. Poincaré and Sir Austen Chamberlain. This does not protect them any longer from the original danger; it does expose them to another and more ghastly fate. One is reminded of the two old men in New York who were so afraid of burglars that they barricaded themselves in their house, fell ill, and died of starvation.

This kind of irrational politics is always justified by a great show of insight and erudition. Hence Mr Dulles's way of proudly bringing out quotations from Lenin to prove that Communism means military aggression. Anyone really familiar with Lenin's life and writings knows that he was one of the greatest opportunists (I use the word in the dictionary sense, not in that given to it by Communist jargon) who ever lived. A veteran Communist once told me that, in an argument with Lenin, he quoted a passage from one of the latter's books which contradicted current Soviet policy. Lenin asked him for the number of the page, which he smugly produced. 'When you get home, tear that page out,' he was told. Of course Lenin said that war could serve the interests of Communism. If he were still alive now that the hydrogen bomb has made it impossible for war to serve the interests of any system, he would say: 'Tear that page out.' To admit this, however, would spoil the perfection of Mr Dulles's obsession—nor is it very easy for Mr Krushchev, to whom we shall come in a minute.

The Dulles line of argument, or more exactly of reiteration, is unluckily very persuasive to the man in the public bar as well as the man at the Cabinet table. There is nothing that the obstinate and rather stupid home-made expert likes better than a fact or a quotation which is new to his listeners. It saves him the trouble of thinking. It may be irrelevant, but if it is authentic, that is enough. It confers the ability to say: 'Those guys may fool you, but they can't fool me—I know the score.' This is a favourite attitude of shallow thinkers the world over, but it yields special prestige in America, and Mr Dulles is no doubt widely admired for his acumen every time he denounces another Soviet proposal as 'propaganda'.

To make matters worse, it is notably difficult for Communists, and especially for Russian Communists, to see that an opponent may be acting irrationally. Prisoners of the past as much as their Washington counterparts, they suppose that the men of Wall Street still 'dream' (a favourite *Pravda* word) of launching an anti-Soviet war in which Wall Street's own skyscrapers would become radioactive dust in a day, exactly as they hoped for a return on their subsidies to General Wrangel in 1919. But Wall Street men don't dream; they figure.

It is hard to believe that Krushchev, although as ignorant and doctrinaire a ruler as any since Philip II of Spain, really thinks that Western monopolists look to war to increase their profits, as he wrote in his amazing letter to the *New Statesman*. Probably there are moments when he does and moments when he doesn't. What concerns us is that, with both powers holding the safety-pin half-way out of the grenade as a 'deterrent' to their own fantasies, disaster may come because both happen to be equally remote from reality at the same time.

Part of the answer to our inquiry, then, is to be found in the power of dead ideas. Among supporters of the present British Government, this is augmented by guilt caused by the blunders of the past.

It is now generally agreed that the Second World War could have been prevented by something very like the policy of deterrence. Indeed, to hear some Tories talk, you might suppose that 'Stop Hitler—Save Czechoslovakia' rallies were organized from the Carlton Club, and that non-intervention and Munich were the work of Oxford undergraduates. So now, determined to get the sum right even twenty years after the exam papers have been marked, they urge—collective security. Everything has changed : the nature of the antagonist, the balance of forces, the weapons, the likely effect of war. But that doesn't matter. They just carry on, like the generals who had the Maginot Line ready for 1940 because it would have been useful in 1914.

Another dead idea is that of defence. Though refuted by Mr Sandys in the plainest terms, many people still think that our weapons are intended to keep out the Russians, as Drake kept out the Spaniards, the navy kept out Napoleon, and the Spitfire boys kept out Hitler. This has been such a constant theme in our history that one can't really expect it to be forgotten simply because of new facts.

Then there is the idea of keeping up with the progress of weapons. From the invention of the longbow to the latest clamour for supersonic fighters, the assumption—perfectly valid in its own terms—has been that our weapons must be better and more numerous than the enemy's. The fact that it just doesn't matter any more, that the only real factor in a nuclear war is vulnerability, that when you've killed everybody you can't kill them twice with more and bigger bombs—this likewise takes a bit of dinning in.

The greatest dead idea is that of war itself. For all its horrors, war was a contest, decided by the exercise of such qualities as skill, courage, and careful planning, as well as by material equipment. There will never again be such a contest; there will be peace or massacre. But, since war is older than civilization or even agriculture, or any other human activity except reproduction, it is naturally hard to imagine a world without it. The failure to do so is shown by two aspects of current controversy. Advocates of nuclear disarmament are stigmatized as cowardly, as if it were brave to fire a missile from a concrete shelter fifteen hundred miles from the enemy. Soldiers are still praised for their courage, and generals promoted (officially, that is) for their professional skill, despite the obvious fact that in a nuclear war the former could all be as brave as Horatius and the latter as brilliant as Marlborough without this making a scrap of difference. Then the argument is carried on in terms of the old debate between pacifists and their opponents, whereas it is manifestly a quite different argument. The pacifists maintained that violence was not justified even in pursuit of a desirable aim, such as the defence of democracy, national independence, or indeed survival. About this there was clearly much to be said on both sides, but it is all of purely historical interest when the use of the hydrogen bomb can serve none of these aims, and for that matter puts a dead stop to all three.

All this looks very simple. But I am under no delusion that what is needed is merely for this book to come to the notice of those who put their faith in the nuclear deterrent, whereupon they will blush at the obvious fallacies they have been cherishing. They are as intelligent, for the most part, as people who share my outlook. The inquiry must go further. I have already used such everyday psychological terms as 'obsession' and 'delusion'. If it were more generally recognized that neither rational thought nor self-interest are all-important in human affairs, the rulers who hold the keys of peace and war might revise their view of their 'diabolically clever' opponents—rating them lower and fearing them less.

I have always profoundly regretted that the discoveries of Freud were not made at the same time as those of Darwin. There is absolutely no telling what difference it might have made to history if Marx, or more likely Engels, had given the same attention to them as to Darwin's work or that of the anthropologist, Morgan. (It is interesting that, in the early period of intellectual liberty in the Soviet Union, Trotsky and Radek urged acceptance of much of Freud's teaching.) Humanity is in danger now, among other reasons, because men possesesing the vast power and limited intelligence of Stalin and Krushchev have reduced Marxism, once a powerful aid to free inquiry, to a closed and antiquated system of economic determinism.

A fact which is sedulously shunned or heatedly denied in Left-wing circles, though both the psychologist and the man in the street will vouch for it, is that the human male likes killing. It is only the very exceptional man who will kill except in war, and only the exceptional soldier who will kill in defiance of what he is taught to regard as the rules of war; but the ordinary man, when he feels himself licensed to kill, does it not as a repugnant duty but with gusto.

I have twice had the experience of being nearly killed, and each time, as it happened, I was able to note the emotions of the men who were in a position to kill me without, on either occasion, any risk to themselves. When I walked right up to a concealed German position in Holland in 1944, a young sergeant, before taking me prisoner, half withdrew the pin from a grenade. When he saw that he couldn't possibly justify himself in throwing the grenade at me, he put it back; but I vividly remember the gleam of excitement in his eyes, and then the pout of disappointment when he decided not to kill. He didn't treat me at all unpleasantly during the hour I spent in his custody, and I have no reason to think that he was anything but a quite ordinary young man. The second incident was similar, though I was in greater danger. It was in Bombay during the general strike that accompanied the naval mutiny of 1946. I was in the mill district in civilian clothes, when an army truck drove through a street crowd firing a Bren gun. Everyone ran for the doorways, except those who were hit. I forget how many were killed—half a dozen, probably. I looked at my compatriots who had fired; they were laughing.

In Alexander Baron's book *The Human Kind*, based on his war memories, there is a chapter about two subalterns who are about to blow up a pillbox in Sicily, when the Italians in it show the white flag. This so irritates the officers that they blow it up anyway. Baron adds that this was told to him as a joke, and comments: 'Sometimes, when I hear myself making free with expressions like "the humanist outlook" and "the sanctity of life", I remember that for a couple of years after the event, I too continued to tell it to other people as a funny story.' There is nobody who was in the war for whom this does not ring true.

That the masses, or the workers, or ordinary chaps, loathe war and get nothing from it but suffering is one of the most hampering of the many sentimental illusions of the Left. In 1949, while collecting signatures for a peace appeal, I got into an amicable argument with a policeman. Seeing his impressive array of campaign medals, I said: 'Well, you've had enough of war, haven't you?' 'Me?' he answered in genuine astonishment. 'Best time I've ever had.' And I'm sure it was, what with the company of good friends, travel, freedom from routine, rapid promotion, responsibility, and just enough danger for excitement. Here he was back on the beat, with five years of boredom before he could hope to be a sergeant.

We must remember, too, that the last war offered more scope for irregular action, initiative, and adventure than any other for a long time. For the British and American armies, the periods of gruelling battle were short and the casualties generally low. Except in a few episodes like Cassino, there were none of the sickening experiences of 1914–18. It was only the German and Russian armies that were given cause for a real loathing of war, the kind of loathing that united the world after 1918. It is instructive to compare the literature of the respective post-war decades. After the First World War, there was for a while nothing but escapism, followed by a series of powerful pacifist novels and plays, whose depiction of the horrors of war met with respect (and big sales). Since 1945, the public has shown an insatiable appetite for books that, while not actually glorifying war, put the accent on heroism, adventure, and the lighter side. It may be that their popularity is due in part to a realization that there can never again be a war in the old sense; perhaps the tommy-gun and the booby-trap have acquired the same period charm as the longbow or the cavalry charge. I don't think, at all events, that one could describe the post-war atmosphere at any stage as militaristic. Still, few of these recent best-sellers would have escaped in the 1920's without shocked protests in the liberal and Socialist press.

Anyone whose memory goes back twenty years must admit that the ordinary man accustoms himself easily to new and worse standards of violence. The hydrogen bomb is appallingly novel in several decisive respects, which I need not detail; but, if one still hears it sincerely said that 'it's no worse than any other weapon', this is because it is the climax of a process. One thinks of the thrill of horror that greeted the news of Guernica. Who would be shocked today at that amateurish onslaught? In 1939 it was considered atrocious to bomb a town. The Royal Air Force raided Germany with leaflets; during the Finnish war strenuous efforts were made to prove that the Russians had bombed Helsinki, which they denied in accents of outraged virtue; the bombing of Coventry was regarded as a wanton crime, though, of course, it was a major centre of war industry. However, as soon as our own bomber force was big enough, we gave up pretending to drop bombs 'plop down a factory chimney', and invented terms like 'area bombing' and 'pattern bombing', which simply meant that German towns were being treated like Coventry. A specially trained force breached a dam and flooded a thickly populated valley, an action that might have caused Tamerlane to raise his eyebrows; the leader was decorated and the exploit was described in a book which you still see on any station bookstall.

There is not really much of a step between the final raids of the war, which created what was proudly called a 'fire storm', and the first atomic raids. In point of fact, the biggest conventional raid on Tokyo killed as many people as the Hiroshima bomb. And these raids had in common one obscene quality—they were unnecessary even by the lax standards permitted to the bomber chiefs. The destruction of Dresden, for instance, had no military purpose whatever. The Hiroshima bomb was dropped when the general state of the war, the fire raids, and the Russian sweep into Manchuria (which the bomb was designed to forestall) made a Japanese surrender more than likely. But before the Japanese, like the men in Baron's pillbox, could effect their surrender, another atomic bomb was dropped on Nagasaki. This was a test pure and simple, and it makes a sour jest of the claim that the nuclear tests have done no damage to life.

And all this we have accepted, while yattering away about the humanist outlook. Indeed, one important reason why the campaign against the hydrogen bomb is urgent is that it still causes a sense of shock. If it remains with us a few more years and is made by a few more countries, it will be regarded as an unpleasant but inevitable item in the contemporary scene. It will be, in the delicious phrase applied to the atom bomb by Dr Adenauer, a further development in artillery.

For when people say that there is nothing new about the H-bomb, there is one sense in which they are right. Neither the revulsion caused by its first appearance, nor the attribution to it of a decisive role in war, is unprecedented. When I was a boy the bombing plane was spoken of as the final abomination. It was widely believed that German raiders could make London uninhabitable. A book appeared, and was gravely discussed, in which Britain was bombed into impotence and surrender in one afternoon, by simultaneous attacks on Hendon aerodrome, the B.B.C., Battersea power station, and a few other places.

Likewise, if you will cast your mind back to 1946, when John Hersey's book and the first medical missions gave us the sobering truth about Hiroshima, you will recall that the feeling of shock, and the conviction that humanity faced the final choice between peace and utter disaster, were as strong as they are now that we know about the ten-megaton hydrogen bomb.

Yes, this time it is true; but the successive false alarms, and the fact that the last war was not as bad (for us) as we expected, have given an excuse for disbelief, just as many people distrusted the accounts and even the photographs of Belsen because the Belgian atrocity stories of 1914 turned out to be fakes. So the truth about our predicament can be shrugged off, and the dead ideas coaxed back into the semblance of life. So, too, our prospective guilt can be assuaged. For if what *they* can do to us may turn out to be not so bad, then what we plan to do to them is not so bad either. Having reached this point, we can justify ourselves in feeling that to make the bomb is an achievement—especially if, like Britain or France, we have been down on our luck of late years. It compensates us for the loss of India, for Dien Bien Phu, for the humiliation of Suez. Hence the drivelling speeches, otherwise inexplicable in a cultured and intelligent man, made by Mr Macmillan about how the H-bomb 'increases our influence' and 'puts us where we ought to be—in the position of a great power'. Hence the headline with which the *Daily Express* greeted our first successful test, and on which only a psychiatrically trained nursery-school teacher could comment adequately—*OUR* H-BANG! For let us beware: while this headline expresses all that is abominable about the Beaverbrook papers, it also goes far to explain why they sell so many copies.

They don't sell exclusively to Conservative voters. It is also among Socialists, both humble and famous, that the illusions, the dead ideas, and the irrational responses to shameful emotions can be detected by the candid seeker.

It may seem strange to have a leader of the Labour Party who says that the Tories were right to equip the country with a weapon of massacre. Very strange indeed, William Morris and Keir Hardie would have thought it. But here again, understanding is more useful than mere reproaches.

The pioneers of British Socialism, except Blatchford, were paci-fists as a matter of course, and took it for granted that Socialists must be opposed to wars between capitalist states, including their own. In this attitude there was an element of clear insight into who made the wars, and why; and an element of simple humanitarian feeling. There was a third element not quite so easy to define. These men were not interested in politics, but purely in creating a new society. They did not want to get into the ritual activity conducted by the older parties, but to put an end to it. They would have been appalled by the idea that a Socialist Party, once it had won the allegiance of the workers and of a good half of the population, should go on indefinitely playing at ins and outs with the Tories. What they expected was what Morris called 'the change'.

Similarly, they were not interested in foreign policy—by no means because they were lacking in internationalism, but because the alliances made by the rulers of Britain with other rulers did not concern them. They had no views, so far as I know, on the great foreign policy issue of the turn of the century: whether Britain should line up with France and Russia or with the Central Powers. It followed *a fortiori* that they could not support a war waged in alliance with either, nor conceive that its outcome would benefit the workers of any country.

This outlook appeared laughably *simpliste*, not only to the Labour leaders whose idea of politics was to show that they could do everything the old parties could do (a tradition founded by Ramsay MacDonald and still dominant), but also to the Marxists. Marx, who was interested in everything, was utterly fascinated by politics and knew a great deal about it, including the kind of politics that had only the remotest impact on the lives of the workers. Since he could not be indifferent to any political event, and a war in those days was still a political event, he used to analyse every war and pronounce on the question of whose victory, on balance, would be of benefit to the proletariat. His views were far-sighted and somewhat arid, for he insisted that each nation must pass through various stages before reaching Socialism, and these stages often had few obvious attractions. History, however, has shown that he was usually right. For example, he thought the suppression of the Indian Mutiny a historically progressive event, because it destroyed Indian attachment to the old princely houses and cleared the way for industrialization and hence for a real popular movement—an icy comment at the time but, as Indian historians now agree, a perceptive forecast.

The harm done by this attitude, regardless of whether Marx was right or wrong in each case, was to involve the working class in the squabbles of its masters, and especially in war. The workers were taught to base their attitudes, not on a simple and unchanging principle, easily understood and preached because it answered to both self-interest and morality, but to meticulous logic and close analysis of a swiftly changing situation. In practice it is almost impossible to direct a mass movement in this way, unless of course the movement has some hope of seizing control of events. Marx supported the Prussians in the war of 1870 until they continued the war after the overthrow of the French Empire; then he supported the French. On the logical plane, I for one find his reasoning convincing in both phases. But had he been obliged to lead a Socialist Party in either Germany or France—or, worse, to co-ordinate the policies of both—he would have got into a first-class mess and lost most of his members.

Lenin, in 1914, was, of course, opposed to both sides in the war. But this did not make him feel kindly toward the British Labour men who were against it simply because they saw no justification in the process of shovelling men in khaki into trenches to hurl steel at men in field-grey. He scorned them as bourgeois pacifists. Here he showed the want of imagination that sometimes betrayed his brilliant intellect. They were not revolutionaries like him, but neither were they simply conscientious objectors. They were what they claimed to be, Socialist pacifists.

In the ensuing decades this valuable tradition became less and less influential in the Labour movement. Communism became increasingly doctrinaire, and also increasingly concerned with the armed defence of the Soviet Union. The dominant trend in the Labour Party got thoroughly entangled with ruling-class politics, and propounded either exactly the same foreign policy as the Tories or a more intelligent policy within the same orthodox framework: this, clearly, is still the case. Then came the enormous exceptional event, a conflict with a foreign power in which it was simply impossible for the working class not to take sides and to ally themselves with Liberals and Churchillian Tories in supporting, first a precise programme for diplomatic action, then a partisan attitude in a series of foreign wars, and finally the British and Allied side in a world war.

I am not for a moment saying that it was either wrong or ignoble to fight Hitler, either in Spain or in the world war. What I am saying is that it was extremely hard to fight Hitler and yet keep alive the idea of a distinctively Socialist, a 'pure' attitude to foreign policy and war. The wartime atmosphere—the coalition, the electoral truce, the lack of protest against either political barbarities like the slogan of unconditional surrender or moral barbarities like the raids on German cities—all this killed a tradition whose loss, unremarked at the time, can now be seen as tragic.

So we come to 1958. We find not only Mr Gaitskell but also Mr Bevan unable to offer us anything but a set of ingenious diplomatic schemes, all naturally conditional on bargaining by our next Foreign Secretary, whose freedom of manœuvre we are begged not to circumscribe by dictating any specifically British—let alone specifically Socialist—line of action.

The trouble with the foreign policy in which Mr Bevan believes, and to which Mr Gaitskell subscribes, is not that it is misdirected (it is not), or even that it is unlikely to succeed (though I fear it is). No, the trouble is that it is incapable of rallying the enthusiastic support of a popular movement, and therefore defenceless against the thousand cuts to be inflicted both by Ministers who don't really believe in it, and by the other forces of pressure in our semi-democracy. In short, it is not a Socialist policy.

Not only this; but it presents no opposition to the ugly emotions, prejudices, and obsessions of which I have written, and which must be attacked by anyone who refuses to rely indefinitely on the protection of the bomb. That refusal is shared, I hope, by sincere advocates of conference disarmament, as well as by believers in unilateral renunciation. Why, therefore, cannot the attack be made at all by the former, or with decisive success by the latter? Because all of us, in varying measure, lack a durable ideology to underpin our immediate policy.

I am persuaded that the only hope for the Labour Party and for our country is a revival in modern terms of Socialist pacifism. As I use the term, it is not necessarily to believe that passive resistance and the techniques of Gandhi (though one is surely bound to respect them) are universally applicable. Few of the Socialist pioneers would have condemned a striker for using a stick if the police used truncheons. Nor is it to oppose all military action. I think the Jews will be right to fight if the Arab States start a 'second round'. But the thing to which we cannot reconcile ourselves except at the cost of spiritual death is the bestial mass-murder of the latter-day great power. It was self-evidently immoral, and purposeless for the working class, when it was a matter of hurling platoons of conscripts on to shell-torn barbed wire along the Somme. It is self-evidently immoral, and purposeless for all mankind, in the age of the hydrogen bomb.

Nobody would suggest that the Aldermaston march, for instance, was an enterprise to stand comparison with the grand gesture of Socialist youth a generation before—volunteering for Spain.

However, in one important sense the cause that has attracted the best of this young generation is ethically superior to the cause which provided the holy water for my own political baptism. The speeches and pamphlets of the thirties never got far without lavish use of the words 'fight', 'beat', 'destroy'. In the circumstances, this couldn't be helped. There was a war in Spain, and Franco had started it, not us. Still, a war is not an elevating affair—least of all in Blighty, where the meetings with flags and drums, letters from the trenches read in lump-in-throat voices, and spotlights on mothers of heroes, bore an alarming likeness to jingo rallies in any ordinary war.

It is a measure of what we had lost and are now regaining that young people in the last decade are supposed to have had no cause. The next sentence always was: 'In the thirties, of course, there was Spain.' A cause, by implication, was a motive for firing a gun, or sending bandages to those who fired guns in your behalf. Possible causes, such as Cyprus, were appraised, but none quite fitted the bill. The real cause was there all the time, and as soon as it was brought to their attention it had people walking fifty miles at Easter. It is the cause of the human race.

The difference between the Aldermaston march and any other demonstration I have known was accurately expressed by a young man who was walking along with a big home-made placard. It said: STOP AND THINK. There were others which, less concisely, said much the same. For this is a campaign that urges people to reflect, not to destroy; to march a silent mile, not to shout; to dissent, not to obey; to be themselves, not to take sides; to love, not to hate; to live and let others live, not to kill or die.

It is about violence itself, and the corruption it works both on the individual and on the community, that we need to think afresh —to think as we did not and could not think when Hitler blocked the view. For, deep down, the argument about the hydrogen bomb is not an argument about any particular weapon, however 'different'; it only seems to be so, because the bomb has swallowed up what was previously called war and violence. The argument is about the place of violence in our lives, and the alternatives to it. And as Socialists we must say once and for all that we have our own binding rule. We may resort to violence, exceptionally, when something can be achieved and there is no other way out, though in doing so we must not forget that it constitutes a defeat and implies an acceptance of moral dangers, But if we consent to live by violence, within its protecting arm and by its leave, to depend upon it and to lose control over it, then we have gone hopelessly astray.

For want of any such basic principle, conscience in the Labour Party has become an 'extra', licensed on application, instead of a guide to policy. On July 16 of this year Mr Gaitskell advised his parliamentary colleagues not to vote against Western brink-walking in the Lebanon, because 'a conscientious minority' (Mr George Brown and his friends) would find it hard to obey the whip. Those who felt equally strongly that a vote was needed failed to earn this consideration. True, the old guard of total pacifists are permitted their scruples, which are regarded, not as having anything to do with practical politics, but as harmless little quirks, like not eating meat. Those who merely object to genocide must march as ordered, like would-be conscientious objectors who fail to impress the tribunal.

As I remember the 'emergency thinking' of the conscript generation, I am embarrassed by the phrases and concepts used by the Left to inspire resistance to Fascism and now taken up by the Right to excuse the H-bomb as a 'deterrent' to Communism. It would be easy to say that they were completely right in the former context, and have lost their virtue solely through their latter-day abuse. But was there nothing in the heart of them that made this exploitation possible? Was this not the acceptance of violence, even at times its exaltation; the lazy belief that violence unaided can not only avert evil, but advance good; finally, the failure to seek other and better protection for what we valued?

One such phrase was: 'It is better to die on your feet than to live on your knees.' I don't know how old it is; it was attributed, at the time of Spain, to Passionaria. Then it was employed, rather less nobly, in the world war. A few weeks ago I heard some pip-squeak of a Tory candidate drum it into line to make genocide look like glory.

At first I was angry at its exploitation; then I examined it afresh, and it seemed to be incomplete and superficial. If you have lived by killing, I asked, can you (morally) die altogether on your feet?

If your ideals are untarnished, on the other hand, can it be said that you live on your knees? I know no certain answer. I do know that the questions must be asked.

Socialists can claim no exclusive right to this kind of thinking, and still less to opposition to nuclear war. Many who are devoted to the existing social order will strongly object to being massacred, and why not? But we ought to claim that we alone can frame a worthy and effective retort to the braggart cries of the killers.

The thousands who have set themselves to do this are Socialist pacifists. Unless I am much mistaken, the simon-pure pacifists of the Peace Pledge Union haven't greatly increased their numbers; it is from the 'new Left' that the thousands came for the jam-packed meetings and the Aldermaston march. To be a Socialist today one must be a pacifist, in the broad sense—one must be in total opposition to the beastliness that has absorbed what was once called war. And to be an effective pacifist one must be a Socialist, for one must seek to render powerless all those persons and institutions which hold for us no other promise than death. Out of their decay, new life can spring.

A sense of outrage

For me, politics have been a comparatively late love-affair. Like most people, I have an instinctive aversion to public life. It is financially unrewarding. It is, in many ways, morally distasteful. It forces us to pose problems in terms of irreconcilable opposites, at the cost, not merely of intellectual niceties, but often of truth itself. It absorbs our energy and passion —usually fruitlessly—leaving only an empty husk of ourselves for private enjoyment. It erodes or even totally destroys our capacity for introspection, for self-analysis; so that most public men become, sooner or later, moral invalids, unable to seek treatment because they are unaware they are sick. Few of them can lead a good life, fewer still a full life. Politicians often refer, with unctuous insincerity, to their 'sacrifices' to the common weal. But there is a grain of truth in the claim. Politics offers the highest worldly rewards of all professions; but political success—and political failure, too— have to be paid for in terms of happiness.

No intellectual reasoning can persuade a man to enter this world. Reason never creates powerful motives. Only emotions are strong enough; and of the emotions, only two can drive men into politics : love of power, or the capacity for outrage. One drives them to the Right, the other to the Left. Power, of itself, has never greatly attracted me, though I must not speak too soon : the urge usually comes in the middle years of life, when earlier ambitions have receded into doubt. Most dictators—or would-be dictators—Stalin, Mosley, Nasser, Hitler, Salazar, have been in their late thirties or early forties before they finally sacrificed all principle for the pursuit of pure power. True, to the upper-class Englishman, taught from the cradle to confuse power with a sense of natural duty, the instinctive wish to exert it may come much earlier. Gladstone, Lord Randolph Churchill, Balfour, Eden, Harold Macmillan were doomed to the pursuit of power from their early twenties; but all had protracted honeymoons with principle before the middle-aged itch set in. But then I was born into the middle classes, and if they have a public passion it is the desire, not to exert power, but to administer—quite a different matter.

Power, therefore, never tempted me; but equally, for a long time, I was immune to the sense of outrage. My father was an artist, and most of my early energies were spent painting. Now painting, of all occupations, most effectively insulates you from the outside world; your absorption in it is complete; it is the perfect antidote to politics. Nearly all painters are not merely selfishly preoccupied with their own concerns, but stupid and ignorant as well; and their rare excursions into politics are never more than reflections of their professional ambitions. Hence, 'modern' painters are superficially on the Left, academicians superficially on the Right. But none of them really cares very much, and I have never heard a painter express an intelligible political opinion. Only three really gifted painters have been deeply concerned in politics—Goya, Courbet and Picasso. One became insane, the second a bad painter and the third a millionaire joker.

The studio, then, is a bad breeding ground for politics, and that is where I grew up. Indeed, in so far as my family had political opinions at all, they were projections of their religious views—for all were passionate Catholics. In this country, practising Catholics, like Orthodox Jews, live in a little private world of their own. The phenomena of the outside world—whether they be men or actions, books or plays, ideas or opinions—are judged solely in their relation to the Faith. A Catholic doctor always wins the high regard of his co-religionaries, no matter how many of them he kills. A Catholic actress—and they are, for obvious reasons, a rare breed—is judged on her sanctity, not her talents. A Catholic author, no matter how turgid, will always get favourable notices in the Catholic press.

Politics, too, are seen through the spiritual spectrum. Just as Communists are tied to the vagaries of Soviet foreign policy, so Catholics are eternally strapped to the rotting corpses of the clerical states of southern Europe. My earliest political memory is the Spanish Civil War; here, so it seemed, the very physical existence of the Church was at stake : Barcelona, Madrid, the Guadaljara, filled our house like a whirlwind. They even changed my way of life, for there came the terrible moment of anger when my father cancelled his subscription to the *Daily Express* and changed to the *Mail* as the only British newspaper which openly supported Franco. For me, this meant a disastrous switch from Rupert to Teddy Tail.

But Catholicism influences the opinions of the faithful not only on current issues, where the Church's interests are believed to be involved, but in their entire approach to politics. It is not merely that the Church teaches that, in the last resort, human welfare in this world is subordinate and irrelevant; it also implies that change, if spiritually negative, is dangerous. Very few Catholics have even read so much as a page of St Thomas Aquinas; but all believe, or are taught to believe, that Aquinas favoured a stable, hierarchic society, of unequal rights matched by unequal duties, the earthly model of the celestial pyramid whose apex was God, and whose dynamic was *noblesse oblige*. And Aquinas, for most Catholics, is regarded as the unchallengeable authority on politics. As it happens, this popular Catholic view of Aquinas's political teachings is totally erroneous. Aquinas was not greatly interested in political theory; indeed, as a student of the Sicilian court, he was a sensible empiricist. His references to politics are widely scattered throughout his voluminous writings, and the orthodox Catholic view is based on a tendentious selection of them. If Aquinas had one political principle which was peculiar to him it was his contention that the function of the State was not merely negative but positive: that its duty was actively to create conditions in which the good life could be led. Now this, as near as makes no difference, is what I understand by Socialism, and in that sense I am a confirmed follower of St Thomas. But it is not, as I have explained, how most Catholics are taught to see him; instead, his writings are employed to provide the highest theological sanction for unrelieved Conservatism.

My education was entirely in the hands of the Church: first at a kindergarten run by nuns, then a secondary school in the hands of the ferocious Irish Christian Brothers; finally at a Jesuit public school. The English Jesuits are very civilized, subtle and able men, who provide an excellent academic education along traditional lines, and are neither so foolish nor so unjust as to resort to the indoctrination of children of which they are accused by those who know nothing about them. My passion was history and I was taught it with considerably more skill by the Jesuits than by any one of my nine tutors at Oxford. They imparted to me whatever belief I possess in the paramountcy of objective historical truth. Nevertheless, the Jesuits are perhaps the most totalitarian organization the world has ever known; and no one who has read the Rules of St Ignatius—which state the objects and methods of their society in plain, almost brutal, terms—can conceivably have any doubts on this score. To the Jesuits, obedience and submission to duly constituted authority are the principal virtues. Politics are never discussed in their schools, but the atmosphere they inevitably—not deliberately—breed is one of political quietism, of acceptance of the existing order, provided it does not conflict with the Church's interests. It is only a short step from this to regarding the Conservatives as natural and ordained rulers, and the Labour Party as the symbol of illicit rebellion. During the war years, of course, political issues did not arise; but when the 1945 election came, I remember only one boy who chose to admit he supported the Labour cause, though with reservations as he confessed himself a 'neo-Marxist'. The rest were violently Tory and booed the election returns as they came over the wireless. The Jesuits themselves professed political neutrality in principle, though they reserved the right to vote against any candidate whose personality or programme seemed undesirable from a Catholic viewpoint. I am afraid Mrs Barbara Castle, who stood in the local division, came into this category; and my earliest memory of British democracy in action was to see, on polling day, a caravan of Jesuits set out to vote against her : two large black cars, loaded with senior Jesuits, in front, followed by the lesser fathers pedalling furiously on bicycles. (Incidentally, the Jesuits, unlike virtually everybody else, except Aneurin Bevan, prophesied a Labour landslide.)

With this background, it is scarcely surprising that I took little interest in politics at Oxford. I went to one meeting of the Socialist Club, then, I think, dominated by fellow-travellers, but found the teacups too thick and the girls as plain as nuns. I went also to a cocktail party given by the ill-fated and infamous Corporate Club, of avowedly Fascist leanings. But here there were no girls at all; and the atmosphere of bitter intrigue was meaningless to one who had not known the savage conflicts of the thirties. The other clubs were well-meaning but dull, and, indeed, Oxford as a whole in the later forties was politically apathetic. The up-and-coming young men, bred and nurtured in the Welfare State, were busy getting their bad degrees and having their first, squalid love affairs; they had not yet gravitated to Beaverbrook, TV, the advertising offices of Berkeley Square and the New Right; the hand they were later to bite was still feeding them. But, of course, with Labour then triumphant and austerity still hanging over the countryside like a fog, our feelings naturally leaned towards the Right. I was totally obsessed by history and, to some extent, social life; but I think I heartily disliked Mr Attlee's administration. For one thing, during my first winter at Oxford the fuel crisis led the Government to issue orders not to use electric fires except at certain hours; and my scout, who combined blatant snobbery (he contrasted me unfavourably with his last pre-war tenant, a Hohenzollern prince, who had provided his own sheets, carpets and curtains in the national colours of the Reich) with doctrinaire Socialism, insisted that these rules were observed in my rooms. Nobody else's scout did this.

I went down with no political views, though I found mild pleasure in the news of the Conservative electoral victory in 1951. I still lacked a sense of outrage. Nor did I find it in the army. Many young intellectuals are driven to the Left by barrack-room discipline, by the brutal stupidity of life in the ranks. But I found the army considerably less awesome than the school O.T.C., and I soon grew to enjoy it. War has nothing in common with democracy and neither, therefore, have the instruments with which it is waged; it is naïve to imagine that any army can be run on trade union lines. Provided one accepts this from the start, there is no reason why army discipline, 'jankers', Queen's Regulations, courts-martial and the rest, should seem in any way irrational or unjust. I liked being a rifleman, I liked being an officer, and I thoroughly enjoyed being stationed at Gibraltar, where I spent most of my time running gramophone record concerts, teaching oil-painting and producing appalling plays. My life had no seeds of discontent; I was well paid and had ample leisure. True, I became for the first time conscious of an outside world; in Spain, I saw the grimy misery and cruelty of the Franco regime, and I was in Morocco at the time of Marshal

Juin's abortive *coup d'état* against the Sultan (which his creatures were later to repeat, with greater success, in 1953). But such things excited at the most dislike, never moral disapproval.

I returned to England at the end of 1951, a mild, uninterested Conservative. And—this is my point—I have no doubt that I would have remained so, if I had chosen to live in London. On the assumption, however—and I still think it is a valid assumption—that no young man's education is complete without a year or so on the Left Bank, I went to live in Paris. There, at long last, my political emotions began to stir. I had a job on the editorial staff of a glossy Paris magazine. It was vaguely right-of-centre, superficially progressive in its approach to industrial and economic problems, pro-E.D.C. and Little Europe, but basically a tarted-up opiate for the wealthy, *bien-pensante* bourgeoisie. Those who criticize the British Press should first of all examine, at close quarters, the French variety; they would then realize how lucky they are.

My work on this paper bred in me a distaste for the French Right, but it was not yet sharpened by anger. Then, in May 1952, came the vital incident. Eisenhower had just left SHAPE to return to Washington for the first stages of his election campaign. General Ridgeway, hated by the Communists as 'the germ-warfare monster of Korea', was appointed to take over at Fontainebleau. He arrived in Paris at the end of May, and all hell was let loose. These were the last big demonstrations the C.P. staged in Paris, and they were very formidable indeed. Every day for four days, huge battalions of workmen armed with clubs assembled in the suburbs and tried to force their way into the centre of the city. Police and *gardes mobiles* were brought to Paris from all over France, and there were bitter fights even on the Grands Boulevards. The students were also active on the Left Bank, and the day the rioting reached its climax —Jacques Duclos had been arrested the day before, accused of having carrier pigeons in his car!—I was walking home from work when I was swept up in the conflict near the Carrefour d'Odéon. Along with a crowd of other innocent bystanders, I took refuge in a cheap students' restaurant, called, I think, *La Petite Source*, where a plate of sausages and chips could be bought for 80 francs. Through its plate-glass windows, I watched a head-on clash between students and a battalion of *gardes mobiles*, wearing steel helmets and carrying rifles. The clash lasted less than five minutes; then the students broke ranks, leaving scattered groups of their comrades isolated in the square. The police descended on them with a ferocity I would not have believed had I not seen it with my own eyes. Students were hurled on the ground and battered senseless with rifle-butts. Only a yard or two from where I stood watching, two policemen seized a young girl, tearing her skirt, and then jumped on her stomach and chest until she vomited blood. Two students tried to take refuge in the restaurant, but the proprietor had locked the door, and they were dragged away screaming. The whole incident might have occurred in Tsarist Russia.

To me, at any rate, it was a cataclysmic experience. Coming from Welfare State England, where the worst fighting word was groundnuts, where political passion was muffled in the foggy boredom of the House of Commons smoking-room, I had never met political evil in physical form. From that moment I possessed the capacity for outrage. Naturally, the full process of conversion to the Left spread over many weeks and months; it involved a great deal of reading, and endless arguments in Left Bank cafés; but it followed inevitably and inexorably once this personal experience had supplied the initial momentum. Before the year was out, I was a Bevanite and a contributor to the *New Statesman*.

I relate this personal case-history, at inordinate length no doubt, not because I think it has any intrinsic interest, but because I believe a number of morals can be drawn from it. And the most important is this: if I had not gone to live in France, and if I had therefore missed the opportunity to observe, at close quarters, militant, aggressive and fundamentally anti-democratic forces in action, I very much doubt if I would ever have taken up strong political attitudes. Nowadays, I base my political beliefs on a wide, coherent and interlocking series of rational arguments, and I should be very much insulted if anyone told me that my Left-wing views were based on emotion. But I am quite prepared to admit, that, without this emotional impetus, I would have no political beliefs at all.

What, then, of the thousands of young Englishmen, of my age and education, who lack this emotional impetus? They have not seen the British Right in its heyday, before Labour's 1945 victory drew its teeth and claws. They have seen a Toryism tamed and timid, whose one desperate gamble in political savagery—the Suez war—was brought to an ignominious close within a week. They have had no personal experience of how Franco subdued the Asturian miners in March 1958, of how the French parachutists tortured Henri Alleg in June 1957, of how Salazar ended the Portuguese salt-mine strike in October 1956; they know nothing of conditions in the Belgian coalpits—whitewashed by a 'Socialist' Government—of the *latifundia* farming system in Southern Italy, of those little-heard-of concentration camps on the Greek Islands— which include the largest in Europe. All they see is the perpetual shadow-boxing between Tory and Labour front benches over marginal issues—sixpence on Health charges, an extra £1,000,000 a year for Malta, part-time directors of the Bank, agricultural subsidies and two more elective seats on the Kenya Legislative Council. They know perfectly well that every major issue which has divided the House under the Tory Government—with the one exception of Suez—had also been faced, in comparable form, by their Labour predecessors, and that in no case was Labour's answer significantly different to that of the Tories. How, then, can they develop the sense of outrage?

It is no use pretending that current political issues *are* important; if they were, they would not be current political issues. The Rent Act is causing a good deal of hardship, and has therefore provoked shrill Labour abuse; but one does not have to be a cynic to suspect that Labour's leaders are silently grateful to the Tories for passing it, and that they have not the slightest intention of repealing it when they are returned to power. Equally, whatever protests the opposition front bench may make about Government defence policy, they quite clearly have every intention of continuing it, in all important respects. How many people really believe that Mr Callaghan would solve the Cyprus problem any quicker than Mr Lennox-Boyd, or that he can effect any but marginal changes in the racial policy of the Central African Federation? Superficially, the contrast between Mr Selwyn Lloyd and Mr Bevan could not be greater; but do we really think that Mr Bevan is going to bring peace in our time? Will the basic principles of national accountancy—the ratio between defence spending, welfare and investment—undergo any radical transformation when Mr Heathcote Amory hands over to Mr Harold Wilson? Doubts about the answers to these questions have led many young people to believe that British politics have reverted to what they were in the mid-eighteenth century: fundamental agreement on principles, concealed by a fierce squabble for places.

But, it may be said, if the logic of this argument is pursued, then only two conclusions follow. Either there must be an organized breakaway from the two-party system of politics—a descent into Poujadist fragmentation, leading to shifting coalitions whose sole beneficiary would be the right—or we must accept that the present political armistice reflects the true interests of the nation and be prepared to forgo a sense of outrage once and for all. Many people in this country have already accepted one or other of these conclusions. Thousands of young, middle-class men and women have plumped for the first—and joined the Liberal Party. Hundreds of thousands of working-class people have accepted the second—hence Labour's total failure to capitalize the Tory decline. But I believe there is a third alternative: that what is required to end the political stalemate is not a sharpening of the divisions over present issues—on the lines of the Victory for Socialism ginger group—but a movement to bring into the arena of political change issues which have scarcely been discussed at all. To put it bluntly, I think it is about time we destroyed the British class system.

This may seem a surprising statement to make. The Labour movement, ever since its inception, has been bitterly accused of waging class-warfare. It has, moreover, been the means of passing legislation and of conducting budgetary policies which have greatly altered the economic relationships between the classes. All this is true; but it does not alter the fact that the British class system has not merely survived the 1945 experiment, but is now actually stronger than it was before. There is one very simple explanation of this. The British Labour movement, though reformist in outlook and nonconformist in favour, has always accepted the Marxist assumption that economic change is the key to history and that society can be transformed merely by the manipulation of incomes. This may be true, provided you are prepared to employ totalitarian means and suspend—for a long period—the machinery of democratic criticism. But it is demonstrably nonsense if you both rule out confiscation as a legitimate act of government—thereby ensuring that the transfer of economic power is as gradual as possible—and, at the same time, submit to periodic elections which inevitably reflect the accumulated discontent of wide sections of society.

Yet this is precisely what Labour attempted to do after 1945. It thought that vertical nationalization of key industries could place the centres of economic power in the control of the public, and that a limited redistribution of incomes would destroy the class structure. Neither of these things happened. Nationalization gave the State only a marginal increase in control over the direction of the economy, whilst high income tax merely increased the power and importance of capital. Public ownership became discredited as a social objective because it was presented as merely an alternative system of management. Under high taxation, possession of inherited wealth, or any form of property, became not less but more valuable. Labour effectively prevented the poor or the hardworking from becoming rich, while allowing the rich to become richer.

Nor has even the limited redistribution of income in the years 1945–58 produced any corresponding changes in the social structure. Where economic barriers between the classes were lowered or demolished, they have been speedily and effectively replaced by social ones. During the 1930's, certain features of the British class structure were in perceptible decline. The dominance of Oxford and Cambridge in the field of advanced education was being successfully challenged by the provincial universities, which were growing rapidly in relative size and influence. In secondary education also, there was a distinct movement away from the public schools towards the new grammar and secondary schools. In middle- and upper-class circles, snobbery was becoming, for the first time, a social handicap, and the literature of the time places it in the same category with anti-semitism. The mechanics of the social pyramid became an object of increasing contempt : it is notable, for instance, that the number of débutantes presented at Court fell progressively throughout the thirties. No doubt, some of these phenomena were superficial and reflected the gathering darkness of the international scene rather than any fundamental change in British social morality. But the trend—slight though it may have been—was there.

Now it has been reversed. Labour's timid assault on the economic foundations of the British class structure evoked a powerful and successful counter-attack. While Labour's economic and fiscal policy was slowly lowering the financial barriers separating the classes, the middle and upper classes were rapidly erecting fresh social ones—more solid by their very nature, for they are largely immune to legislative attack. Social behaviour, as opposed to the distribution of wealth, is not a legitimate or even practicable field for political policy, but it is a vital factor in the distribution of political power. In this metaphysical citadel, which Marx and all his followers had ignored, the British class system was able to rest, recuperate and emerge stronger than before.

For it is stronger. Our class structure has survived for two reasons. First, it is complex and finely graduated: the yawning chasms which breed violent jealousies, and therefore violent changes, have never been allowed to emerge. Second, it is inclusive, not exclusive. Rising economic groups have always been allowed to find their natural level in the social hierarchy, and the upper tiers have always taken care to come to terms with, and subsequently annex, emergent institutions. This dual process has been hard at work since the war. As full employment and higher investment have increased the national income, so the dominant classes have welcomed new recruits and thus broadened their basis of acceptance. Equally, they have accepted and neutralized the new centres of power. The leaders of the Labour Party and the trade union movement have been given their natural places in the Establishment. It fought, to be sure, commercial television tooth and nail—just as it had earlier fought the popular press—but once the battle was lost, as was inevitable, it neatly climbed on to the shoulders of its conqueror, like some Old Man of the Sea. The Monster emerged—but with Sir Kenneth Clark presiding over its first faltering steps; and when he went, what better choice than Sir Ivone Kirkpatrick?

The new graduates of the Welfare State were slowly and carefully digested. Many of them, of course, went into science and technology, still totally excluded from social and political power. But a number—too few to dilute the spirit of the existing structure, but enough, when converted, to bring it a perceptible accession of strength—went into those central citadels: the executive grades of industry, the Press, wireless and television, the Treasury, the Foreign Service and the law. As with working-class entrants to the public schools, the proportion was never allowed to exceed ten per cent. For, though the higher classes have always opened their ranks to new recruits, they will never tolerate an influx of sufficient magnitude to produce a real change of character.

The continuity and future of the class structure having been thus assured, its beneficiaries were able to sharpen and flourish the traditional instruments employed to inhibit political change. The essence of a class system is that property, birth and upbringing, rather than virtue or ability, determine status, power and income. Since the war, the image of such a society, as one which is natural and therefore just, has been projected on the minds of the British public with all the resources of modern mass-communications. A number of factors contributed to the success of this operation. The British newspaper industry, vastly over-inflated, and subsisting largely on the portrayal of sensational personalities, provided one channel; the fact that Britain is, geographically, a 'natural' television nation, another. The actors were there, too: a young and reasonably presentable royal family, large numbers of impoverished noblemen, keeping their creaking country houses together and willing to cavort to anyone's tune for money, annual crops of débutantes, growing up in a world where wealthy husbands were scarce and where life in a Knightsbridge dress-shop—or worse— lies just round the corner, all were only too anxious to pose before the cameras and supply the paragraphs. The public, too, emerging only slowly from the austerity of war and the Labour experiment, had an insatiable appetite for glamour.

The intellectuals have provided no check on this stampede of Gadarene swine; on the contrary, where possible, they have joined in the mêlée. Since the war, our literary and academic estabishments have been controlled largely by men who were 'lefties' in the thirties, whose Socialism has turned sour, to whom the arrival of the Welfare State brought no rewards, and who have turned, with some bitterness, on the idols of their youth. They have found only too willing associates among the intellectuals of the welfare age, who climbed—assisted by a benevolent State—on to the promised land of the middle-class plateau, only to find it stripped of its old delights and privileges. All this has bred in the intellectual milieu a ferocious hatred of equality and a desperate, almost comic, quest for the traditional certitudes of a hierarchical society. Mr Cyril Connolly provides a case-history of the older generation, Mr George Scott of the younger. Hence a book, whatever its merits, can have its reputation made at a few fashionable dinner-tables, and, for the first time in British literary history, the judgements of duchesses and men of letters have become virtually identical. It is some token of the degeneration of our literary standards that the monthly review *Encounter* never caught on until it published Miss Nancy Mitford's now celebrated essay on U and non-U.

Hence the class system flourishes as never before. The 1958 season was the most brilliant in living memory, undimmed by the Queen's gracious concessions to Lord Altrincham and Mr Muggeridge. In greyest suburbia, the honest wives of shopkeepers shudder painfully when their husbands—who haven't yet caught on—speak of serviettes and notepaper. In the Tory party, the Etonian element is more than ever dominant, so that Mr Macmillan can refer to his Foreign Secretary as 'that middle-class lawyer'. In the Labour Party, the class struggle is fiercely waged, with Mr George Brown's conviction that all middle-class intellectuals are doubtfully loyal matched only by Mr Richard Crossman's belief that few trade union leaders are fit for office. Lady Violet Bonham-Carter exercises more real power than when her father was Prime Minister, and even the Royal Court Theatre—that alleged nest of revolutionaries—finds it convenient to have a cousin of the Queen on its board. The public schools have their longest waiting lists in history. The provincial universities sadly watch the flight of their intellectual capital to Oxbridge, and a brilliant young teacher may turn down a professorship in Sheffield in favour of a junior fellowship at Trinity.

Snobbery is a specifically English disease: we have, as a nation, a peculiarly low resistance to it, in the same way that the French suffer from destructive individualism and the Americans from the conformist instincts of the herd. To this extent, of course, it cannot be legislated against. But this need not make us despair. For that matter, it is not the function of politics to proscribe sin, merely to reduce or eliminate the occasions of sin. We cannot enact laws which will end the class system, any more than we can prohibit poverty: but we can destroy its institutional framework, in the same way that we can introduce legislative correctives to the natural laws of capitalism, and so reduce the incidence of poverty.

But the destruction of this framework will demand a ruthless singlemindedness and a sense of urgency which the British Left, at any rate since Chartist days, has never possessed. I remember once discussing the public schools with Aneurin Bevan and stating, bluntly, that the correct policy here was the obvious one: a straightforward State take-over. He replied: 'You are confusing cause and effect. The public schools exist because people can afford to send their children there. Take them over and they simply reappear in another form. But eliminate economic differentials and they will gradually wither away.' With all respect, this belief seemed to me to suffer from the characteristic and central fallacy of the Labour movement which, along with many others, stems from Marx. Institutions are far more important than money, because they possess metaphysical qualities which legislation cannot correct. France has systematically returned Left-wing majorities for the past seventy-five years; but it remains a profoundly Conservative, even reactionary, country, because its great institutions—the Préfecture, the École Normale, St Cyr, the Académie, the Collège de France, the Bourse, the Haute Cour—have preserved their continuity. No doubt there is something to be said for continuity: but the desirable consequences of this choice must be balanced by its attendant evils: 5,000,000 Communist voters and fifteen years of disastrous colonial wars.

Much the same could be said of England. The British Left has, rightly, preferred constitutional change to violence. But it has also assumed that change is most effective and most acceptable when it is most gradual, that the institutional framework of nineteenth century society can be imperceptibly absorbed into a new order, until it reflects the interests of the working class while still preserving its historical continuity. This is erroneous. A new society cannot expect to inherit the institutions of the old—superficially attractive though they may be—without accepting their social characteristics. It must create new ones, which embody its own social, economic and political beliefs. Such a process entails a great deal of hard work and the willingness to sacrifice much that is beloved, or even valuable. Labour failed in 1945–51 because it tried to take the easy way out: to conduct a social revolution without hurting anyone's feelings or infringing any prejudices.

I am simple-minded enough to believe that we will never get a Socialist society in Britain—that is, a society based on the Christian principle that each individual is of equal worth, and has equal claims and duties—so long as we preserve historical continuity in our institutions, or indeed, and this may seem a hard thing to say, so long as we evaluate institutions in terms of their intrinsic merit and not in terms of their social consequences. I would therefore abolish the monarchy and House of Lords, dispossess the corporate bodies which control the public schools and the Oxford and Cambridge colleges; end the regimental system in the army, and destroy Service 'traditions' by amalgamating all three; disestablish the Church; replace the Inns of Court system with a central law college directly responsible to a Government department; unify the chaotic hospital administration system, so that the Ministry of Health takes direct charge of training; and, finally, abolish the Honours List. What is more, we should take the offensive on all these fronts simultaneously: for, if the apostles of social change eschew violence, they must embrace speed. Our society is a many-headed hydra: it is no use chopping the heads off singly, for while you are dealing with the second or third, the first will grow again. Transforming society is rather like bombing a factory complex: if, on each raid, you concentrate on one workshop, you allow the others to employ their resources on rebuilding it in the intervals. You must destroy the whole simultaneously, otherwise the complex will survive. The British Left—whether Liberal or Labour—has tinkered with our institutions in the past, but singly and timidly, and on the assumption that what is old should command respect. It should not; it should inspire fear. A better society can only be bought at a price; we should not be afraid of inflicting damage. After all, it is no accident that wars herald and permit social transformations.

To secure electoral approval for such a programme will not be easy; it may well be impossible; and certainly, the Labour movement, as at present constituted and led, could not conceivably undertake such a task. I have no illusions on this score. But equally, I have no illusions that anything of real social value is going to emerge from its current policies, based as they are on the fallacy that the attitudes of human beings to each other can be transformed merely by changing the amount of money in their pockets. Broadly speaking, Labour has acted on the assumption that short-term materialism pays the biggest dividends. Up to a point, this is correct, and the movement in Britain has accomplished far more than its branches on the Continent, which have been handicapped by their preoccupation with ideology. But a heavy price has been paid: the abandonment of the concept that the function of Socialism is not to improve, but to change society. Having consented to operate within the framework of nineteenth-century society, Labour now finds that it has accomplished most of the tasks which this limitation allows. It therefore has the choice of becoming a party of government, concerned primarily with administering a social structure to which it has become reconciled, or attempting to change the structure. I believe it must and will choose the second, even though this involves a retreat into the political wilderness. But if it finally surrenders its sense of outrage, and allows the power-motive to become its political dynamic, it will cease to be a progressive movement, and something else will take its place. For the sense of outrage, like the love of power, will continue to draw men and women into the political struggle.

IRIS MURDOCH

A house of theory

THE SOCIALIST MOVEMENT in this country is suffering from a loss of energy: and this is a misfortune which touches the whole community. The Tories are, by their nature, not a party of ideals and moral inventions. It is rather their function, a function which liberal-minded Socialists must welcome in general even if they often deplore it in particular, to check and criticize the more abstract visions of the Left. But now the salt itself seems to have lost its savour. The more progressive section of society seems able, in this time, to provide very little in the way of guidance and inspiration. There is a certain moral void in the life of the country. How has this come about?

It does not seem difficult to analyse the sources of moral energy which fed the Socialist movement in the past. First and most primitive was the desire for human equality, the valuing of the poorest he with the richest he: a desire made more intense by the miseries of the Industrial Revolution. Developing later, and giving to the movement its most characteristic and probably most profound motive, was the conception of exploitation, whose technical form was the Labour Theory of Value. Joined with this was what one might call Benthamite efficiency, the desire to tidy up society, sweeping away metaphysical obscurantism and out-dated tradition, and plan rationally for the happiness which was so patently lacking. To be compared and contrasted with this was Marxist efficiency, closely knit theoretical scientific Socialism, offering a more complex philosophy and a more revolutionary vision. A product of this confident science was a certain determinism whose appeal was religious as well as scientific: the apocalyptic belief that capitalism was doomed, the Messianic belief in the role of the proletariat. Independent of these sources of power but mingled with all of them was a general revolt against convention, the resistance to the nineteenth-century father-figure in his many

guises, the revolt against sexual taboos and restrictions, the movement for the liberation of women. With this one may connect the
hatred of industrial civilization which certainly moved many
people and which sometimes led to nostalgia for the apparent
simplicity of the medieval world: all that poor Morris had in mind
when he cried that 'Shoddy is king!' Consolation and promise were,
however, to be found in the sheer energy generated by the working
men's associations themselves, the discovery of active community
and common purpose, the warmth of proletarian solidarity. While
common in some way to almost all, and equally Christian, Marxist
and anarchist in its inspiration, was the vision of an ideal community in which work would once again be creative and meaningful, and human brotherhood would be restored; whereas now the
working classes were deracinate and disinherited, human nature
both in them and in their masters mutilated and divided: all that
could be summed up in the Hegelian concept of 'alienation'. These
—and the list could doubtless be extended and the items sub-
divided in different ways—were the complex and various ideals
and motives of Socialism.

Nearly all this great accumulation of energy has now been dis-
sipated, by the achievement of goals which satisfied the desires in
question, or by the achievement of something which made the
desires less sharp. As a result largely of the working-class movement itself together with the development of new economic
techniques we have the Welfare State. Many of the most obvious
injustices and deprivations have been remedied. The rich are not so
rich nor the poor so poor, and there has been a serious attempt to
create equality of opportunity. The sense of exploitation has faded
and the struggle for equality tends to take the form of the struggle
for higher wages. It now seems possible that capitalism is not
doomed after all, or at least not doomed in the dramatic manner
once envisaged. On both the theoretical and the practical plane
economists have led us to believe that capitalism can (perhaps)
overcome its tendency to periodic crises, and does not inevitably
(and, as was thought, increasingly) grind the faces of the poor:
thus removing the sense of impending cataclysm, destroying the
attraction of the Labour Theory of Value, and blunting the Socialist
claim to provide the only true science of society.

219

The appeal of Marxism as a body of doctrine, never strong in this country, has diminished with the lengthening history of the U.S.S.R. Marx and Marxist theorizing have been left to the Communists. The revolt against convention which was a sacred duty in the nineteenth century and between the wars was at least still fun, is now, as a result of the greater flexibility of society, not obviously either. Shoddy remains king, but nobody bothers much. The vision of the ideal society, which, outside Marxism, was often associated with opposition to parliamentary methods, lingered a while in Guild Socialism, and perished with the development of the parliamentary Labour Party. The sentiments of 'proletarian solidarity' have given way to the sentiments of the trade union movement. Socialism no longer seems (as it seemed to certain favoured spirits) something essentially and profoundly Christian. The anarchists are gone. What has triumphed (with many results for which we are profoundly thankful) and what is still largely with us is Benthamite efficiency, the spirit of the Fabians. Socialism, in the course of its rapid and successful development, has lost even the oddments of theory with which it started out.

It will be argued that the absence of Socialist theory is neither surprising nor deplorable. The British were never ones for theory in any case. We have always been empiricist, anti-metaphysical in philosophy, mistrustful of theoretical systems. It is true, indeed, that our political thought has been almost entirely sceptical, and could be summed up under the three heads of Tory scepticism, scientific scepticism, and Liberal humanist scepticism. Hume and Burke would represent the first. (Don't theorize: let habit and tradition solve your problems.) Bentham, with some assistance from Hobbes, would represent the second. (Don't theorize: theories are troublesome metaphysical nonsense. What matters in society is the mechanics of satisfaction.) Locke and Mill, with Kant in the background, would represent the third. (Don't theorize: empirical truths are unsystematic and moral truths can't be demonstrated; so be an undogmatic but rational respecter of persons.) However, all these thinkers were themselves theorists in the minimal sense that they invented certain concepts, presented certain schemes and pictures, in terms of which we can understand their differences and conceive them as constituting a conversation. The Liberals particularly set before us, unsystematically but with a power which has kept its hold upon our imagination, certain spiritual values 'fixed' in concepts such as that of Natural Rights.

Now 'Socialist theory', in so far as it existed here, was not directly a product of academic thinkers. It was not in its nature to be. It consisted rather of overlapping sets of ideas argumentatively put together by bodies such as the Socialist League and the Fabian Society. We have never produced a great Socialist philosopher, and we have paid very limited attention to the one whom we had in our midst. However, our Socialist thinking was strongly nourished by philosophical ideas which had become to some extent common property: the ideas of Locke and Utilitarians, as well as modified versions of Marxism and Utopian theories imported from France. A Socialist philosophy does not, and should not, grow independently of the main stream of philosophical ideas. With this in mind, we turn from the 'conceptual conversation' of the past to look at the contemporary scene, where we notice, of course, a marked contrast. Developments in mathematical logic, the influence of scientific method, the techniques of linguistic analysis, have combined to produce a new philosophy even more anti-theoretical than its sceptical predecessor. The creative aspect of philosophy is reduced almost to nil, or rather tends to be limited to the invention of what one might call 'logical gadgets'. (Russell's Theory of Descriptions would be a distinguished example.) The instrument that results is for its purposes excellent, and the critical task of philosophy, of great importance in a liberal society, has never been performed with greater exactness and rigour. Many persistent philosophical problems have been solved by the new method, which represents a genuine advance and discovery. One consequence, however (and I shall argue an unnecessary one), is that a certain area of thought which was formerly influential is becoming denuded. As philosophy is steadily drawn in the direction of logic and becomes increasingly a matter for highly trained experts, it separates itself from, and discourages, the vaguer and more generally comprehensible theorizing which it used to nourish and be nourished by; and the serious student who is either studying philosophy or is influenced by it (and there are many of the latter) develops an almost excessive fear of imprecision. 'Everything that can be said can be said clearly'. Outside the small area of possible clarity lies the dangerous region of 'mushy' thinking from which attention is averted. The ideal is a demonstration, however tiny, which is clean, sterile and conclusive.

In considering the way in which the modern techniques have affected moral and political theory, and through them affected a range of less specialized theorizing, it is necessary to consider in more detail the 'elimination of metaphysics'. In the past philosophers had invented concepts expressive of moral belief and presented them as if they were facts concerning the nature of the mind or of the world. Philosophy since Hume has, in opposing dogmatic rationalist metaphysics in general, been critical of this tendency, but in varying ways. Briefly, criticism of metaphysics may proceed along Humian, Kantian, or Hegelian lines. Hume, who wished to maintain as rigorously as possible that we know only what our senses tell us, denied the existence of moral 'facts' or 'realities', analysed moral concepts into non-rational feelings and imaginative habits, and was prepared to let basic empirical concepts suffer the same fate. Kant, anxious to defend both the reality of our empirical knowledge and the dignity of our moral intimations, changed Hume's habits of imagination into 'categories', or fixed formal modes of apprehension which if directed upon empirical data would yield knowledge. Other matters, such as the moral law and the destiny of the soul, could only be objects of belief, although the reality and something of the nature of the spiritual realm were suggested by the demands of conscience. Hegel altered Kant's criticism in a fundamental way when he conceived the categories as the forms not only of our knowledge of empirical objects, but also of our apprehension of social, psychological and spiritual realities, and subjected them to historical treatment, taking the pattern of their development initially from the history of the changing ideas of the human race.

These philosophers were all critical of dogmatic rationalist metaphysical arguments (such as those used by St Thomas) and so put a question mark beside moral beliefs (ethical, political, religious) which rested formerly on such arguments; but they differed significantly in the place which they assigned to beliefs of this kind under the new regime. Neither Hume nor Kant had any interest in variety of belief, nor, for these purposes, any historical sense; and they virtually removed from the scene of rational discourse all theories except those specifically accredited by their own philosophical methods. Hume, whose 'elimination' followed the simple lines of atomic empiricism, regarded all beliefs as equally irrational, but some as inevitable and convenient. Civilized life after all rested on moral instincts, and Hume described those of his own society. Kant more systematically attempted to show why our knowledge was limited to certain kinds of object, and in doing so pictured the mind as solely concerned with the objects of empirical observation and science. He allowed in addition one belief (the belief in Reason, with the related and tentative belief in God); and all other theories were classed together as superstition. Hegel differed from Hume and Kant in that he did not regard the fact that a belief or theory had rested upon a discredited type of philosophical argument as automatically denuding the theory of philosophical interest or even of truth. He did not class theories as either whole truths or total errors, but allowed to all the influential beliefs that men have held the status of interpretation and discovery of the world. All three philosophers are, of course, vulnerable themselves, though not in the essentials of what they have to say, to attacks by modern critics; all three, in different ways, can lay claim to the title of 'empiricist'.

Modern British philosophy is Humian and Kantian in inspiration. It follows Hume and Kant in regarding sense experience as the only basis for knowledge, and it follows Kant in attempting more specifically to show that concepts not so based are 'empty'. Moral and political philosophies, never the centre of modern developments, have followed in the wake. Attention was concentrated upon the error by which former philosophers imagined themselves to be making quasi-factual discoveries when really they were preaching. Since morality could not be 'proved' by philosophical argument, philosophy now aimed at studying it in a non-partisan manner, analysing the 'logic' of moral discourse in general, and leaving moral exhortation to others. Moral judgements, since they did not admit of empirical verification, were first said to be 'emotive' (a Humian position). Later they were likened to imperatives (a Kantian position). In this second and more subtle phase Kant's single belief in Reason was re-fashioned into a formula which purported to give the defining characteristics of any moral judgement as such. A certain rationality, universality, consistency, was thought of (with minor variations) as defining the *form* of morality irrespective of its *content*. The variegated area of moral belief or ideology (the special religious and social concepts which guide choice, and which are in many cases a legacy from the metaphysical philosophers) was usually treated, together with the actual patterns of choice, as part of the *content*, the region of morality which is a matter of personal decision and not a proper subject for analysis. Such beliefs were not, of course, demonstrable by philosophical argument (it was the mistake of the old philosophers to think that they were) and they came to be seen as the idiosyncratic 'colour' of a moral attitude, something nebulous and hazy, which for purposes of exposition and example was best analysed away into actual choices at the empirical level. The moral agent is thus pictured, in a manner which remains essentially Kantian, as using his reason to survey the ordinary factual world, and making decisions therein which he will defend by reference to facts and to simple principles offered as patently rational. He is *not* pictured as using his reason to explore the intermediate area of concepts. Moral action, in short, is seen as the making of sensible choices and the giving of sensible and simple reasons. It is not seen as the activity of theorizing, imagining, or seeking for deeper insight.[1]

Such a situation could hardly be promising for the department of ethics which deals with political concepts; and indeed whereas moral philosophy survives by the skin of its teeth, political philosophy has almost perished. Whereas some sense (misleading perhaps but just comprehensible) can be made of the idea of the 'fundamental logical form of a moral judgement', very little sense can be made of the idea of the 'fundamental logical form of a political judgement'. The 'form' of political thinking cannot be thus

[1] *See especially R. M. Hare* The Language of Morals, *and also articles by Hampshire, Urmson and others. It will be noted that this position is curiously existentialist in flavour. Popular existentialism is Kantianism with Reason in the veiled role of Kierkegaard's God. All positive beliefs stand in danger of* mauvaise foi.

plausibly divided from its 'content'. It is impossible not to regard political philosophy in an historical manner; and it is very difficult to extract from it the type of compact philosophical problem whose statement and attempted solution now alone count as really 'doing philosophy'. Exercises in political philosophy consist usually in carefully restricted discussion of a well-known concept (such as the General Will), attempting with brief and undetailed historical reference to illustrate the nature and 'function' of the concept. These discussions are often valuable; but they are not popular because they necessarily lack precision of a logical or near-logical variety, and their atmosphere is such as to suggest that 'political concepts' are things of the past. They are, after all, metaphysical beliefs, or, to be more exact, they are personal evaluations and social recommendations disguised as truths about the nature of man. It is the (logical and morally neutral) task of the philosopher to pierce this disguise, and to separate the solid recommendation from the conceptual mask which comes away, as it were, empty. The giving of actual political advice and the suggestion of moves in definite political dilemmas are, of course, not the business of philosophy. Here again, political activity, like moral activity, is thought of as the making of empirical choices, and not as itself an activity of theorizing. The most consistent exposition of this generally favoured view is in T. D. Weldon's *The Vocabulary of Politics*. A curious result of this development is that liberal and progressive thinkers who are touched by modern philosophy come on what they take to be logical grounds to the same conclusions about political theorizing to which conservative thinkers come on frankly moral grounds. Berlin and Weldon and Popper agree with T. S. Eliot and Michael Oakeshott that systematic political theorizing is a bad thing.[1] The former think it so because is it 'metaphysi-

---

[1] *Mr Eliot forms in fact a curious counterpart in this respect to Bertrand Russell. Both share the view that real thinking is highly systematic (for Russell, mathematics, for Eliot, Thomist theology) and accept the implication that thinking about society is another matter. Russell, when acting as a social critic, drops his rigorous philosophical persona and is clearly engaged in a quite different kind of activity. Mr Eliot, who reserves a unique pinnacle for Dante*

C.—P

cal' and opinionated and obscures the scientific business of altering our society for the better. The latter think it so because it interferes with the deep operation of traditions which should not be tampered with by critical reflection. Bentham and Hume are still with us; but we are losing touch with Locke and Mill.

The discrediting of theory has, then, taken place as a result of a combination of different tendencies: Tory scepticism, Benthamite scepticism, a Kantian protestant fear of 'superstitions', and more recently a dislike of Marxism, all apparently supported by the anti-metaphysical destructive techniques of modern philosophy. It is moreover felt that theorizing is anti-liberal (an idea which it is easy to extract from Kant) and that liberal-minded persons should surround their choices with a minimum of theory, relying rather on open above-board references to facts or to principles which are simple and comprehensible to all. Here it is important, in accordance indeed with the clear-headed methods of analytical philosophy, in order to see what one is doing, to separate neutral arguments from evaluations. The point, briefly made, is that the 'elimination of metaphysics', though it shows that moral beliefs were often supported by erroneous arguments, does not *ipso facto* 'discredit' the area of moral belief, properly understood as an area of conceptual moral exploration. All that the anti-metaphysical arguments make clear (and one would not wish to deny this) is that moral theorizing is not the discovery of bogus 'facts', but is an activity whose purpose and justification are moral. Hegel understood and displayed this, though he also sinned by picturing moral exploration dogmati-

---

because (unlike Shakespeare) he combined literary ability with a background of real (i.e. systematic theological) thought, denies the name of 'thinking' to social analysis such as that practised by D. H. Lawrence. Mr Eliot's theology is, however, more relevant to his social criticism than Lord Russell's mathematics is to his, and this in itself is an advantage. Right-wing thinkers may be shy of system at the political level but they are not shy of moralizing. Whereas Left-wing (non-Communist) utterances must be 'scientific' or else offered as fragmentary personal notions. The greater moral solemnity of the Right (and of the extreme Left) makes them, I suspect, in certain ways profounder critics of our society at present.

cally within a rigid hierarchy of ideas. There is no philosophical (or scientific) reason why there should not be an area of theory, reflection, meditation, contemplation, *between* ourselves and the simple empirical levels of action, so long as certain arguments are eschewed, and so long as it is clearly recognized that the purpose of the theorizing is moral clarification and understanding: and moral, political, and religious theories have, after all, often served this purpose in the past and have not always been 'mere superstitions'. It therefore emerges that the choice made by our intellectuals against the development of theories is a moral choice.

Is it a right choice? I think not. There is a serious and growing void in our thinking about moral and social problems. This void is uneasily felt by society at large and is the more distressing since we are now perhaps for the first time in our history feeling the loss of religion as a consolation and guide; until recently various substitutes (Socialism itself, later Communism, Pacifism, Internationalism) were available: now there seems to be a shortage even of substitutes. The claim of Socialism to be a 'science' has become, after many setbacks, a trifle less confident, and has certainly lost the spiritual appeal which it once had. Of course Socialism will continue to attempt to constitute itself a science, in the sense of a highly organized investigation of the mechanics of society. But, and especially since it cannot now claim to be the scientific study of an inevitable quasi-biological development, it should, in my view, also far more frankly and more systematically declare itself a morality. Our Socialist ancestors had ideals but no techniques. We are often amazed at their naïveté. We have the techniques: *these* we can explain clearly. But we can give only a rather brief and denuded explanation of our ideals. We have reached a stage where the amount of theory is decreasing while the social need for it increases. The danger represented by what is called the 'managerial society' is the danger (already diagnosed by Marx as characteristic of capitalism) of the division of the population into experts and ignorant (though perhaps contented) masses with no communication between them; and we have now the additional spectacle of the division of the experts into mutually non-comprehending groups. What is needed is an *area of translation*, an area in which specialized concepts and recommendations can be seen and understood in the light of moral and social ideas which have a certain degree of complexity and yet are not the sole property of technicians. There is a Tory contention that theorizing leads to violence, and there is a liberal contention that theories are obscurantist and blinding. Now on the contrary it is the absence of theory which renders us blind and which enables bureaucracy, in all its sense, to keep us mystified; and as for violence, the absence of civilized theorizing can also lead in that direction. It is dangerous to starve the moral imagination of the young. We require, in addition to our 'science', a social analysis which is both detailed and frank in its moral orientation. A more ambitious conceptual picture, thought out anew in the light of modern critical philosophy and our improved knowledge of the world, of the moral centre and moral direction of Socialism would enable those of us who are not experts to pick up the facts of our situation in a reflective, organized and argumentative way : would give us what Shelley called the power to imagine what we know. Socialist thought is hampered, and the appeal of Socialism is restricted, because our technical concepts are highly esoteric and our moral concepts are excessively simple and there is nothing in between. We need, and the Left should provide, some refuge from the cold open field of Benthamite empiricism, a framework, a house of theory.

In response to these ambitious desires it may be coldly argued that 'Socialist theory' was a product of the working-class movement, and that the working-class movement no longer exists, whereas the trade union movement does; and that it is impossible to call up moral visions in a situation in which there is no material incentive to make people lift their eyes to the hills. Further, it will be said that a perfectly good Socialist theory of a down-to-earth kind does exist and indeed fills many volumes. Those who ask for information about Socialism are not left unanswered : what more is required? If it is a 'philosophy' that is wanted, that can hardly be produced on the spur of the moment and would in any case be itself something esoteric and technical.

It is doubtless true in a sense that the working-class movement as a dynamic theory-generating body with immediate objectives does not at present exist. There is less appetite for ideas. Education is no longer seen as the road to freedom; it is seen as the road to a higher salary. However, the working class exists, and with it many of the ills of capitalist society which were a scandal to our fore-fathers, and a large body of increasingly vague but loyal Socialist opinion exists, too. The question must be continually asked: how are we to keep *thought* about Socialism and *moral concern* about Socialism alive in a Welfare State? Spiritual unrest and even decisive moral reactions are not lacking. 'Public opinion' is the name of a force which should control and check the development of bureaucracy; and public opinion has shown itself of late, to the dismay of certain Tories, to be still both lively and powerful. Its activity, however, has been limited to the sudden assertion of some absolute value (usually in the field of foreign affairs), obscurely grasped, without any connection of a theoretical kind being established between the occasions. A religious and moral vocabulary is the possession now of a few; and most people lack the words with which to say just what is felt to be wrong is wrong.

If in the hope of finding such words we turn to the available Socialist 'literature' we are likely to be disappointed. In the old days professional and amateur philosophizing fed the public mind with ideas. Now, for a larger vision, we have to look back to Laski or Tawney, or search for hints in eccentric and little-known works by Christians or Marxists. What we have plenty of, and what we find officially in the centre of the picture, are detailed technical books and pamphlets in which the author tells us briefly that we need public ownership in order to bring about equality, and then hurries on to the details of investment policy. The motive, the passion, in much of this literature is patently that of an expert making an efficient plan. Needless to say one is glad of such experts, and it would be an impertinence in the uninitiated to criticize what they cannot understand. But what one requires as well is a little more pausing at the first stage, a little more analysis, in terms which are not those of the economist, of an idea such as that of equality: which is, in fact, in danger of becoming the only influential 'general idea' of contemporary Socialism. More theoretical exploration of the aims of Socialism, those aims to which all techniques are properly subordinate, would benefit both sides of the specialist barrier. The expert would gain that unifying vision which is needed to prompt more inspired and imaginative uses of technique. He would be less isolated, more responsible, more often compelled to explain; and having to explain, to connect, to translate, deepens understanding: while the average person would gain a more complex, and hence more influential, grasp upon what is being done on his behalf, instead of coming straightaway up against the blank wall of economics.

It is not true that 'everyone knows what is wrong with our society' and differs only over a simple choice of solutions. What we see as wrong, and our ability to express what is wrong in a profound, subtle and organized way, will influence our conception of a solution as well as providing us with the energy to seek it. We have not mended our society since its mutilation by nineteenth-century industrialism. There is less poverty but no more (in some ways less) true community life. Work has become less unpleasant without becoming more significant. The gulf remains between the skilled and creative few and the unskilled and uncreative many. What was formerly called the proletariat has lost what culture it once had, and gained no true substitute. A stream of half-baked amusements hinders thought and the enjoyment of art and even of conversation. Equality of opportunity produces, not a society of equals, but a society in which the class division is made more sinister by the removal of intelligent persons into the bureaucracy and the destruction of their roots and characteristics as members of the mass. In short, a proletariat in the fundamental sense intended by Marx still exists: a deracinate, disinherited and excluded mass of people. Only this mass is now quiescent, its manner of life largely suburban and its outlook 'petty bourgeois', and it increasingly lacks any concept of itself as deprived.

This list of grievances, whose items would be regarded as obvious in some quarters and eccentric in others, suggests to me the following, which again will seem obvious to some. The Socialist movement should most explicitly bring back into the centre of its thinking its original great source of inspiration and reflection, the problem of labour: the problem, that is, of the transformation of labour from something senseless which forms no real part of the personality of the labourer into something creative and significant. To do this would involve a re-thinking and re-grouping on the theoretical plane of concepts such as 'exploitation' and 'alienation' which were formerly gathered about the Labour Theory of Value. The familiar ideas of 'equality', democracy', 'freedom' need to be understood anew in the light of the problem of labour and not treated as independent 'absolutes' whose meaning is taken for granted. To treat them so is ultimately to imperil them. Theory is needed to refresh the tired imagination of practice. Our available techniques seem uninteresting because we lack the vision to grasp their possibilities. A line of thought such as I have in mind leads very directly to problems that have been immensely discussed and considered. Can we maintain educational standards while making education more 'democratic'? Can we make technical training more universal and more humane while still meeting the demands of industry? Is the 'opposition' role of the trade unions a hindrance to 'industrial democracy''? It is not that these matters have not been studied; it is rather that they have been studied on too severely practical a level and without a sufficient consultation of our final aims. We should profit by widening the area in which they could be discussed with intelligence and interest.

A study of nationalization, such as *Industry and Society*, for instance, representing an official attitude, combines complexity at the technical level with question-begging simplicity at the moral and theoretical level. 'Nationalization' is spoken of in terms of redistribution of wealth, making important powers socially responsible, and enabling the State to profit from the present structure of our economy. 'Equality' is envisaged as the abolition of private shareholding and inherited position. Keynes is quoted to show that with the dissociation of ownership of industry from its control there is a 'natural line of development' in the direction of State Socialism. There is a momentary reference to 'joint consultation'. Nothing whatever is said about conditions and nature of work. Whereas critics (the authors of *The Insiders*, for instance) who rightly suggest that 'public ownership must be seen in the context of the original Socialist goal of industrial democracy', and who point out the extent to which *Industry and Society* takes our present economic and social structure for granted, still conceive the problem in terms of 'the democratization of power', rather than in terms of what such a shift of power would be designed to achieve.

But the fascination of the means should not obscure the end; and to *see* the end we must to some extent separate it from the often seemingly barren complexities of the means; we must to some extent lend it the remoteness and flexibility of a 'theory'. The problem of the transformation of labour is not only the original centre of Socialist thought, it is the problem of the managerial society. Even to pose it with enough clarity would help to counteract the movement of talent and interest toward the levels of bureaucratic control and to send it back toward the levels of the unskilled. But for such an idea to be fruitful, a source of inspiration and controversy, it needs to be presented as an autonomous moral conception, independent of, and ultimately sovereign over, the mere notions of efficiency and rational 'tidying up' of capitalist society into which Socialism is in danger of degenerating.

If we seek here for inspiration in our own tradition we have not far to look. The Guild Socialists dissented on precisely this point from their less ambitious and more purely Benthamite colleagues, in that the latter were concerned with the damage done to the consumer and the former with the damage done to the producer. The Guild Socialists were deeply concerned with the destruction of community life, the degradation of work, the division of man from man which the economic relationships of capitalism had produced; and they looked to the transformation of existing communities, the trade unions, the factories themselves, for the restoration of what was lost. Such ideas were and are easy targets for mockery, and in the old Guild Socialist form were doubtless quite impracticable; and they faded from the scene partly because they were tied to inadequate techniques, and partly because the conception of the Welfare State presented an easier and more obviously urgent and attractive target. With its achievement it is necessary to renew our study of the more difficult and fundamental problems of capitalism. We cannot live without the 'experts'. But the true 'open society' in the modern world is one in which expertise is not mysterious; and the only way to prevent it from becoming mysterious is continually to subordinate its activities to a lively and *interested* public opinion : and this in turn will languish without 'theories'. The Welfare State marks the successful end of the first road along which the Socialist movement in this country elected to travel. It is time now to go back and explore the other road, to go back to the point of divergence, the point not so very far back at which we retained as a living morality ideas which were common to Marx and to William Morris.

Biographies

NORMAN MACKENZIE

Born 1921. Married, with two children. Educated at Aske's School, Hatcham, and London School of Economics. Member of the editorial staff of the *New Statesman*. Labour candidate for Hemel Hempstead, 1951 and 1955 elections. Author of *Socialism: a Short History, The New Towns: the Success of Social Planning*, and other books and pamphlets.

PETER SHORE

Born 1924. Married, with three children. Educated at Quarrybank High School, Liverpool, and King's College, Cambridge, Political economist. Labour candidate for Halifax. Author (with A. A. Rogow) of *The Labour Government and British Industry*, and of *The Real Nature of Conservatism*.

BRIAN ABEL-SMITH

Born 1927. Single. Educated at Haileybury and Clare College, Cambridge. Lecturer at the London School of Economics. Member of the National Executive of the Fabian Society, of a regional hospital board, and of the Nurses and Midwives Whitley Council. Governor of St Thomas's Hospital. Author (with Professor Titmuss) of *The Cost of the National Health Service*, (with Peter Townsend) of *New Pensions for the Old, The Reform of Social Security*, and (with Professor Titmuss and Peter Townsend) of Part II of *National Superannuation*.

RICHARD HOGGART

Born 1919. Married, with three children. Educated at local grammar school in Leeds and Leeds University. Senior Staff tutor in Literature, Department of Adult Education. Hull University. Member B.B.C. Advisory Council for North Region. Visiting professor of English, University of Rochester, New York, in 1956–57. Author of *Auden, The Uses of Literacy* and *W. H. Auden*.

PETER TOWNSEND

Born 1928. Married, with three children. Educated at University College School and St John's College, Cambridge. Sociologist. Author of *The Family Life of Old People*, (with Brian Abel-Smith) of *New Pensions for the Old*, and (with Professor Titmuss and Brian Abel-Smith) of Part II of *National Superannuation*.

RAYMOND WILLIAMS

Born 1922. Married, with three children. Educated at King Henry VIII Grammar School, Abergavenny, and Trinity College Cambridge. Staff tutor in the Delegacy for Extra-Mural Studies, University of Oxford. Author of *Culture and Society, 1780–1950*, *Drama from Ibsen to Eliot*, *Drama in Performance*, *Reading and Criticism*.

NIGEL CALDER

Born 1932. Married, with three children. Member of editorial staff of the *New Scientist*, formerly a research physicist. Educated at Merchant Taylors' and Sidney Sussex College, Cambridge. Author of *Electricity Grows Up*, *Robots, and Radio Astronomy*.

PETER MARRIS

Born 1928. Single. Educated at Bryanston and Clare College, Cambridge. Sociologist, formerly a District Officer in Kenya. Author of *Widows and their Families*.

HUGH THOMAS

Born 1932. Single. Educated at Sherborne School and Queen's College, Cambridge. Novelist, formerly in the Foreign Office. Labour candidate for Ruislip-Northwood. Now working on a history of the Spanish Civil War. Author of *The World's Game* and *The Oxygen Age*.

MERVYN JONES

Born 1922. Married, with three children. Educated at Abbotsholme and New York University. Novelist, and member of *Tribune* staff. Labour candidate for Chichester, 1955. Author of five novels, including *On the Last Day*, and co-author with Michael Foot of *Guilty Men*, *1957*.

PAUL JOHNSON

Born 1928. Married, with one child. Educated at Stonyhurst and Magdalen College, Oxford. Member of editorial staff of the *New Statesman*. Author of *The Suez War* and *Journey into Chaos*.

IRIS MURDOCH

Born 1919. Married. Educated at Badminton and Somerville College, Oxford. Fellow of St Anne's College, Oxford, teacher of philosophy, and formerly in the Treasury. Author of *Sartre, Romantic Rationalist, Under the Net, The Flight from the Enchanter* and *The Sandcastle*.